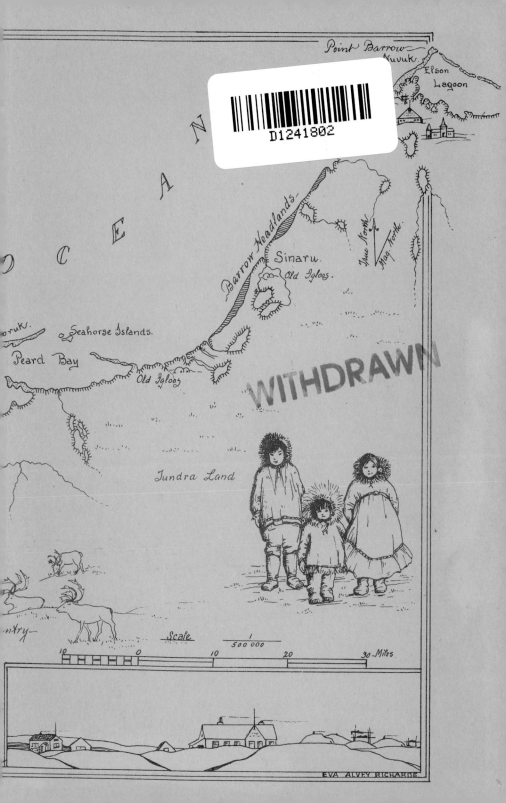

Point Barrow
Nuvuk.
Elson Lagoon

OCEAN

Barrow Headlands
Sinaru.
Old Igloos.

True North.
Mag. North.

oruk.
Seahorse Islands.

Peard Bay

Old Igloos

D1241802

Tundra Land

ntry—

Scale
1
500 000

10   0   10   20   30 Miles

EVA ALVEY RICHARDS

ARCTIC MOOD

Arctic Mood

A Narrative of Arctic Adventures

BY

Eva Alvey Richards

"It is the time of life, the circumstances, the mood, which at that moment fell so happily together."
—George Gissing

The Caxton Printers, Ltd.
Caldwell, Idaho
1949

Printed and bound in the United States of America

To

The Dearest Ones

MY FATHER

MY SON   MY DAUGHTER

ACKNOWLEDGMENTS

But for the kindly and encouraging insistence of a good friend never met, Dr. George Miksch Sutton of Cornell University, this book would never have been retrieved from the dusty pages of my Arctic Journals. My sincere thanks to Dr. Sutton.

To the late Dr. Wm. Thomas Lopp, former Chief of the Alaska Division, United States Bureau of Education, builder of the first school on the Arctic coast, pioneer teacher and friend beloved of all Eskimo peoples living today in that northern territory, as well as others in the Baffin Land, Ungava and Hudson's Bay regions, I here inscribe my debt of gratitude for the loan of material relating to the early schools, particularly for the generous excerpts I have taken from a paper on *Pioneer Education in the Northwest,* one of a series compiled by himself and other pioneer teachers, at the behest of Dr. Francis Powers of the University of Washington, for the archives of the College of Education.

I am also grateful to the late Mr. C. L. Andrews and to Mr. Peter Vander Sterre for permission to use their excellent photographs.

Portions of this book have appeared in *The Lamp,* Standard Oil (N. J.) house organ, and in *The Trained Nurse and Hospital Review,* New York City. The author thanks the publishers for their release of copyright.

E. A. R.

Trading Station. Ice house. The Schoolhouse. The Igloos. Meat racks.

PREAMBLE

Tooruk and I were talking over cups of tea, and many slices of bread, and a great dish of jam. Also there was a big bowl of sugar. Tooruk likes sugar with tea. He likes it with blubber too, and with seal meat.

Tooruk had just brought in the ice for the water barrels. He usually did this in the mornings, but now it was summer and Tooruk came in whenever he thought about the ice—or maybe it was the sugar he thought about—well anyway, we were talking.

We were talking about a sled trip we had taken together. It had been a great trip. We had talked about it many times and now we were at it again, our words running to gay comparisons. I had been saying, "It was such fun getting ready for it, Tooruk, freezing the bean soup; packing the sled; and then the going—all those miles of going—beautiful miles. Then that night in the old igloo! And our home-coming!—remember, Tooruk, how glad we were—the village people running from their igloos to meet us—shaking hands with everyone— all laughing and talking together?" (And now Tooruk is talking. His words come between sips of syrup.) "Yesh-yesh, Missus Eva, that going is good—and that time we comes to village is plenty fine—and now I tells you something—I thinks time we tells about that trip is better—is like when we tells about that trip—we goes again."

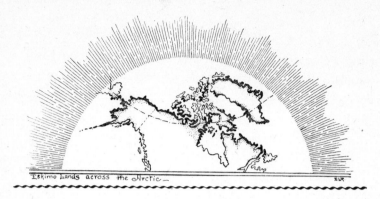

Eskimo Lands across the Arctic

INTRODUCTION

For those who have been to the Arctic:
I do not need to declaim.
You are forever gathered to its beauty;
to its long winter of night days with their swift
crackling phenomena of Northern Lights;
to its bright beautiful summer with the never setting
sun and far frozen distances with pageant of incredible
color; to its bewildering bird and animal life filled
with strange interest;
forever holding in admiration the little people who
have made the Arctic their own, the Eskimo, who have
by their nimble wit wrested from its desolate wastes
all things for happy living.

All of these will no more let you go than that the Pole
Star should fall from its place in the vault of heaven.

For those who have not been to the Arctic:

I have endeavored to tell you of it as I knew it;
of events that came in to crowd each day of living

in an Eskimo village;
in a village of low mounded igloos snuggled close to the
tundra at Wainwright, on the Arctic Ocean.
And if I succeed in the telling,
so you may know the kindly Eskimos,
I shall be well content.

Here then, is a year of the Arctic in all its moods,
as lived by a schoolteacher (yes, she had to be a nurse,
        too)
who went to this village to do what was written in her
government contract to do, (and much that was not)
for a little people—a little happy people—
the happiest in the world
with the least to be happy for.

Now Tooruk will be jubilant, for he will know when
he reads these pages, what a truth I have learned from
        him: that
"Time we tells about that trip is better—is like when we
tells about that trip—we goes again."

BOXER at Wainwright
Unloading Supplies

SKAL Tichards.

LIST OF ILLUSTRATIONS

ILLUSTRATIONS CONTINUED

ARCTIC MOOD

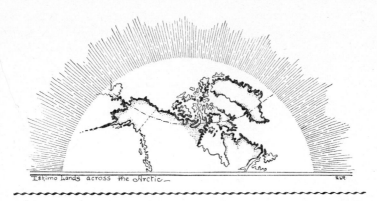

Eskimo Lands across the Arctic—

ARCTIC MOOD

For years I had been going to the Arctic; in all manners of ways I had been going; in books—in dreams —my finger on a map—and always with the wild geese in the spring.

And then one day (for dreams do come true) I received my appointment to the Alaska Division of the Native School and Medical Service (Department of the Interior) with assignment to the Eskimo village of Wainwright on the Arctic coast. I lost no time looking it up on the map. There it was, a mere pin point of a place, just below Point Belcher, about one hundred miles southwest of Point Barrow, far up on the northwest coast of North America. And now for the nth time I was tracing the curve of a shallow bight there, wholly absorbed in the tiny blue indentation marked Wainwright Inlet. I circled it with a red pencil—possessively.

So now I was going to the Arctic again.

This time I was really going.

With mounting anticipation I read my appointment letter. "In addition to your salary," it went on to say, "you will be furnished with living quarters in the Government School there, together with light and fuel. . . . Information regarding food supplies, clothing requirements, time of sailing, etcetera, may be obtained at the Bureau Office in Seattle." In the afternoon I was there.

The place was a hive. Typewriters were clicking a merry pace—papers crackled in and out of files—a clerk breezed by—telephones buzzed—a ship's officer dashed in waving a sheaf of blue and yellow bills—a young couple hurried in to consult at once a large map on the wall: "Here we are, dear," he says, pointing with enthusiasm. "I wish there wasn't so much ocean between here and there," she observes—but here I had reached the secretary's desk, credentials crisp in hand (and congratulating my good fortune on entering a service that could hum with such efficiency and precision), when I was met by a quiet voice, "Looks like you hold the ticket for Wainwright!" I was shaking hands with William Thomas Lopp, genial Chief of the Alaska Native Schools. He was just leaving the office, his pockets bulging with bureau business. It was a neat interview, sheared down to "Can you make good bread?" The elevator gates cut in on my answer, with noise enough to make any wavering "yes" sound convincing.

Two hours later I was reading the directions on a package of Compressed Yeast while mentally overhauling my wardrobe.

The bureau ship *Boxer* was scheduled to sail July 18. I had ten days in which to make ready; to shop for and fashion suitable clothing; plan and order food supplies for a year; see an oculist and dentist; collect blankets and pillows, utensils and tableware; arrange for the banking and investing of my salary—whew!—ten days!—in mid-July! The task loomed illogical!—shopping for Arctic cold in the swelter of summer!

Never again will I attempt to buy woolen underwear in the month of July. Such an upsetting of department store shelves and astonishment of clerks I never wish to be party to again. "Did you say *woolen* underwear, Madam? Say, Josie, where will I find the wool unions?" "*Wool unions!* Wool—! Say, Maisie, who's kidding you? Beg pardon Madam, I'll take a look in the stock room."

Blessings on the stock rooms! Out of their cedar and camphor recesses came such comforts as woolen gloves and knitted caps, felt shoes and soft moccasins, sweaters and a warm robe (Ooh! what a scorching day that was!), together with blankets and yarn for knitting, and the "wool unions" and hose. And bless all the willing Josies and Maisies! For more reasons than that of woolen clothing I knew I was going to be warm in the Arctic.

Every morning—nearer truth to say every hour of the night—found me with pad and pencil jotting down every possible need I could think of for the year before me. Things to work with—things for living—for comfort—while my trunk yawned in a melee of more things —toilet articles, a clock, water colors and brushes, desk fittings, songbooks, notebooks, all waiting to be packed.

I took time off on one of these bustling days to hear a talk by a missionary nurse, on furlough from some northern mission hospital. From her I learned of outing flannel pillow cases and of sleeping garments with hoods attached, "sure comfort for fifty below." These I made, wondering no little about such frigid nights. I thought of the holidays, Thanksgiving and Christmas to come, and provided for their joy to myself: bright candles— table linen—maraschino cherries—red and green crepe paper—and gay artificial flowers with a bowl of shiny pottery to place them in.

One sultry afternoon I put by the pad and pencil to sit awhile with friends who came to say farewell. (Ostensibly, for secretly they were cherishing the notion, "we must persuade her from this mad purpose.")

"If this isn't sheer folly!" one began, "I declare I believe you've lost your mind," and then another chimed in, "Eva Louise, you're burying yourself alive in this crazy scheme! How in the world are you going to keep house, be your own cook, teach Eskimos all day, and nurse Eskimos all night!" Dear gentle ladies all shouting at once, "Well, new babies always come at night, don't they?"

In storming babel they croaked a lively chorus about "shoveling coal" and "freezing to death" and "a perilous foolhardy undertaking," until—with purpose still intact —I sought my pencil again to remark: "My dears! you know so much about the North; what would you suggest to take the place of lettuce and celery, parsley and such green stuff?"—for all the while you see, my mind was on my planning—balanced menus plus full quotas of vitamins—computing 365 x three meals a day with never a diverting notion of freezing to death.

From the culinary experiences of the teachers who had pioneered in the school service, the Seattle office had compiled a number of quantitative lists of the staple supplies, together with suggestions pertaining to the uses of concentrated foods, such as powdered eggs (glory be! how would I poach a powdered egg!) and powdered milk and other similar products, prepared it would seem, especially for northern kitchens. Suggestions for packing personal effects were included—"the saving of weight

or space aboard ship or ease of handling in the cargo
slings is all to the good." And since one economy leads
to another, I was soon taking part in conversations like
this: (when teachers meet in the Bureau office they go
into a huddle over supplies.)

"I just must have jam with my toast—that's
my breakfast, that and coffee."

"How are you taking it?"

"Oh, in small glasses packed in sawdust."

"How many cases?"

"Oh, about four I guess—assorted stuff."

"Why not make your own jams up North?"

"Make jam up North! How would you do
it?"

"With dried fruits: apricots, peaches, prunes,
apples. Apricots and raisins make a delicious
conserve—sugar travels best in a sack, you
know, and one can spice dried peaches—it's
easy, soak 'em overnight—mighty tasty with
meats—cheaper than buying them already
glassed plus no risk of breakage in the bargain."

"How about berry jams?"

"Do without. Leave something to enjoy
when you get back to the States again."

It was a big help to know what others had tried and
found good while living under strange conditions, indeed
for one going to an isolated station for the first time such
lists and suggestions came nigh to being indispensable.
It was the red typed caution, CHECK YOUR SUP-
PLIES CAREFULLY, that I gave heed to. There could
be no traipsing to a corner grocery for some forgotten
can of cinnamon or something, much less run to the

next-door neighbors for a cup of this or that. My eyes were beginning to see double, but I persisted in checking and counter-checking until at last my nights were no longer troubled with dreams of making bread with pickles or mixing an ocean of vanilla with hominy.

A firm specializing in and shipping foodstuffs to the North did the rest. And what a consignment of eatables it was!—tinned, dehydrated, powdered, evaporated, condensed, compressed, preserved,—with not a vitamin or a calorie missing, nor one complaining for being thus processed.

"The Bureau of Education usually pays (reading my appointment letter again) the transportation of its newly appointed teachers from Seattle to their destination in Alaska. Transportation does not include meals, hotel bills, excess baggage, or miscellaneous expenses of travel." Since the July sailing of the bureau ship is the one directly to the far north stations, I had only "excess baggage" to worry about. "It is advisable," I was told, "to hold freight and baggage to a minimum. There are difficulties in certain ice seasons, getting the stuff ashore."

The day came to count noses: I was taking a sewing machine and a small Victrola—its records traveling snug between blankets and quilts—a comfy chair, a two-burner oil stove and a typewriter, and a small mirror. The chair crated awkwardly. On second count it loomed ponderously "excess." I decided to consult the office.

No one could say just what the furnishings consisted of in the quarters at Wainwright, that is, no one could say exactly. Now and again teachers contributed, usually something of their own handiwork, a bookcase, a desk—made while teaching manual training likely—it was hard to tell; one might run into luxury and again one might have to sit on a packing case. Mrs. Knox, the office secretary, (and blessed angel to every new teacher), pulled out her file drawer. "Perhaps these recent requisitions from Wainwright may uncover a clue," so I sat me down to study a sheaf of yellow papers and promptly forgot all about the chair in an intriguing maze of new stimulus.

Dear me! of all the lovely surprises! Here was a requisition for a school organ but this: this order for five hundred *sacks, twine,* and *sack needles!*—what could they be for?

"For your fuel coal at Wainwright. The Eskimos mine it from open seams along the banks of a river up there, where they sack it for hauling down to the village in their canoes or sleds. It's a co-operative arrangement. The native store buys the sacks," and she went on to tell me, "your 'light,' of course, is kerosene and gasoline."

I found a new kitchen range had been requisitioned. Would it be possible to learn the size of the oven so the bread pans and covered roaster I intended purchasing would fit? Another file quest and the dimensions were in hand, or rather down with other scribbled memoranda of requisitioned "furnishings," lampwicks; panes of glass and putty; innumerable lengths of stovepipe (I pictured them stowed in the ship's hold like cordwood); a set of sadirons; washboilers and brooms; mantles for the acetylene fixtures; oilcloth and tacks; and countless other items, all very necessary (I was to learn) to one's domestic comfort in the Arctic. With such attention as the Seattle office was giving to details, not alone for Wainwright but for every native school in the North, I was satisfied a comfy chair would not be lacking, and anyway it would be fun to experiment with hammer and saw on a packing case.

What books to take proved *the* problem. I was not forgetting that no "corner grocery" meant also *no* public library. But books are heavy things and my favorites were no feathers. A round of the bookshops proved discouraging. The old classics were not running any too generously, much less inexpensively, to thin-paper editions as yet, and I had not attained to one Arctic explorer's altruistic disregard for fine bindings to the point of tearing off handsome tooled covers to lighten the weight of supplies. I decided to take fewer books, but to choose these few from the many I loved, tantamount to some latent Arctic mood, I longed for the vision of a seer. This wishful speculation drew every book off the shelves before the chosen few, ten in the lot, were stacked ready to be boxed. (A hearty chuckle halts my pen here as I recall the sober study I gave to this business, the importance I attached to—but wait, this is no place to digress.) Two of these were stowed into my carryall, to serve as Baedekers when I should reach the Arctic coast. They were Beechey's *Narrative* and an old blue bound government report of the first schools in the North. The others were old stand-bys, well thumbed with memories, sentimental wings for thought excursions home perhaps, or to the garden I was leaving in the fullness of its fragrance.

You know how one always finds room for one more thing when a trunk is already filled to overflowing? Just so did I squeeze in some extra kindergarten crayons and a folder of sheet music (inspired by the new organ), a few yards of chintz, and the host of little trifles every woman will take with her when she plans to make a home in some far land.

Trading Station. See house. The Schoolhouse. The igloos. Meat racks.

WAINWRIGHT, ESKIMO VILLAGE

THE NAME WAINWRIGHT DATES BACK TO THE TIME when white men first sailed up this desolate coast, the year 1826, one of those heroic years of long searching for the Northwest Passage. A new route, it was to be, to the fabulous wealth of old Cathay—to the expedition of Captain Frederick William Beechey, one of England's noted hydrographers and a skillful navigator of that time. Beechey's voyage up the Arctic coast, through Bering Straits, in the summer of that year was made chiefly "to co-operate with the expeditions of Parry and Franklin, with the flattering expectation that the three commanders might meet in northern seas,"[1] at the same time, he was to make additions to the then known knowledge of the geography of the polar regions.

The "three commanders" did not meet, though Franklin and Beechey came within one hundred and sixty miles of doing so, but knowledge of the polar regions did go forward. You have only to glance at the map, noting there the names of many who had accompanied the expedition, to learn the extent of Beechey's survey. In

[1] BEECHEY (Capt. F. W.) *Narrative of a Voyage to the Pacific and Bering Strait* to co-operate with the Polar Expeditions performed in His Majesty's Ship *Blossom* in the years 1825-28. (London, 1831.)

mapping the wide inlet just south of my village, Beechey honored his gallant Lieutenant John Wainwright, and marked it thus on his polar chart of that long ago year. At Point Lay, the naturalist of the expedition was re-membered—another lieutenant at Point Belcher—and so on up the coast to "the farthest tongue of land which they reached, conspicuous as being the most northerly point yet discovered on the continent of America, and it was called Point Barrow, to mark the progress of northern discovery on each side of the American conti-nent, which *had* been so perseveringly advocated by that distinguished member of our naval administration."[2] (Sir John Barrow.)

Now, long before naval administrations were advo-cating polar exploration, the Eskimos had a name for this place Wainwright. An Eskimo name for a place is full of meaning: much more useful than some person's name on a map, or for a post office. When you hear it, if you understand the Eskimo language, it will tell you something. It may say, "this is the end of land," or "here the sun comes quickly," or may tell you "the place where the wind is made," and suddenly you will think of Laughing Water at Minnehaha, remembering other primitive peoples.

And then one day you arrive at "the place where storms are not very bad." You will be at Wainwright. I mean at *Al-gon-nik*.

You can see this is a name full of meaning. You would know it for certain, had you come to it at the end of thirty-four days of sailing, weary of heavy seas and adverse winds; sick of waggling in a narrow bunk in a

_____
2 Beechey's *Narrative*.

ship hove to—in a ship dragging anchor (dragging two anchors and losing one). Then to arrive at a "place where storms are not very bad," you would say that the Eskimos manifest a neat precision in this matter of naming their villages. However, Wainwright or *Al-gonnik*, I ran in luck to reach the place at all.

Few ships reached their destinations in Arctic Alaska in the summer of 1924. Three were caught in the ice pack and wrecked in the vicinity of Point Barrow during the first fortnight of August of that year. One of these, the fine Hudson's Bay Company's supply ship *Lady Kindersley*, was full cargoed and on its way to the trading posts of that company in the Canadian Arctic. The Liebes Company ship *Arctic*, was crushed thirty miles south of her destination, Point Barrow, while the small trading schooner *Duxbury*, met a similiar fate a few miles east of there. The veteran coast guard cutter *Bear*, always at hand to aid disabled vessels in these waters, had been nipped in the ice off Kotzebue early in July, damaged her rudder, and was obliged to return to a southern port for repairs; a humiliating retreat surely, for a gallant ship flying proud colors of undaunted valor in northern seas.

Thus it developed upon *our* little Bureau of Education ship *Boxer* (everyone in the school service possessed this little ship with their affections), to perform a twofold duty in the Arctic that year; her own, that of transporting teachers and supplies to the government schools and native villages along the coast, and the more arduous one, one for which she was not equipped, that of coast guard duty. How well the little craft performed this duty is now recorded in the annals of valorous deeds done in the Northland.

The thrilling rescue of twenty men, officers and crew of the *Lady Kindersley,* has been told by others who have faithfully pictured the harrowing experiences and the splendid heroism of the event. It comes into this story of Wainwright solely as the stirring incident which served as my introduction to the polar wastes. I met the Arctic in its most dreaded and unrelenting mood.

On the morning of August 16, *Boxer* slowly wedged her way through masses of floating ice debris to anchor before the tiny village I was to know as home. Even while the leadsman was calling the soundings, "half-five —quarter-five—five—," wireless dispatches were received from the *Lady Kindersley,* saying she was hopelessly fast in the ice, that her crew was building sleds preparing to abandon the vessel. At that time she was fifty miles east of Barrow, drifting with the northeast current, held in a vast moving swathe of ice, known as the "graveyard-drift" of the polar ice fields. Ice fields, in this part of the Arctic, extend to the Pole, and, save for short lanes of open water threading the face of the pack, are impenetrable.

In less than an hour *Boxer* was off for Point Barrow, and with as much speed as the tedious navigating through ice would permit, made her way up open lanes to within four miles of the wrecked ship.

The rescue was made on August thirty-first. Six Eskimos, accompanied by the second officer of the *Kindersley* and a representative of the Hudson's Bay Company, who had left his ship to secure a supply of fresh reindeer meat when she stopped at Barrow, set out from *Boxer* in a large native skin boat. And from the doomed ship came the men, mere black dots crawling over gray distances; men, who had been at the ship's pumps night and day, were now dragging ship's boats over a maze of floebergs; finding some relief in the short turns when they paddled across the narrow stretches of black water, only to drag the boats again over ice wastes—seemingly impassable at times—to where they met the rescue party. A brief halt for stimulants and first aid and they came on again. Hours of gruelling hardship—eons of tense and watchful waiting on *Boxer*. At last, one by one, over the rail they came, haggard and weary, an ashen nameless anguish there on their faces. Crumpled heaps of men on deck—away off in the gray silence, two masts marked a sinking ship—two masts and a bright British ensign.

Boxer returned to Barrow through an eternity of ice —through floebergs careening with deafening roar against the bow, hurling frozen spray, clattering like hail, over the ice-covered deck. The night lengthened to a day, and in the first quarter of the next midnight we were at Barrow taking on the crew of the wrecked schooner *Arctic,* together with eight men of the United States Geographical Survey, (they had charted the Meade River that summer and had expected to return south on the cutter *Bear*), and once again *Boxer* headed for the village of Wainwright. In a few hours we were running at half speed, in loose ice, rounding Point Belcher. A saffron horizon half veiled in wispy fog told us it was morning. Far to the south, the Stars and Stripes fluttered from a white building, the Wainwright schoolhouse. I made my way through the little salon, where exhausted men were crowded in sleep, to my stateroom to gather my belongings.

I was going to miss this little ship. Still more was I to

miss her goodly company of officers and crew. *Little ship*
indeed—one hundred and twenty-five feet long, thirty-
foot beam, limited quarters for the crew, four tiny state-
rooms for passengers—this was our *Boxer,* and when
smothered in cargo, as she had been for much of this
voyage, you may guess that all hands were bound to
frequent the one clear space on board, a small dining
salon below deck.

Here we assembled to eat "windjammer" specialties
served up by Barney three times a day, or his whopping
spice-sugared doughnuts with hot coffee at any hour.
Here we found snug comfort and relaxation. We played
cribbage, smoked fragrant (?) pipes, read the daily
"Radiogram," scribbled in voluminous notebooks, and
applauded our captain's genial tales, retold to beguile the
long hove-to hours, from his old logbook of adventures.
Here, on Saturdays, a barber shop was set up and a tai-
loring establishment (neat flour-sack patches on blue
dungarees), while Manuel, the Portuguese mess boy
strummed gay fandangos on his "ol' countree" guitar.
Here too, we spread bandages and aseptics and glittering
surgical instruments the day Barney's finger was crushed.
Ten gales blew in that day—havoc on deck! Terror in
the galley—Manuel on his knees imploring "Madre Dios
e Santa Pietro" to loosen Barney from the vice of a
jammed flour bin—a very devil of a day!.

And we talked shop too, lolling in those swivel chairs
around the captain's table, and wrote letters—reams and
reams of letters to the dearest ones—posting them at
every village where happened a post office.

All these we did and more, in the small dining salon
of *Boxer.*

In fair weather—"scarce as whale-feathers," the boatswain opined—we put up lines from deckhouse to masts and washed our clothes and aired the blankets, glad as any land housewife for the fine day. We rubbed sprouts off the potatoes, drying the sodden sacks in the sun, and cut spotted leaves from cabbages, thrifty of our supply of green produce, rarest of luxuries in the Arctic. In idle moments we loitered at the taffrail, feeding the roving kittiwakes, captivated by their grace and motion— or delighted in the antics of the tiny sea parrots, so astonished as they were swept spinning like tops in the swirling waters of our wake. Suddenly we would go tearing pellmell over oil drums and crates, dizzy in the rigging, whooping it up with, "Thar she blows," crazier than loons, whenever a spouting whale hove in sight.

But more often we were wrapped in furs, comfy in the shelter of the dory, intent on the unfolding panorama of Arctic shores; the ancient Silurian drama of limestone and chert, shale and marls. On the hills at Cape Prince of Wales curious rock formations lie scattered about, like broken statuary fallen from ruin of antiquity. On a sheltered ledge of this bleak rocky hillside, standing windowless and forlorn, gleams a small white building— the first school erected on the Arctic coast, where little brown savages first looked upon the printed word and called it "paper talk." Wales is the farthest point west on the continent, where we had only to turn our heads to see the mountains of Siberia across the Bering Straits.

We crossed the Arctic Circle at Kotzebue Sound, a vast basin for many rivers, where we saw amber-colored skin canoes filled with jolly Eskimos on their way to the fishing carnival at Kotzebue. Great village, Kotzebue!— where river Eskimos meet coast Eskimos to trade and make merry, while their scarlet hoard of salmon hangs drying in the sun. (I'm not telling of the seasons it hangs rotting in the rain.)

And whom should we meet here, at Kotzebue, but the noted Danish explorer and ethnologist, Dr. Knud Rasmussen, come to the end of his long journey from Greenland; three years crossing Arctic America on the fifth of his Thule expeditions devoted to the study of the Eskimo race. Picture his delight at finding here a great gathering of the little brown people, searching out their old culture, their old tales; meeting Eskimos from Selawik; Shungnak; Kiwalik; Noorvik; and other inland places. From *Boxer's* radio, the news went crackling to Copenhagen, Rasmussen's home in Denmark, for this was the first place from which the telegraphic word could be sent, that he and his two companions, Mitek and Anarulunguak, Greenland Eskimos, were safe and well.

Exciting days at Kotzebue! *Boxer's* diesel was overhauled, timely precaution for ice work ahead. There was a trip up the Kobuk as far as Noorvik, across Hotham Inlet, through the extensive delta waters of the wide gray river, winding between low stretches of dwarf willows and sedgy grasses and gay sweet flowers reeling with color. Forty-five miles up we nearly capsized the small launch at the sight of a few stunted spruces, the first trees we had seen since leaving home. Oh, the joy of branches, tiny fragrant branches, after miles and miles of barren treeless coast! At Noorvik, ninety miles inland, we came to real trees, tall and close as in a forest, and there, on a high glacial bluff overlooking the river, was the village. We came to real mosquitoes too. Or did they come to us? No matter, we survived to inspect the co-operative sawmill and the light plant owned and operated by Eskimos—see the log huts of their model village and the rafts of new lumber, to say nothing of the hospital and the school.

Save for the government superintendent and his family, the model village of Noorvik was deserted. The erstwhile millowners and electricians were gutting fish in high glee at Kotzebue. What of the nurses? Oh, they were at Kotzebue too. You see, the arrival of *Boxer* is the year's one red-letter event, eagerly awaited by the handful of white folks. Saints on high! They wouldn't miss it for a crown. If you could see them waiting for the mail! Sacks and sacks of mail!—the first since the last winter's sled mail, February or March maybe! Such scads of letters to paw through, searching out the fat ones from home, reading the pages between laughter and tears—everyone, teachers, traders, and nurses, contributing a share of the news from the great outside.

"The country is sure riding pretty with Coolidge at the helm" ... "Listen to this! Walnuts come vacuum-packed now, and they're canning celery!" ... "Some swell burg, Los Angeles! Say, that town's boomin' like a Fourth of July! You can fry the Arctic out of your bones down there."

Along with all this there was wry gossip of the coast, picked up here and there and passed around with coffee and cake.

" ... a brave little woman! packing their supplies all night and that big fat husband of hers sleeping like a full walrus" ... "*serves him right!* A missionary has no business trading." ... "My dear, you're not telling me she went alone with him—on a ten-day sled trip? How on earth did they manage at night?"

And you should see the supplies! Tons of supplies— the beach walled with freight—unloaded here at Kotzebue for the river school stations; and then, well, you must know what excitement there can be when handsome officers of a ship are ashore!

Were we really north of the Arctic Circle? How then to reconcile these warm and lovely days with the pictured Arctic Circle of our old geographies? This gentle stirring of tall grasses; this swift mating of birds; muskrats riffling the still waters; and the wild loons calling—the length and breadth of the land responding to the urge of the brief Arctic summer. We forgot old geographies. We forgot the racks of reeking fish along the shore. We forgot everything but the tranquil beauty of the scene which lay before us as *Boxer* weighed anchor and headed northward again.

There, in the receding purple distances, was the wide expanse of Kotzebue Sound, an expanse which seems to cleave the very continent. Small wonder the Russian navigator Otto von Kotzebue, who discovered this body of water in 1816, believed he had found the long sought-for passage to the Atlantic! And very well pleased he was with his exploit, when he landed and had tea on Chamisso Island and declared he had never felt happier than here in this lonely spot. With his tea he had broiled partridge and hare which his men had caught in great numbers. We surmise the welcome change from ship's fare may have been responsible for much of his pleasure. Incidently, Kotzebue remembered the botanist of this expedition, when he named the island Chamisso. And here we may well mention another naturalist, our own beloved John Muir, who enjoyed in this sound, in its environs of inlets, rivers, capes, and islands, the richest field for his observations when he cruised the Arctic in 1881, collecting data for his notable work on the glaciation of the North Islands.

These are the splendid latitudes, where in July and August, the midnight sun gilds a shimmering path down the waters from the north horizon, where rose and lilac mists festoon the highlands of Krusenstern and Thompson, and every little valley is a green and flowered carpet.

Farther north we came to the long low sandspit of Point Hope, like a clean slender finger pointing to westward, where a village of the dead lies under bleaching bones of whale, stark mementos of the old whaling days when women wore "stays," and whale-oil lamps lighted the homes of New England. Here is the ancient ground of an ancient Eskimo people, where larkspurs are likely to build their nests in human skulls, while forget-me-nots riot to make a blue meadow. Eskimos still have a populous village here, and here they still hunt the whale, but the whaling fleet comes no more to seek safe anchorage, nor to meet in accustomed rendezvous.

True north the compass read as we came to the great old headland of Lisburne, its dark outline veiled in the ceaseless winging of countless sea birds, the nesting place for thousands of auklets, guillemots, and gulls. Was it the storm or the sight of an alien thing, our scudding ship, that sent them flying about like heavy flakes of snow, their wild screams heard eerily above the wind?

North by east-half-east now, and fair sailing with the prevailing two-mile current, past Point Lay and the quiet silver waters of the Kasegaluk Lagoon, to come to Icy Cape, the bleakest spot on all the Arctic coast if not the bleakest in the world. As if here the earth were lying still in death, wrapped in winding cerement of dreary glacial plain—the tundra going on and on interminably.

"Where does it end?" and "Why are we?" we asked ourselves, as we contemplated (in the snug shelter of the dory) the impenetrable mystery of creation, the long eroding processes of time, reading in this coastal scene of austere beauty the mighty granitic saga of the glacial ages.

The steady purring rhythm of the ship grew fitful. A block of ice went careening by. Someone shouted from the pilothouse—Heavens! we all went dashing over the oil drums again to be awed by a strange light on the north horizon—white and glittering, as if one million Super-Mazdas were sweeping a field of lilies—the Iceblink! Clear sunlight reflected from the infinite facets of the ice pack, a phenomena one of us had never seen before.

Beautiful days—fair weather on *Boxer*. Yes! I was going to miss this little ship.

Everything happened at once. Manuel led off by taking my luggage on deck. Barney came up with a pot of hot coffee. "Ship or shore, 'tis a long wait to breakfast— I tell ye, a mug of black Java. . . ." I drank it gratefully. (Had I known what the day was to bring I would have drained the pot.) *Boxer* rattled her anchorage in floe ice, a veritable floating jigsaw puzzle of floes. The fog had lifted. The village with its low mounded igloos appeared as a huddle of weathered brown haycocks, sepia dark against the lemon sky of early morning. The school-house, standing apart and on somewhat higher ground, seemed to be floating on its purple shadow which lay like a dark pool before it. The one bright spot in the picture was Old Glory. I could have counted every star, so taut was it held in the steady blow of the northeast wind.

The Eskimos came from everywhere—bobbing up between the igloos like children playing hide-and-seek, dashing down to the shore shouting as they leaped over the shore ice into their canoes, to race in noisy excitement out to the ship. Other canoes hurried from an open lead beyond the drift ice where their crews had been hunting walrus. With a deft swish of paddles they shunted the ice and brought their skin boats alongside. And how these Eskimos could climb a ship's ladder! Nimble as squirrels—and just as chattery. The arrival of *Boxer* was something more than a mere red-letter day at Wainwright. Here was a real event, the town out and giddy with color, a festive rainbow holiday with the women and children decked in bright flowered calicos and circus-pink ginghams, ribbons in their hair and tassels on their boots. What if the colorful cotton garments were worn mainly to protect their more sombre furs, they cut a dash all the same. And *Boxer's* deck hummed with gala merriment.

A jolly receiving line we made, captain and crew, everybody shaking hands—the Eskimos shaking and bowing—and learning, without any effort at all, the Eskimo expressions of joy and gladness—*"Ah-re-gah!"*— *"Na-guruk!"*—*"Aiyah!"*—*"Aiyah ah-regah!"* The Eskimos went into a huddle around the captain, greeting him as the brave *"Oo-malik,"* and ran their hands over the deckhouse and railings, saying, *"Boxer, oo-miak-puk na-guruk! Ah-regah!"* No one had to interpret that for us. Plain as plain that *Boxer* was a fine ship.

And the children! Brown as hazelnuts, their round faces half tucked away in the hoods of their garments, one eye on the lookout for Barney's domain where they were sure of a treat. Barney delighted in these children of the igloos. "Ain't they the shy little devils," he would say, "I gives 'em a plum, and they runs to their mithers like a deer shure frighted." But the next minute the mothers were pushing their dears forward and he was filling greasy little fists with raisins and prunes, telling them how I had made his finger well—that I was going to teach them how to read and write and care for their fingers too, going on with his talk, as if they had been the children of his own county Kilkenny, understanding all his blarney.

Meanwhile the winches were rattling freight out of the hold and lowering it to the native boats waiting alongside. Crates, boxes, the organ, school and medical supplies, food supplies, my sewing machine and Victrola, drums of gasoline and drums of kerosene—all were taken to shore by the Eskimos and carried to the schoolhouse. Presently my luggage was going over the side. A slow lump gathered in my throat as I made ready to follow it.

It wasn't easy to say farewell—not to Captain Whit-lam and fine officers, nor to Barney and Manuel, or to the Eskimo boys who made up the crew. One does not meet up with such fellowship every day—every day for thirty-four days—pressed down and running over, enough to assure the grand memory of it a joy forever.

No, it wasn't easy and besides I was too suddenly aware that five thousand miles lay between me and home. Throughout the long journey, in some inexplicable way, *Boxer* had held me—as a lengthening chain can hold—to home, anchored there round a hearth, safe with the dearest ones. Now, here above the seventieth parallel, I was letting go the last link reluctantly and with a numbing dread for what lay before me: the untried experience of being an only white woman in a village of nearly three hundred Eskimos.

It proved an unsteady moment, an inkling of which had never clouded the joyous days of packing and planning. Not that there hadn't been times for sober reflection—with the warnings of friends on all sides! Ten days of their babel! So here it was, their croaking chorus of "I-told-you-so's," caught up with me! Well, I would let them know—write them that I kept my handkerchiefs dry and with a gay bravado.

But ships do not tarry in these waters, and teachers do not loiter on deck when luggage is waiting in a skin boat alongside. We come to bless such exigencies of Arctic leave-takings. The difficult farewells are lost in a jamboree of banter; in a firm handclasp through the pilot-house window; another at the rail; then a long reach from the ship's ladder for a last glad hand, and it's "Good Luck," and "Don't eat too much blubber," and "We'll be seeing you next year!" Heartening gestures! "Bye, captain! Bye, everybody!"

One is not pre-occupied with nostalgia for long when facing fifteen brown smiling faces—eyes shining through mere slits with all their smiling—glad, happy Eskimos paddling their new teacher to shore. The ice clinked like musical glasses about us. We could have walked ashore had we dared to jump from one floe to the next, so full of ice was the stretch of water between ship and shore. The beach was strewn with muddy ice debris. The late southwest storm had swept new ice over this, clean blue slabs of it like enormous sapphires, piling up a bulwark of them all along the shore. We landed on the slippery stuff. One of the men carried me over the knee-deep slush. He waded through it with sure stride—despite his awkward burden—and never let me down until he had reached the path atop the bluff which led to the schoolhouse. Somewhat bewildered I turned to thank him, but he had disappeared below the bank. I wondered if I would recognize him to do so later. Eskimo

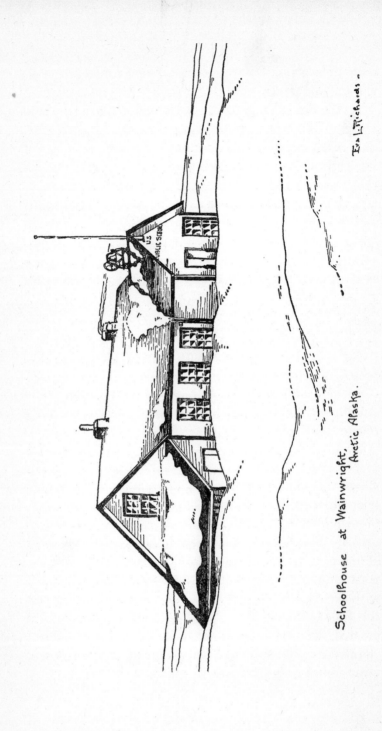

Schoolhouse at Wainwright,
Arctic Alaska.

Eva L. Richards.

men all looked alike to me. But I remembered that he was tall and strong-armed and walked on young feet.

At the top of the bluff the path made a sharp turn and there, on a tussock of tawny grass, sat an old woman. She looked like a little live mummy, as if faded old brown silk had puckered around her sunken lips and keen old eyes and over the tiny bird claws of her hands. As soon as I came up she let loose such a babble of glad little sounds as I had ever heard. And no end to shaking hands again. She pointed to *Boxer,* rubbed her legs and hobbled about, back and forth as if in great distress, moaning too as if in pain, then pointed to the ship again. All this pantomime was to say:

"Tooklamora is full of desire to journey out to the ship ... but Tooklamora has now many years in her bones ... a ship's ladder is a rack of pain to old bones and there is no pleasure in pain ... a tussock of grass in the sun is like a pillow of duck down under young lovers ... a warm place for glad waiting."

And all the while her tongue was alive with glad little sounds, the inflections of the Eskimo language revealing the joy in its welcome.

I waited near the path for the men to come up with my luggage. Along the bank were the mounds of the igloos and high racks that seemed alive with a ragtag assortment of skins and furs flapping in the wind. Near the igloos were piles of dark bloody meat. It was walrus time in Wainwright. On the ship the natives had told of the unusual catch this season, the winter's supply of meat assured for men and dogs in plenty. The raw skulls with their gleaming ivory tusks lay in tumbled heaps on the grass. The intestines of these animals, cleaned and inflated, were strung about the village like ballooned clotheslines. The stomachs and bladders too, were blown, great amber globes swaying in the sun.

Up and down the village the tethered dogs howled and yelped their state of mind over the stranger who was on her way to the schoolhouse. And up and down the bank went a procession of Eskimos still busy carrying boxes and supplies. And with a hearty curiosity for everything they carried. There was no peeking behind lace curtains here, to comment on what the neighbors were moving in. Theirs was an open-and-above-board sincere inquisitiveness to learn more of the wonderful (?) white man's possessions. So they turned the boxes this way and that; they traced the letters of whatever was stamped upon them, calling on the ones who could read for the interpretation, which, more often than not, proved more puzzling than ever.

"What was this, 'Handle with Care?' Was it the teacher's name? *Na-ga!* Teacher's name on that big box (my trunk). Maybe something to eat. And what that mean, 'Keep in a Cool Place?' Maybe that box for other village. Maybe ask captain. 'T-h-i-s s-i-d-e u-p.' *Ai-yah!* white mans make funny words." So they turned the box over to see what was on the other side, and they set it down so in the schoolroom. They held a long deliberation over the organ crate. They walked around it solemn like. Whatever could be in a box shaped like that? This teacher had queer things brought to Wainwright. But it wasn't so queer when the crate was opened. A touchdown in the last minute of an Army-Navy game might come up to what followed. The very tundra melted under the warmth of the tumultuous song-and-dance welcome they gave that organ. *"Aiyah! -ai-yah!! Moosik! Moo-sik! Aiyah-ai-yah!"* On my word, it was as if the population of the village had suddenly doubled, so eager and happy were they to carry that organ to the schoolroom right side up with care. Altogether, moving in at Wainwright was as exciting as a circus come to town.

In these far northern settlements the transfer of teachers is always accompanied by more or less confusion due to the uncertain time of the ship's arrival. The season of navigation is short, open ice from about August first to September fifteenth, but even then adverse winds may close the open leads in a few hours, making delays inevitable. The retiring teachers are obliged to leave, of course, on the same ship which brings the new teachers, and their departure must necessarily be a hurried one. Trunks and bags are rushed out when the first mast has been sighted and there is a wild scramble. My arrival at Wainwright was no exception to this customary albeit hasty routine.

The out-going teachers, a young man and his wife, were tearing around in frantic circles. Their breakfast had been a snatched meal. Burnt toast and bacon aromas hovered in the entrance hall where all was disorder. Boxes were being packed and nailed, trunks yawned with a confusion of clothing, dishes and books about them, while, from some inner sanctum, their baby demanded attention with no small voice. To add to their distress, the Eskimos were busy lightering the freight from the ship, leaving few natives at hand to hustle their luggage to the beach.

There was nothing to do but wait and presently I found myself seated in the dim schoolroom surveying empty desks and the jumbled assortment of boxes, crates, and bales, which the men had piled high against the walls, in front of the windows, sharply crowding the cupboards and doors. In front of me gaped the new kitchen range, lidless and doorless, as if mutely begging for a few warming coals—a bleak and cheerless sight. I wondered where the lids and doors could be, where to begin the search for them. From the dark smoky ceiling a broken mantle hung from the acetylene fixture. Soot dripped from the sections of stovepipe which led off in zigzag angles from a huge cannon-ball heater in the center of the room. I thought about the children who would occupy the desks next to the huge thing: roasting on one side, freezing on the other, maybe. Around the grimy walls stretched the smudged blackboard spaces with their troughs of chalk dust and worn erasers. Hairs shed from fur clothing strewed the floor like bits of straw in a threshing barn.

The task of evolving order out of this chaotic muddle quite overwhelmed me. It was all so unreal, so difficult and complicated. There swept over me the feeling that the easiest way out was to escape. And this, I well knew, was the surest way of plunging head on into greater difficulties—but such an arm-chair-before-the-fire philosophy completely eluded me on this cold gray morning. Thin shivery icicles began to prickle up and down my spine. To ward off a chill I got up to examine the cupboards, but with boxes jammed against them, the doors would not budge beyond an inch and I was in no mood to move freight. But in that inch I made a discovery.

The walls had been painted white and not the dingy gray they appeared to be. What they needed was a good scrubbing and with plenty of soap and hot water. The thought of something *hot* revived my courage. I went on to the blackboards. They were fabric boards and much worn. Useless to wish for new ones in this hour. Black paint would improve them, but I had not noticed black paint on the requisitions. Perhaps *Boxer* had some aboard. Given paint and soap and time, things would soon look different. I wondered what needed to be done in the teacher's quarters. Where was I to sleep and eat? It was nearly eight o'clock and breakfast still as remote as if I had been lost on some desert. I thought of Barney's hot pancakes all luscious with butter and strawberry jam. I thought of the cold ones too, I had pilfered to coax the gulls with. Even burnt toast was beginning to smell like all heaven.

I was sorting pencils in a littered desk drawer when Nasholook came in. I had met Nasholook on *Boxer*. He was the interpreter for the village and we had talked about the freight. He had just come ashore. "Please, Missus Eva," he began, "you come see that Anakok's boy what got sick arm. Please you make that boy for hospital on ship *Boxer*. Captain say he take that boy. Captain say teacher see boy and medicine that arm." No time for questions and "medicine" always a part of my emergency kit, I picked it up and followed Nasholook through the hubbub of the hall into the fresh cool morning.

Three minutes later I was crawling into an igloo. (Old geographies did better with the igloos. You can see the entrance will not permit the more dignified (?) way of entering this queer inverted bowl of a dwelling). I made no attempt to identify the smells which rolled up as I crept through the long passage. I was too intent on the job before me to notice what could be raising such a ruction, what might be sticking to my shoes or maybe on the hem of my skirt. And then I saw the boy, about ten years of age he was, lying on a heap of skins in the middle of the place. Nasholook explained how five hours before the child had caught his arm in the flywheel of the trader's launch. It was a messy fracture, with a case of shock to treat besides. God! how long had I been in the schoolroom—entertaining thoughts of escape—fussing with pencils—and here a child in agony!

The plucky little fellow never uttered a cry while I redressed the arm, for someone had applied a splint of sorts and with it a crude bandage. Working over the discolored and twisted flesh in the dusky dimness, lighted only by an amber-colored gut window just over my head, it was as if I had suddenly stumbled upon the broken child in some dark nightmare. The air was thick and heavy with peculiar smells, like as wet green hides and mouldy wood together. I longed to bury my face in the pack of gauze and cotton I was shaping. Never had the stuff smelled so clean, so bracingly clean.

After what seemed an interminable time, I came to the last strip of adhesive. The lad's mother had gone to the trading store for a new shirt, pathetic errand revealing a primitive mother's love. Her child was hurt and *they* were taking him away—she might never see him again—and his fur shirt was ruined past mending. She returned with a man's size undershirt and pridefully smoothed the gray folds of it as I cut the sleeve and fastened it about with safety pins from the kit. The child smiled wanly as I dried his face and told him how quickly he was going to be well with the good doctor at the hospital. (You remember Nasholook is interpreting.)

His father contrived a toboggan of a reindeer hide to take him through the passage, then carried him to the waiting dory. A profound sense of relief came over us, when, after watching the dory struggle with the ice, we saw him lifted to the deck, safely in the ship's sling. At once his mother wanted to know when her boy would return home. It would be a year before a ship could come again. Would he come with Panigeo on the first winter mail sled? She scarcely understood about X-rays and the urgent need of surgical attention for such an injury, or how distant was the hospital at Nome. *Boxer* was to make a non-stop run to Nome; the shipwrecked men were to be transferred to a steamer there. The mother looked out to the ship again, long and wistfully.

When the dory returned, the teachers and their baby (fast asleep now) were ready to go aboard. "Gosh! but we're glad," they declared, "so glad to be going home —back to God's country." They looked tired. Having their baby in the Arctic had been an exhausting experience for the young couple. Something they said too, about leaving the "rooms in such a mess." Lucky they did. It put me in mind of the paint. I waded through slush to ask the boatswain about it. Said he thought they had some funnel paint. "Would that be good for blackboards?" "Shure, I painted my Ford with it once —I'll drop it in one of the native boats—there's a couple of 'em out to the ship yet." With that they shoved off, all of us shouting across the ice, waving our arms like so many animated semaphores, "Good-bye—Good-bye!"

The natives had come up on the bank now, the children still munching their precious prunes and raisins. The men and boys sat down on the grass, weary (so I thought then) of hauling freight and poling ice. The women crowded round, as women have a way of doing when they would comfort a lost child—or welcome a new minister. (Perhaps I had taken on the aspects of both.) The busy excitement on the beach was over. Together we watched, as the glad teachers climbed the ship's ladder, heard the rattle of the windlass as the dripping dory was hoisted to the deck, then the "Anchors aweigh!"

Slowly *Boxer* made her way to open water, gathering speed as she turned southward, gathering speed and growing smaller, until all we could see was a tiny nick cutting the bright horizon.

Godspeed, and a fond farewell, little ship!

"Boxer, oo-miak-puk na-guruk!"

The next thing was to search through the motley of crates for rolled oats and canned milk, coffee, bacon, something—anything—for breakfast. What a time! The natives were just wonderful. Every one of them offered to help: every last two hundred of them. It was then Nasholook took matters in hand, like one accustomed to smoothing out a new teacher's dilemmas, and for the next few minutes I was spending my time in this wise: "Now see if I can remember—your name is Akadrigak—and yours is Sungaravik—and yours—oh dear, have I forgotten—yes, of course, you are Mayuenna." "Yesh," and suddenly the sun was shining on snow. No slip of my memory was ever rewarded by so ravishing a smile. Oooh! the dazzling dental health of it! Mayuenna shyly hid it in the fur of her hood. She was a young girl, one of the belles, I guessed, of the village. Sungaravik was a lively lad, bright and pleasantly aware of the importance of his English vocabulary. Akadrigak was a man of family, a very numerous family. He told off the names of his children—seems

they would all attend school. Before he finished I knew
I was going to dispense with roll call of mornings. Roll
calls were instituted for Mary Jones and Tom Brown,
never for Kangataluk, Ahmayurak, Nuleachuk, and
Kavisikluk. Just the same, I went on repeating—Akadrigak—Sungaravik—Mayuenna—over and over again.
These three, Nasholook assured me, were "very helping
quickly people." They were.

They opened the boxes, carefully removing each nail.
Sungaravik straightened the crooked ones, and sorted
them in neat piles on the window sills. They smoothed
and folded the packing papers, saving every little scrap,
for later use in kindling fires. With elaborate patience
they untied each length of cord and twine to carefully
coil and wind it as fishermen wind small lines. They put
by every piece of wood, pausing now and again to admire the fine boards of the organ crate, commenting on
their width and thickness and their smooth surface, and
were curious too, about the metal strips which had rein-
forced it. Finally, they uncovered a case of packaged
figs and rye crackers. Had someone yelled "Thar she
blows," I could not have been over the desks any faster.
Finding ready-to-eat food in such confusion of boxes
and in a melee of schoolbooks, bedding, drugs, and stove
lids, was to say the least nothing short of miraculous.
My "helping quickly" guests were as excited as children
round a cookie jar.

Mayuenna's smile came out of her hood to beam on
figs. Akadrigak put down his hammer to investigate
this pressed fruit. He separated the layers with eager
expectancy, like a man who lifts pie crust to first feast
his eyes on the filling. Sungaravik spelled the words on
the packages. F-i-g-s, which he somehow made out to

be "sriks." C-r-a-c-k-e-r-s, "clackus," pleased to learn these new words. Pleased to eat figs and crackers too. The pet notions I had always held about Eskimos eating nothing but seal and whale blubber, vanished like snow in hot water. I hasten to spread the news that Eskimos eat figs and rye crackers. Saints! with what a grand gusto they eat them!

And with what keen connoisseuring of flavor! Akadrigak was full of praise (I almost said figs) : said figs had "the good taste of young birds that have been long cured in seal oil." He talked slowly as if he were eating small portions of wings between his words. Not so Mayuenna. Her words fairly bubbled together—soft Eskimo words with little quick accents here and there coming from between her cheeks—to say that figs tasted more like the fine fat shrimps her grandmother had found in the stomach of the big walrus that morning. *"Aiyah na-guruk—na-guruk!"* Came a rousing cheer of *na-gu-ruk-s,* as if Mayuenna had conjured up a full platter of these tasty kickshaws with her words—smacking good stuff Mayuenna could think of—*na-guruk!* I opened another package of figs, as if I were pouring another cup of coffee, just to prolong this unique breakfast with its convivial talk of pickled birds and pre-digested sea food —the hors-d'oeuvre, the caviar, you could guess, of the igloo banquets. No French chef beaming over some culinary masterpiece ever radiated such gustatory delight as did these brown faces praising the wonder and goodness of white man's food: praising it in flattering simile of their own delicacies. It was no moment to turn pea-green squeamish over juicy morsels garnered from walrus innards. *"Sriks—na-guruk!"* It was time to pass the figs again.

English to Eskimo—Eskimo to English—conversation
flowed in and out of Nasholook—a merry lot of it. We
talked about everything—just the kind of talk you
would expect when folks are getting acquainted. I
seized upon it as a preliminary introduction to my
village—to the forty families who lived in Wainwright
and about twenty more from the near villages of Attanik and Icy Cape and Point Lay who come to Wainwright every summer for the walrus hunting, not to
mention, "they likes to see ship *Boxer*, Missus Eva";
they come every winter too, for the "good dancing" at
Christmas time. They were pleased to tell me that my
little "live mummy" friend was Tooklamora, the oldest
woman in the village, and that someone named Tomaichuk was "that very old man of Eskimos." It needed
no interpreting to perceive the respect they held for
these old people, or to feel their quick sympathy when
they told me of Tingook's mother, who, they said, had
not "walk that many long time of days now." Nasholook would take me to see this invalid.

With open-eyed admiration they told me of Captain
Roald Amundsen, and of his two airplanes down at the
inlet; how his Lieutenant Omdal had built the skis for
one of the planes, "sled runners to runs on that ice for
time they comes down for land." It proved a costly
experiment (the world knows) ; a cruel disappointment.
Akadrigak happened to be down at the inlet getting
coal the day Lieutenant Omdal made the test flight and
had witnessed the mishap: the improvised gear shattered
to matchwood when the plane grounded. Akadrigak
said it made a noise like "many breaking duck eggs."
"They wants to fly to Pole places, Missus Eva," and
from the tone of Akadrigak's words, stressed in Nasho-

look's trick of interpreting, you could just know that flying had better be left to the birds—winged machinery for going places was much too uncertain.

A team of dogs now, or reindeer—*Aiyah!* that was traveling! Goodness! a good sled deer could take one places fast enough. Koosik or Matook or Anashugak could tell me about that: "those herder boys knows to drives that sled deer many places all the quickly." But Nasholook did tell me about the dogs. "All the families owns dogs, Missus Eva. The peoples drives to the trapping places and to whale camp and they likes to see their cousins down to Point Lay. Peoples has parents sometimes. They gets very lonesome for happy talk to parents. Now the peoples has to own good leader dogs. Those good leader dogs comes from puppies. The womans feeds those puppies plenty soup. They grows big for knowing many good trails."

Nasholook went on to tell of Otoiyuk's leader, what an intelligent dog he was, and how fast Neokok's team could travel, and Kootook's fine dog "that female is eight puppies now." So there we were, brushing crumbs off the desks and planning trips—sledding to Attanik and to the inland country—with reindeer up the Kuk River—with dogs down to the inlet, a sled trip to Maudheim, as Amundsen had named his depot on the inlet. "That is not far places, that Maudheim, is good trip for puppies when comes first time to harness— that is good trip for teacher, Missus Eva, you likes that trip." I wasn't so sure when Sungaravik added, "those puppies gets plenty tired."

We made great strides getting settled in the afternoon. The men carried the flour and sugar, rice and such foods as would not be affected by zero temperatures, to the convenient storage upstairs. As a fire precaution, some of these supplies were stored in the icehouse. The canned fruits, vegetables, and milk, would need to be coddled in warm storage, so we lined the wall spaces of the pantry and kitchen and remembered the advice of the superintendent at Noorvik to "stack your cases with the label ends out . . . when you want grapefruit you don't want peas." And it surely looked as if I was stacked up for ten years.

What with seeing to the storage I soon made the rounds of the building. It was downright cheering to have schoolrooms and living quarters—yes, even a huge bin accommodating over four tons of coal—all under one roof. I had been hearing so many stories about Arctic weather interrupting school work—snow-smoking blizzards days on end—teachers floundering through drifts, lost, half-frozen—that sort of thing. I recalled the separate cottage housing the teachers down at Shishmaref[3] and the great iron chain suspended from its door to the schoolhouse, something to grope for link by link, your head bowed before the blizzardy wilderness— something to keep one awake too, they said, with the wind a nightmare, wishing the clanking jangling thing could be silenced deep in the snows forever. And at Sinuk[4] they marked the way with sacks of coal and the teachers spent half the winter digging themselves, to say nothing of their fuel, out of the drifts. Well, I would not be tussling with chains or shovels of mornings, not with quarters just around the corner from the schoolroom, if three halls between breakfast and the blackboards can be called a corner. It certainly was

---

[3] Eskimo village sixty miles north of Wales.
[4] Methodist Mission thirty miles northwest of Nome, now abandoned.

cheering. And that coal bin looked awfully good in the entrance hall.

In the middle hall, where the stairs went up to the storage loft, there were primus stoves and lanterns on a shelf, and some queer, broad-bladed tools Nasholook said were ice knives and, because I knew nothing about ice knives, he went on to explain that "the boys needs those ice knives when they cleans the teacher's water." I wanted to ask another question but he had opened the door of a storage closet under the stairs and was telling me about the kegs of nails and extra panes of glass and coal buckets, and some ice saws hanging just inside. I pretended to know all about ice saws.

The third hall (so many halls had me guessing too) opened directly on my combination office-dispensary-living room with its small bedroom alcove and of course, the large kitchen and pantry. Here the painted walls were really white, and a heavy linoleum helped to keep the wind under the floors. There was another smaller schoolroom at the north end of the building, serving that year as temporary quarters for the native co-opera-tive store. Adjoining was the dog shelter and a shed for sleds and equipment, a good place to store kindling and packing papers, we decided.

Besides the spacious loft on the second floor (Nasho-look conducted me all over the place), there were two extra sleeping rooms furnished with small heaters and army cots. Would you believe it! Guest rooms in the Arctic! for "sometimes the missionary doctor he comes when young peoples likes to marry, Missus Eva."

"And when will that be, Nasholook?"

"Those young peoples likes to marry all the time, but that doctor he say he come time for resurrection."

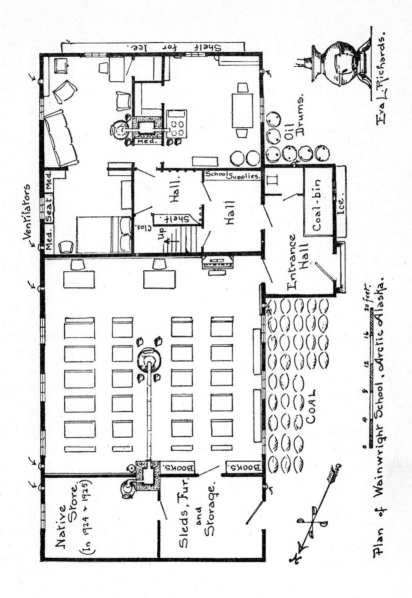

Plan of Wainwright School, Arctic Alaska.

Eva L. Richards.

From a roundabout question or two I learned that I could look for company about Easter time. Making a home in the Arctic was surprisingly exciting!

I set Mayuenna to washing the shelves in the pantry while I hunted up an apron and the brooms and the roll of white oilcloth and a package of tacks, and found the pillows to make the bed, and—oh, but before this I had to open the windows. What with the stuffy days of closed portholes and a nose full of dust from packing cases—right away I stepped across the room to open them. And right away I was ready to tell the builders of Arctic schoolhouses any number of things, but I'll skip these remarks (we forget bruised flesh), and go on to tell you that up in this corner of the world windows are fixed affairs, thick glassed and stoutly framed, never opened for fresh air. We open ventilators instead: tight little boxlike chutes set into the walls, high up near the ceiling in each room, with adjustable shutters worked with a pull-cord gadget. Talk about effective air conditioning! Whew! how the air did blow in!

Mayuenna had the time of her life washing those shelves. Soap and water was a combination of kitchen aids entirely foreign to Mayuenna—somewhat rare, as I had seen, around an igloo: all the same, she knew what to do with it. Her first timid swishes were soon venturing a mountainous steam of suds. Oooh! it was fascinating stuff!—smooth as blubber to sweep across a shelf in sleek and swirly patterns, or dabble from her fingers in dripping chains of bubbles, or swoop up in one blobby handful and squeeze out again to little, light, whipped puffs, like creamy pudding she could make with reindeer fat and seal oil, kneading and beating them, a foamy mess together.

Mayuenna would make one of these puddings every time Sulik came to the village. He would come to get a supply of tea, or tobacco, or it might be a bottle of liniment, for his aged parents who lived up at Attanik. Sulik liked fat puddings, very especially Mayuenna's. He liked those toothsome bits of seal flipper she always put in them, nippy like currants in plum duff between his teeth.

"I gets lonesome for that seal flippers," he would say. "Honest, Missus Eva, my eyes grows full of crying for that flippers." All the time I knew the passage to his mother's igloo was lined with wooden pots full of seal flippers—but dear me! what I started to say was, the shelves were shining. And in no time at all they were full up with an assortment of groceries in glass jars, tins, and canisters, and I was hearing a chorus of *na-guruks* again. Figs? Oh no! Just a picture of tomatoes on a can.

Every five steps I was at the windows. The igloos— the dogs—those curious up-in-the-air platforms—were all an intriguing sight. Mid-distant, I could trace the dark line of shore curving down to the inlet; beyond that, the blue-gray smudge of lonely distances. It gave me a comfortable feeling to have the igloos so near: three of them near enough to be just across the street, only instead of a street there was a swampy pattern of coffee-colored puddles with patches of tawny grasses between.

Something was going on in the village. I could see the women hurrying to the edge of the bank, and the children, so shyly teetering on their heels just outside the kitchen windows, were running off now to join them. Nasholook, halfway to the icehouse, came back on the run to tell me the last of the oomiaks had come in loaded with walrus. I wanted to see a walrus—a complete walrus, not a pile of meat. But I wanted to see the new range set up more, so I stood by with lengths of stove-pipe and pieces of wire, lending a hand to Akadrigak who was carefully busy with all this. Sungaravik was waiting with kindling and paper to start the fire. He had filled six buckets with coal, three for the kitchen, the others he set beside the cannon-ball heater in the living room.

When the range job was finished my helpers went down to the beach to help unload the walrus. The boys who had rolled up the oil drums were down there too. They got away before I could ask them where they had put the kerosene—where the gasoline? I staggered on the thought of filling a lamp with gasoline. Thanks to the homeward-bound teachers, the lamps were filled well enough for the night, so I collected yeast and salt and got around to the making of bread. I could hardly wait to experiment with dehydrated potatoes and dry yeast and to try the twenty-odd bread recipes I had collected on my way up the Arctic coast. Every teacher, yes, and the traders and missionaries, each had their own pet method for making bread or making yeast and all sorts of schemes for keeping the sponge warm in winter weather. One teacher used hot water bags, another warm sand, still another had a shelf for her pans up under the chimney and one of the nurses down at Kotzebue declared, "You can't make good bread in this country unless you sleep with the sponge," and because I was taking this for a bit of a jest, someone chimed in, "Believe it or not, she really did—used to put the mixture in a big roasting pan, fix the cover with adhesive tape, wrap it up in a quilt and take it to bed. 'Beats a husband,' she would say, setting it down in the kitchen next morning, all light and ready to be made into loaves."

In all these discussions no one had mentioned a good oven. I thought it half the battle and was mighty glad a new range had been requisitioned for Wainwright. And high time too, I thought, with the top of the old one so warped the kettles sat askew and the oven a makeshift of patched tin. (Precious little did I know what a new stove could look like at the end of a year in the Arctic.)

I set my sponge and then made corn bread for supper. Something of a culinary innovation to be using powdered eggs and powdered milk, sifting them, if you please, with the more familiar dry ingredients of flour and meal, salt and baking powder—simply adding water to make this hot bread—and it was all done in a twinkling. It looked as if the work of cooking my own meals was going to mean nothing more than opening a can. I would not have to peel potatoes, or wash spinach, or weep over the onions—not even a milk bottle to set out—just hang a gunny sack up in the hall to catch the empty tins—when full dump them out, away out on the sea ice for the foxes and polar bears to sniff over.

With a blue linen cloth on the table, a jar of marmalade and a pot of tea, oh, and a little yellow bowl filled with the flowers a friend had pinned on my coat the morning I sailed (they last longer when artificial, she had said) the evening of my first day found me very much at home. Perhaps, *At Home,* would be more like it, for I had no sooner cleared away the supper things when my first callers arrived—the hunters from the oomiaks come to shake hands with the new teacher and

to bring (Heaven bless the boatswain!) the paint for
the blackboards. And who should be with them but the
tall young-footed lad who had carried me ashore. His
name was Tooruk. It was he who had brought the paint
and he lost no time telling me that he knew very well
how to paint blackboards. The hunters had had adventures aplenty after *Boxer* had sailed—hunting and
shooting walrus. No one could tell how many big ones
had gotten away. What with the wind shifting the ice
and hauling their boats and meat over the floes—what
a time they had getting back to the village! Nasholook,
of course, came in to interpret all this, and soon half
the village was trailing through the halls.

They crowded in, sat on the floor, the benches and
boxes—they cramped onto the window sills until I
wondered if there might not, after all, be some truth in
what the croakers had said, about being buried alive.

My helper Akadrigak came with his wife Kittik and
all their children and Angashuk with his wife and his
wife's sister, all padded in fine lustrous parkas.[5] I wondered if these might be the first families of Wainwright.
There was venerable Otoiyuk with his wife Ekalook and
their adopted daughter who presented me with a frozen
fish while she hid her pretty face in her furs. Old Tooklamora came and Keruk from Attanik. There was Negovanna and his family, with apologies for the absence
of two of his sons, "herder boys at reindeer herd No. 2,"
he said, and promised to send them in next time they
came to the village for seal meat. Shyly following after
came four "sweet debutantes," Tigalook, Nowlik, and
Anavak, and my Mayuenna, her smile more dazzling
than ever, all of them lovely and as graceful as fawns,

---

[5] Fur garment—sometimes called an artiga, tiga, or teegee.

TIGALOOK.

Eva Louise Richards.

NOWLIK

Eva Louise Richards
1925

"the sea," no doubt, "calm before their dwellings." To-komek, a neat and comely widow, came with her three small daughters. They made no more protest than stuffed dolls when she bunched them together on her lap to make room for old and crippled Ahgeepaluk, who was brought to the schoolhouse on a small sled and trundled in to add his native good humor to the party.

The room was a sea of faces and brown shoulders and arms for some of the men had slipped off their parkas. When they had moved over and shifted the children, so that all were comfortable, old Kootook, looking like some contemplative bronze Buddha come to life, got up to make a speech. I had come ashore in Kootook's oomiak. He was *the* mighty hunter of the village, a man of great knowledge concerning whale and walrus and polar bear (he knew something of women too, as I was to discover from time to time) and it was said, that he could tell from the *feel* of snow, just what the calms or blows of weather held in store. But tonight Kootook did not speak of these. He had come to voice a welcome for the village. Evidently, all the handshakings had not been enough: he wanted me to *know* that "all the peoples now is happy for that school—all Eskimo peoples likes that school—they likes for helping that teacher—all the children likes that school—peoples is many happy you come Missus Eva." The applause was spontaneous, a chorus hubbub of "*Ah-regahs!!*" every face bright with smiles and glowing with friendliness. It made me feel glad all over and I told them so.

The stars were shining on a landscape white with frost when my callers said good night. The clean cold air rushed into the halls from the open door. I couldn't breathe enough of it. You see, I had been up to my eyes in smells—all new smells—walrus blended with seal mostly. Honestly, there was a healthy tang to it but my nose behaved like a nuisance, as if it had never turned up to a stale morning of society's vaunted tobaccos in a hotel lobby, or day-before-yesterday's cabbage in an apartment hallway. Anyway, the ventilators worked like an inhalator squad and I was so revived that I unpacked a small box of fragiles, clinical thermometers, hypodermic needles and such, and put them away in the medical cabinets before I pinned up some papers at the windows and crawled in for my first night near the Pole.

In a few days, the schoolroom was free of its imposed role as freight depot, and the village women, supplied with soap and water, soon restored the walls to their pristine freshness. They were a merry group, laughing and visiting while they worked, occasionally pausing to slip a wee bantling off their backs to nurse it. They sat on the floor, their babies fussy and noisy until, with a satisfied little grunt they found a full, brown breast. At once, the mother would solicitously begin to pick stray bits of reindeer hair from the small ears and tiny fists, examine tiny feet and buttocks, perform all necessary cleansing with saliva, convenient supply at hand and most adroitly applied. With baby's bath and breakfast accomplished, it was soon snug in the cozy hollow of its mother's back under her warm parka. Tightening her belt to hold the baby in place, an Eskimo mother's hands are free to whatever task she has at hand, whether it be cleaning walrus intestine, cutting seal blubber, harnessing dogs, or washing the walls of the schoolroom.

All this cleaning made drastic inroads in our coal and

water supply. Coal and water—the pearls of great price in the Arctic! At any other village along the Arctic coast, sharp retrenchment would have been necessary, at least as far as coal was concerned. Wainwright is a singularly fortunate village in this regard, for an excellent coal is obtained on the Kuk River, a navigable stream (for canoes) which flows into the inlet. The best of the exposed veins—there are three of good width —is about twenty-five miles up the river, a pleasant jaunt either by sled in winter or canoe in summer. We made a picnic of it, one fine day just before school opened. The entire village sacked coal. And a gay caravan we made, paddling up the calm river, the early frost white on its banks, the brown grasses shining "fledged with icy feathers." At the end of the day over four hundred sacks of coal had been sacked, much of it stacked ready for later sled transportation to the village, when the river and inlet were frozen.

The Eskimos provide all the fuel needed for the school and teacher's use. In open summers they have managed a few extra tons for *Boxer* to transport to other villages. The bureau pays seventy-five cents per sack (cwt.) thus providing this village with a sure revenue and one which the natives have been quick to take advantage of, especially during poor hunting or trapping seasons. Hunting will always take precedence over sacking coal, however, for the keen zest of the chase is a too ever-present and compelling stimulant. To lend its counterpart of breathless excitement to the mining of coal, there was inaugurated a keen rivalry of teams—the boys against the men. The results far exceeded my wildest dreams. It was a marvelously successful picnic. Paddles dipped on the way home to the tune of "Bringing in the

Sheaves," only the Arctic welkin rang to "Bringing in the Coal"—something to sing about in this country.

Some of the natives burn coal in their igloos in queer little stoves fashioned of old gasoline tins. The older Eskimos prefer to burn blubber in the flat stone lamps of olden time. (Wainwright coal is subbituminous—makes a hot quick fire, leaving a residue of light white ash.)

As the coal was reckoned in tons, so was our water. Tons of water? Sounds like the din of a deluge or a mighty moving river, and often enough I would have been glad had the water supply flowed thus freely. No turning of a faucet here, no lavender tinted or chromium plumbing, not even a well sweep with a sentimental old oaken bucket, but literally *tons* of ice, sawed, chopped, and hauled from a large tundra lake, about two miles distant from the village. As the glittering loads came skidding into the village, I recalled the sickening qualmishness I had felt my first morning in Wainwright, when, after dressing the broken arm of Anakok's son, I had asked for water to bathe his face and hands, but the darkish amber fluid they brought in looked so much like old stale rain water, that I could not bring myself to use it—scarcely dared to believe that it could be water. So it was a relief to learn that the first freeze of the season eliminates all brackishness of color and taste; that crystal clear water was to fill the kettles and make my tea, and that my creamy silk and wool flannels would not be sepia-tinted after laundering.

The icehouse was about thirty yards away from the school. It covered an underground cellar dug out of the frozen tundra, about twenty feet square and twelve deep. In the center of its floor of stout planking was a square opening, like a ship's hatch. A ladder gave easy access to the stacks of ice blocks stored below where they remained frozen the year round. In the kitchen, two large barrels, or oil drums, were cleaned and filled with ice. More was melted in the wash boiler, and when hot, poured over the ice in the barrels. Thus was our water supply started. It was Tooruk who kept it flowing. Every morning he would bring in two huge blocks, first scraping off the accumulated frost with the long ice knives until they were sparkling clean. Like polishing glass was this business of cleaning "teacher's water." How the ice would boom and crack when it was first dropped in the barrels! Especially on those bitter cold days when the thermometer hung around forty degrees below. We used to make fair guesses at the temperature by the thickness of skim ice which formed over night.

The small house over the cellar served as a refrigerator. It was soon filled with haunches of reindeer, braces of duck and ptarmigan, and two precious wild swan, Arctic "turkeys" to grace the holiday board.

Before the end of September, about forty tons of ice had been stored, transforming the cellar to a veritable Aladdin's cave of scintillating jeweled fairyland, surpassingly lovely after the Reimthursin (or whatever the mythical frost giants of the Norsemen are called in this Arctic) had put their finishing touches of ice embellishment on every surface even to the satiny wings of the black brant and the plumage of the swans, the delicate tracery of each fimbria beautifully etched in frost.

(From my Journal) September 14th.

Three oomiaks came in loaded with coal today. The men have banked the sacks against the building on the east side, to serve as a wind break there until we have exhausted the fuel on the west side, where the sacks are now layered eight deep up to the level of the windows and around the door. The kerosene and gasoline drums have been rolled to a sheltered corner on the south side of the entrance, protected there, so Nasholook tells me, from being buried in snow drifts.

We are no less busy indoors. The gasoline pressure tank has been filled, new mantles on the fixtures, so that our school lights are now in working order. Stove-polish has improved the cannon-balls and the new stove pipe fits like a silk hat. Tomorrow Tooruk is to paint the blackboards. Akadrigak is mending two desks. Yesterday he built a small cabinet in the kitchen and no Caucasian carpenter could have done better. With my pictures and books in place, it is fast beginning to look and feel like home. Only the windows needed curtains, so this morning I went shopping. That just means going through the schoolroom to the native store at the other end of the building. Some of the old men of the village were enjoying their pipes in there. Nasholook, who serves as store manager, was arranging his shelves.

And what a variety of trading material was here! Cotton prints and calicos,—leading colorful and fore-ground display by the way—combs and hair brushes, safety pins and needles, handkerchiefs, big bandannas red and blue, boxes of dried fruits and cans of milk, sacks of flour, long bundles of thin oaken strips for sled making, rolls of white drilling for "snow shirts," pack-ages of tea,—highly prized by the native housewife,—lanterns and kettles, tobacco and enamel cups, and even bedroom chambers—all these crowded in this little mart at Wainwright—all bartered for with furs.

Instead of putting money in a till, Nasholook will hang furs on the walls. Thick cream-colored polar bear skins light up the dark corners of the smoky oil-stained room. Tassels of sleek ermine lie on the counter beside fluffy fox skins, red and white. Native women come in with spotted sealskins, dressed and smoothly stretched, or a few fawn skins soft as a rabbit's ear, or maybe a pair of sealskin water boots, or boots made of reindeer with brightly decorated cuffs, to exchange for sugar or a package of tea or more likely a few yards of gay calico. Tingook, who has no wife to make boots for him, may take a fancy to those water boots and trade some ivory tusks for them. But mostly the natives trade for the "white man's" merchandise Nasholook was storing away on the shelves this morning. And that's where I found some bright yellow gingham for the kitchen curtains. Tonight they are up. Already the room looks warmer but to get the effect I had to put my feet in the oven as I worked out a daily schedule for the school term. Outside a bitter north wind blows.

A.M. and P.M.	Schedule for Week Days
7 to 8:30	Wet towel rub. Breakfast and housework. Open ventilators while washing dishes. (The moisture in the room would freeze so quickly that the air blowing in was like a shower of talcum powder.)
9 to Noon	Schoolroom. Recess of 15 minutes at 10:30. Out of doors with children.
Noon Hour	Lunch and dishes. Bank fires.
1 to 3:30	Schoolroom. Primary Department dismissed at 2:30.
3:30 to 4	Out of doors. Visiting the natives or walking.

4 to 5	Clinic. Emergency cases at any time night or day.
5 to 6	Preparing the best meal of the day.
6 to 7	Dinner and dishes.

Programme for Saturdays

Laundry. Baking bread, rolls, cookies or cake. Cleaning rooms. Shampoo as needed, and a luxurious bath.

| 4 to 5 | Clinic. |

Evening devoted to preparation of school work, particularly kindergarten material. A walk before bedtime when weather permitted.

Keeping the Sabbath

Sunday morning same as Weekdays.

11 to Noon	Services in the Schoolroom. A short *sermon* to my *congregation* and playing the "moosik" for their hymns.
1 to 3	Cooking. Dining to Victrola Concert Orchestra. Pretty gown, flowers, candle light and everything. (So I planned, but oh! the Sundays when morale was more comfortable in a sweater, a good thick woolly one buttoned up to my chin.)
4 to 5	Clinic for those patients taking medicines or tonics daily—clean dressings, etc.
7 to 9	Light supper—candy making—popcorn—reading or writing letters. (Those everlasting manuscripts to the dearest ones.)
10 P.M. .	Lights out at this hour on all days. (Except when lamps happened to be filled with midnight oil.)

I must digress here to tell you that weekday evenings gave ample time for school records, medical reports, weather reports (at some schools) and so forth—a mere matter of routine, filling out government forms.

On Friday evenings, the village turned out for a community sing—gala nights, when we sang improvised ditties to the good old tunes of "Songs the Whole World Sings." The Eskimos could raise the rafters singing, "Carry Me Back to Ol' Virginny," "Loch Lomond," and the rest of those old favorites. One verse of "In the Good Old Summer Time," was enough to joggle the stovepipe to a zigzag pattern again—the melody, you understand, not the words, for the Eskimos know nothing of "baby mine," or "She's your tootsie-wootsie." Their affections for one another never approach the burlesque, as a consequence their language isn't cluttered with expressions for such gush. But they do know their summertime, and what they lack of "shady lanes," is never missed, when they sing of icy ones.

> Paddling through the open lanes,
>   shooting walrus half the night,
> From Icy Cape to Belcher Point,
>   we have a very good time,
> Hunting meat for winter in the
>   good old summer time.

And just in case you may be curious what the Arctic scene for a Scotch lake might be, here it is:

> By yon mossy banks of Kukpowruk's river shores,
> The reindeer chew their cud in the twilight,
> While herders drink their tea
> All happy as can be,
> On the bonny mossy banks of Kukpowruk.[6]

During the fox-trapping season, from November 15 to March 15, when the men are away from the village,

---

[6] River south of the inlet.

often for weeks at a stretch, these song fests are discontinued. These are the dark days, when the women of the village enjoy more leisure, so were organized for their Mothers' Meetings—not on Friday nights, but on Saturday mornings, to bathe and weigh their babies, and to learn about their care and feeding.

As a general rule, all goes well for an Eskimo baby throughout the nursing period. It is when he is weaned from his mother's breast, and she begins to feed him seal and whale blubber, yes, even frozen fish, that we can expect all kinds of tummy aches, colic and intestinal disorders, too often fatal, as the charts of Eskimo mortality sadly testify. So, on Saturdays the schoolroom became a cooking school where mothers learned and helped to make nourishing soups using the wild fowl or reindeer meat, thickened with duck's eggs beaten until light and dropped by spoonfuls in to the boiling broth, to cook (and taste) very like vermicelli. Sometimes we combined the eggs with flour to make excellent noodles —or cooked by themselves, poached or soft-boiled or scrambled, the children found them smacking good. Towards the end of winter, when their store of wild eggs was exhausted, the women were taught how to use the dehydrated vegetables, or a bit of rice, though a teacher has ever to bear in mind, that while these may be obtained at the trading stores, the cost of even such simple "white man's" fare as a daily ration, is almost prohibitive to the average Eskimo housewife. Better for them to use what they have in great abundance.

I was typing a copy of the schedule next morning to post in the schoolroom, when Nasholook came in to tell me that former teachers had always put up a shelf out of doors for ice. "Sometimes is plenty storm—Akadrigak he like to help with that shelf." I suppose it was one way of having water on tap.

So the preparations for the opening of school progressed. With snow flurries and the sea like milk sherbet for days, it was comforting to see the coal sacks, heaped higher now, around the building and to know that the storm windows were in place and secure. And I had only to open the door a wee crack to read the weather glass. The ice shelf, high enough to escape the casual investigations of the village dogs, was but a step away. Oyalla, one of the schoolboys, was to help Tooruk with the ice and keep the coal bin filled. With ice, coal, and oil drums just outside the door, the entrance took on the aspect of a barricade, a veritable fortification to withstand a seige against Höder, the blind god of winter, who at that very moment had eyesight keen enough, whiplashing his Arctic steeds in wild abandon, seeking his pleasure in wind and frozen sleet—through the darkness of an Arctic night descending.

On September 20 the Arctic ocean was as still as death, and all the space between it and the sky was filled with a surging cold gray portent. The natives had extended the entrances to their igloos, making long low tunnels with blocks of ice. Through the gathering gloom I could see their oomiaks and kayaks high upon the racks.

The storm broke at noon. It came down from the north like a fury blowing, snow flying thick as smoke, heaping itself swiftly in long streamline drifts over every obstacle, piling on until dunelike banks made their appearance on each side of the schoolhouse, the building held between them like a wedge. Ever blowing southward, like sheeted ghosts trailing shrouded arms, was a constant spewing smoke of snow—penetrating, intrusive stuff—sweeping over land and sea, changing the contours of the igloos, burying the coal sacks, snuffing the whining dogs and the village silent beneath.

Thursday—Friday—Saturday—and our world still in the grip of this blowing! Were the trolls on a migrating rampage? I fancied I could hear them hallooing in wicked glee. I looked at the coal bin in the hall with anxious misgivings. Most certainly it was being emptied with a swiftness which rivaled the wind. What use was an empty coal bin under the roof, or full sacks just outside the door, when one hardly dared open the door?

Since I had to keep the range going for warmth, I baked bread and cookies, then more cookies, all the while my eyes on this storm drama of the Arctic. Not a soul stirred in the village. Buried were all the igloos, and for all I knew, buried were all the Eskimos.

Monday, September 22, was the date I had set for the opening of school. Sunday, while the village population was assembled for services, I would make the announcement. My plans were to tell them about the daily programme beginning with the rising bell. Few igloos have clocks so the eight o'clock ringing would serve as an alarm clock for the village. When day is like night, primitive folks know nothing of time. The second bell, at 8:45, would sound the school summons. Forty-five minutes, Nasholook assured me, gave an Eskimo menage ample time to get children ready for school. I would stress clean faces and hands, and hair neatly combed, above all, freed of inhabitants. Mothers needing fine combs for this business could obtain them at the clinic hour. Also, that children must eat breakfast at home, instead of bringing lumps of tallow and blubber in tight fists to be eaten at school.

I rehearsed my little speech, drew the face of a clock on the blackboard to make my talk plain, counted out a few dozen fine combs, tended the fires—how these stoves could consume coal!—and was soon intent on the storm again. The driving snow swept across the window like the sea against a porthole. Saturday night—the steady stream of snow powder continued to sift under the door. The wind was still blowing.

The hurried patter of *mukluked* footsteps approaching in the inner hall, flung me out to the edge of my bed and deep dreaming. What could be so urgent this hour of a dark morning?

The yellow light from a lantern streaked across the floor as the door opened, a clean rush of cold air blowing in with the lad who suddenly stood before me, snow still clinging to his garments. He thrust a crumpled bit of paper into my hand and then held the lantern close for me to read. "that baby he come now teacher come"— labored penciled words on a scrap of torn school tablet— enough to galvanize me into reindeer boots and parka, push my hair into a knitted cap, snatch my bag—always ready for these emergencies—together with a bottle of sweet oil from behind the stove—where it could not con- geal—and we were off. I felt these schoolhouses were pretty well planned as I closed the doors to my rooms and in the passageway. How well the halls served to keep out the intense cold! And going out—each hall several degrees colder—as if to prepare one's lungs in the same way to the severe temperature of the outside. At that moment the coal bin with its gaping near-emptiness had lost its worrying interest. Nothing mattered now but my Eskimo woman in labor.

The steps were free from drift and down these I followed Koonanuck, my lungs sharply protesting the suddenness of breath so cold! A silent place, this Wainwright, at three o'clock in the morning, cradled in the lull of a four-day storm. No sound but the crunching of dry snow as our weight passed over it. The storm had spent its strength.

Deeper and deeper went my nose into my parka, as over the flintlike ridges of snow I followed Koonanuck's lantern. How firmly his feet trod the frozen trail! How certain and sure was his going! Koonanuck knew the Main Street of his village in all its moods and weather. I would have been lost without him. A day or two before the storm I had made the rounds of the village, noting for a landmark the ancient igloo in which Tingook lived with his rack of flapping skins beside it. Noted too, Segavan's dwelling, the peatlike turf piled neatly around it, the skin window secured with willow withes, the entrance protected from the cold with an ice vestibule, his hunting equipment placed within and the stakes for tethering his dogs well fastened. Tegausena, Segavan's wife, pridefully entertained me that day, proud of her clean, freshly scrubbed igloo, proud of her two enamel cups, which she was careful to wipe again before pouring the tea. She had been weaving willow withes into flat trays for meat thawing. The willows had been gathered far inland up the river where Segavan had fished the past summer. Somewhere, in this metamorphosis which the storm had wrought, were these two careful citizens of Wainwright sitting on their clean floor with their cups of tea, eating frozen fish, and somewhere among all the queer moundy places we were passing, was Tingook's ancient igloo, but I could not identify them. It was like wandering over the face of a dead moon, so strange was the gray sameness of half-lighted mystery. We passed the first of the boat racks, ghostly platforms upheld by frosted driftwood, and the caches, queer dark objects piled upon them, loomed high above the drifts.

Suddenly the light made a sharp turn and Koonanuck and his lantern disappeared—then a faint flickering of it came from a low entry and with it the weird howling of many dogs. I bent low and entered the tunnel, a man-made rabbit's burrow built of ice, roofed with stiff dark walrus hides. At the far end my youthful guide was holding a small door open to light my way. Twenty feet of tunnel! Midway a dark figure was subduing the aroused dogs. The swift effective gestures cut across the light with every growl and snarl. Fear rode my spine as I crept past the ugly animals, their eyes glowing like coals in that darkness. Twenty feet of sounds and smells and angry dogs and penetrating stinks that came from heaps of green skins and trays of walrus meat. But the warm igloo was reached at last so crowded with moving life and so dimly lighted that I scarcely knew where to step or place my bag.

For a moment I stood in the center of a circle of brown faces. An old man sat up to reach for a fur garment from a carelessly bundled heap on a shelf behind him. This shelf served as a bunk or sleeping place. Four young faces, studies in curiosity, peeped over the edge of it. For some strange and inexplicable reason I began to count these faces, the human bodies that lay huddled in this primitive dwelling fashioned so cunningly of drift-wood and peat. Fourteen! Fourteen earthlings in this low shelter scarcely nine feet across! The old man shuffled into his garment and left the igloo followed by the four curious ones who tumbled from their places in great hurry. From the dim recess beneath the shelf out rolled two others who shyly smiled, as they too went out through the small door. I added the two to my count.

And then I saw her, my woman in travail, near the wall half sitting, half reclining against the fleshy comfort of a fat woman. Strands of wet black hair matted her forehead and the deepness of agony lay in her dark eyes. Her small moist hand reached up for mine, "I many glad you come," she said, and if there was any word more, it was suddenly held by lips shut tight against ineffable pain.

My thoughts were as busy as my hands for the next hour, from the time I improved the lighting system by fastening Koonanuck's lantern to a bit of driftwood above me, folded my parka for a kneeling pad on the floor beside my patient, opened my bag, all sterile within —its shining instruments the admiration of all eyes—to that relieved and blessed moment when the lively brown infant was receiving an oil bath on my lap (probably the one and only bath of his life). His mother and the old woman were the only ones interested in this rite, apparently, for rising above the baby's lusty cries was the deep sonorous breathing of the others who lay in heavy sleep scarcely three feet away. Such a wee bit of blubber ball, was this baby telling us quite emphatically that he had come to stay, and that he had brought a surprisingly good appetite with him.

The wan half-light of the paling morning came through the skin window as I cleaned up. The old woman folded up the thick piece of heavy reindeer pelt, which had so comfortably served the young mother for a receiving bed. The igloo was warm, human bodies contributing, like so many heating units, to its drowsy comfort. The mother adjusted a soft new fawn skin about her baby as his hungry mouth suckled her smooth full breast. The business of the night was over.

(From my Journal) September 21. New baby in Wainwright. Boy. Guessed his weight around eight pounds. Dark blue birthmark just over the coccyx— thought at first it was a bruise. Duration of labor two hours. Born to Nasealik, wife of Seekearock. Her name should be Rare Courage. Not a moan did I hear throughout the ordeal. Crowded igloo. Two herder boys there for the night. Thought we were going to have an audience but the family went to sleep. Funny, how the old woman wiped the sweet-oil cup with her finger, licking it off with much gusto! Reindeer pads! What a sanitary idea! Thickest part of the hide used. Sort of absorbent too! Darling baby! Strong primitive mother! Could Mary of Galilee have been surrounded by weary shepherd boys I wonder? Could she, do you think, have used a thick fleece for her bed?

I did not need the light of a lantern going home. The stillness over the vastness of gray dawn was strangely moving. On the threshold I turned to listen to the silence. Far to the south a purple and rose horizon bugled the swan song of the sunlight. The thermometer registered 18°, and those blessed boys, Tooruk and Oyalla, had filled the coal bin. If there be any virtue in the work of the teachers, the doctors and the nurses in the Arctic, it is due, let me record now and forever, to the Tooruks and Oyallas who keep the coal bins filled.

It was as if the children had been ready since midnight

to rush out at the first clang of the bell that morning. Tooruk and Oyalla came to ring it at eight. The glad note of it was scarcely on the air when they came running from every direction, shouting and laughing to pile themselves up in a furry bunch about the door. I was in the kitchen stirring oatmeal, when every window suddenly darkened to become a framed picture of curious little faces, each little face surrounded by a halo of fur, each little nose flattened against the pane. Tooruk and Oyalla stood like watchful sentinels waiting to ring the second bell and to open the door to the schoolroom. I wondered if these youngsters had had breakfast.

You may have your memories of first times for many of the dear experiences of life—your first party—your first dance—the first kiss—when all unexpectedly comes one which transcends all the rest. My first day teaching the Eskimos was like that. No happy event since has served to topple it off the high place in my affections. Those round bright faces, pretty teeth and laughing eyes! Eager to learn, to say their first English word, to use a pencil, to sing—to march—to read—to sing again. Oh, pedagogic paradise! Angels for perfect attendance —no discipline—no tardy marks—exemplary conduct —attention and application, (the pencil-chewing type of application). Could any teacher wish for more?

We started the day by hopping around the stove to get warm. It was a good time to note the weather, the direction of the wind and temperature, and whether they had heard the ice booming last night. For the older children, this constituted a practice drill in the use of English words. The child most proficient had the honor of marking the calendar the next day. Then followed special village news; how many seals caught—a new family

Eva L. Richards

South Kitchen Window
School Morning

come from the eastward or from the south—the dogs
Negovanna was taking to Barrow. After this came the
home news; "my fadder's brudder he come down from
river and have fish,"—"my sister make fawn skins boots"
—"my old fadder make whale canoe"—"that sled dog
got six puppies." Their shyness dispelled, we could turn
to the opening morning exercises, the Lord's Prayer—
or that simple little poem "Father we thank Thee for this
day." For my tiny "primaries" these had to be interpreted, a slow but interesting process. Dark eyes would open
wide in little serious faces when Nasholook told them
how some day they might learn to pray like old Kunoodluk did on Sunday mornings. One day, after the school
routine was well established, I asked one of the older
boys, "What did you thank the Heavenly Father for
today?" He gave this answer. "I tanks God Fadder for
good wind, [a warm wind from the southwest]; I tanks
Fadder for happy plenty that my mudder she have can
of milk," then with a long look at the ceiling he added,
"I tanks that God Fadder many business."

These exercises would usually bring us to morning
recess. Fifteen minutes of outdoor play and they were
ready for real work, lessons in reading, writing and arithmetic. Reading meant books, and writing meant pencils
and paper, and numbers meant chalk and blackboard
competition, all very new and exciting. And it meant
too, weeks and weeks of patient interpreting, for a
teacher in the north meets with a unique problem presenting as she must, the lessons in a new language to her
pupils. I do not know how I would have managed without Nasholook.

The first interpreter must have been a most important
fellow. Heaven only knows how the first teachers ever

got along without him, or the explorers, or the captains of the whaling ships, for that matter. As late as 1881, government ship captains were having a sorry time enough. John Muir tells us, while cruising on the *Corwin*, that one day "we inquired of one who spoke a few words of English whether any of their number could speak *good English*." Think of the patience of the pioneers in the missions and schools, zealously striving with signs and objects, to make themselves understood, painstakingly working on a vocabulary, and in time, teaching the natives a few words. An old report throws some light on the labors of these pioneer teachers.

"From words they proceeded to phrases, and from phrases to sentences, teaching the natives to translate the Eskimo into English and vice versa. They gradually added English letters and numbers, together with some elementary geography and arithmetic. Although they had had a combined experience of thirteen years in the schoolroom in the States, the teachers declare that they never had more quick-witted, intelligent pupils than these wild Eskimo children. At the beginning of the school year only a few could count ten in a blundering fashion, and nine-tenths of the pupils knew practically no English whatever. At the close of the first school year they had a good working vocabulary, knew something of geography and map-drawing, understood thoroughly the decimal basis of our numbers, could count up to one thousand, work examples in simple addition, write and read simple English words, and carry on a conversation in English on everyday practical matters. The pupils showed a remarkable desire to learn for learning's sake."[7]

---

[7] From Senate Report on Introduction of Reindeer in Alaska. 1895.

My work in the classroom was simple in comparison. Today, most Eskimo children understand many English words. An interpreter is usually needed to smooth out the conversations between teacher and the older natives. The very old natives would look Nasholook up before coming to see me. He always came with them. The younger men and women speak well enough for most trading transactions, though I remember the sign language was often resorted to, a language quite adequate, I find, between peoples who would be kind to each other.

"Instructions to Teachers" read, "Stress the little courtesies." I had an amusing time with "Thank you." I never could understand why we teach Eskimos to say the English "Thank you." Why not learn their own euphonious word for it, *Kwayanna,* which they never fail to use when obliged to each other or to their teachers? Perhaps it helps to keep some traders calm and unruffled —or maybe some missionary who may come among them with little capacity for recognizing their inherent good manners. The first time I sharpened a pencil for a small son of the Arctic, he learned to say "Tank oo," together with its meaning. Then I turned to chalk some work on the board. Immediately there was a *muk-luk* commotion behind me, and there, giggling at each other, as children will when they are bubbling over with some delicious secret, was every child in my primary class, standing in a line like soldiers presenting arms. Each small fist held a pencil, its broken point upwards. The sharpener buzzed. So did my thoughts. How came these pencils to have points broken as if by one simultaneous crack? The mystery was soon solved. As each small hand reached for its pencil, out piped the newly learned word,

"Tank oo," "Tenk," "Tanku," right down the line, with variations, of course, on the pronunciation. The entire class had been wide awake to the lesson intended for one child. Taking this as a cue, other lessons were taught by the same method with equal success, though I saw to it that no pencils were damaged in the process.

Again, a teacher must often delete from the popular school readers, and relegate to the limbo-of-things-that-can-never-be-seen, the stories of horses and pigs and hay fields, substituting tales of walrus and whale and other objects of an Eskimo child's world. Sometimes the children made their own surprisingly quick-witted applications. For example: along towards spring we came to a story in the third reader about a circus with many little boys carrying many pails of water to an elephant. I puzzled how I was going to explain a circus and an elephant, when quick as a flash, Panick said, "that like big stove in schoolroom—plenty coal buckets." So the cannon ball was dubbed "the elephant," though I'd better tell you here, that in January and February, when the glass registered 54 degrees below zero, carrying coal to that cannon ball was no circus.

In the upper grades, problems in arithmetic were arranged around the value of furs, ermine, and fox skins, whale bone, walrus ivory, eider down, and other commodities which their parents exchange for tea, flour, steel traps, tobacco and so forth. They had a fine time playing at trading, every day putting down the foxes they had caught—or the tea and prunes they bought—their credits and debits as neat on ruled sheets as any bookkeeper's.

Writing was the high light of the school day, a very real joy to them. They would almost write with their noses, in their zeal to copy the lines on the board—"Wash your hands and faces before you come to school"—"Eat your blubber at home"—"Comb your hair every morning," thus combining lessons in hygiene with the writing they loved. In music and singing they quite surpassed the classes of white children I had taught—but there, I have already told you how they could shake the rafters and make the welkin ring.

The building of schools in this far Arctic was a task of no mean proportion, presenting, as it did, problems never met with in milder climes. Yet, paradoxically enough, the very severity of this region—ice-nipped ships and stranded men—had everything to do with the establishing of the first schools.

In the summer of 1889, Lieutenant-Commander Stockton of the U.S. Navy, was ordered to Point Barrow to erect a refuge station for the accommodation of ship-wrecked whalers. At the same time he was to make a survey of the Eskimo villages along the Arctic coast. He found a wretched people. Want and starvation stalked every village. The whalers for over fifty years had been depleting their waters of whale and seal and walrus, all necessary for the subsistence and equipment of this primitive people. Among the recommendations contained in the report of this survey, was one urging the immediate establishment of schools at Point Barrow, Point Hope, and Cape Prince of Wales. Except for a small mission school newly established near St. Michael, there was not a single school between Norton Sound and Point Barrow.

The annual appropriation, at that time, for all white and native schools in Alaska, was only $50,000. With

PANICK

Eva Louise Richards.
1925

this inadequate fund, Dr. Sheldon Jackson, the government agent, assisted by subsidy contracts with the mission boards of the Presbyterian, Episcopal, and Congregational churches, was able to provide for the building and equipment of these three schools. They were located at the villages which Commander Stockton had prescribed.

Point Barrow is the farthest north Eskimo village on the North American continent. Its latitude is 71½ degrees north, so far north, that in the summer one might say nature seems afflicted with a peculiar wakefulness, and we enjoy a midnight-sun period for nearly three months. In the winter we endure a "No-sun" season for about seventy days. (About the same at Wainwright.) Point Barrow has a winter population of about four hundred Eskimos and ten or more white folks. It is an important center of trade for the Eskimos living along the coasts extending to the southwest and southeast of it.

Cape Prince of Wales is the farthest point west on the continent. Here is the largest Eskimo village in Alaska, if not in the world. It is approximately six hundred miles, by sled travel, southwest of Point Barrow, and about sixty miles below the Arctic Circle. Here the sun is visible for nearly four hours on the shortest winter day. The isolation of Wales is somewhat mitigated viewing the mountains of Siberia across the Bering Straits.

At the time of which I speak, Wales was the summer rendezvous for the Eskimos of the Straits region, for those living to the southward as far as Nome, and northward to the great Kotzebue Sound country. Here they would assemble with their great walrus-skin boats to make ready for their annual trading cruise to Siberia. Seventy to eighty of these canoes, each manned by thirty to forty natives, would cross the stormy Straits to obtain from the Siberian Chuckchees, furred reindeer skins for clothing, reindeer sinew for thread, and Russian leaf tobacco. A most adequate native merchant marine, for tons of material were transported to Alaskan shores in this manner.

Midway between Wales and Point Barrow is the village of Point Hope. Its population numbered about 375 Eskimos and eight or ten white people. These natives were accustomed to meet the Wales and the river Eskimos at the great trade fair held at Kotzebue every summer.

On June 6, 1890, the four teachers selected for these Arctic schools, together with their supplies of food, fuel, and school materials, sailed from San Francisco on the *Jeanie,* a small steamer serving as tender to the whaling fleet.

They were Rev. L. M. Stevenson, who started the work at Point Barrow, Dr. John B. Driggs, at Point Hope, and William T. Lopp and Harrison Thornton.

Because a few white people, traders and whalers, had lived at Point Hope and Point Barrow for a number of years, and none had ever lived at Wales, Mr. Lopp and Mr. Thornton were sent to the latter place.

The reaction of these two young men, suddenly finding themselves on a strange shore far from home and civilization, there to organize and teach school among a wild and primitive people, whose only contact with white men had been with those on the passing whaling ships, must be left to your imaginations. But let Mr. Lopp finish the story:

"Our duties and responsibilities were so many, so varied and perplexing, to say nothing of exciting, that we considered the year of 1890-91 the shortest one of our lives.

"Fortunately for us, most of Wales' '500' departed on their summer trading and fishing trips soon after the landing of our supplies and the completion of our house went forward. This gave us, not only a breathing spell, but some very much needed sleeping spells. The aggressive curiosity of our strange neighbors was, to say the least, somewhat wearing on our nerves, and sorely tried our patience on many an occasion.

"After checking and storing our supplies, we opened school in order to experiment on the small population left in the village. Sixteen children came the first day, with more than twice that number a few days later. We soon discovered our school books were useless. We made our own charts of blackboard cloth and large sheets of heavy paper. For a few days we were occupied almost exclusively with an Eskimo-English vocabulary, drilling them on the spelling of every word. Their interest in phonetic spelling was soon aroused, especially of the Eskimo words. The magic of representing sounds by letters and 'making paper talk' gripped them. Their progress was remarkable, and soon we were going on to arithmetic, geography and music with singing.

"Not very long after, we discovered, much to our surprise, that their language, like the Greek, had the singular, dual and plural numbers. Not only that, but we learned that every child of ten or twelve knew how to use the inflected forms of their nouns correctly. For example, when speaking of a ship they say, oo-me-ak-puk; of two, oo-me-ak-pak; of more than two, oo-me-ak-pait. It delighted them to see us write these dual and plural forms of their nouns on the blackboard, as they called them off to us.

"Later we learned that every noun had at least six case

endings, and that the inflected forms of each verb accommodated not only number, person, tense, mode, and voice, but also of many adverbs. With visions of pages of paradigms, of declensions and conjugations, we decided to be satisfied with mastering just enough of their language to enable us to teach them the English understandingly.

"But I recall that we were impressed by the thought that a people who could master and speak this unwritten language grammatically, have possibilities and need never resort to Greek and Latin for mental drills. We estimated that they possessed a vocabulary of several thousand words.[8]

"What our summer pupils told the hunting nomads who returned in the fall, awakened their interest to the nth degree. All the young men and women were eager to learn the secret of 'making paper talk.' To accommodate them we were compelled to divide the school into four sections. Although we advised them not to attend school when the weather was favorable for sealing, fishing, crabbing, trapping and bear hunting, our average attendance was 105, with an enrollment of 172."[9]

In the summer of 1893, Mr. Lopp was appointed superintendent of the reindeer station at Port Clarence, marking the beginning of the development of the reindeer industry to which he devoted nearly forty years, the best years of his life. He inaugurated a system of training native boys to be herders, of which the late Dr. Elmer Ellsworth Brown, chancellor of New York University, says, ". . . the most interesting application of educational

---

8 Peck's *Eskimo-English Dictionary* of the Hudson Bay country Eskimos, published in 1925, contains more than 15,000 words.

9 Quotations from *Pioneer Education in the Northwest—Alaska,* by William T. Lopp.

processes to the fundamental needs of a people which I have ever known." But I'm running ahead of my story.

The idea of bringing reindeer across the Strait was suggested to Mr. Lopp in September, when one of the oomiaks brought in fresh reindeer meat from East Cape, Siberia. "Here was a capital idea, we thought, even if it did come to us from stomachs filled with excellent meat. We did not share this idea with our people until we had learned what we could from them regarding the Siberian Chuckchees and their reindeer. We found that the Eskimos were very familiar with every detail of the reindeer industry on the other side of the Strait, and fully realized, far more than did we, what the introduction of this food-clothing-transportation animal would mean.

"When we suggested the possibility of bringing a small herd across, we aroused a hope, apparently, which they had long entertained, but had never spoken of. It spread throughout the village and to the neighboring villages. Later, when more definite plans were made for bringing reindeer to Wales in their oomiaks the coming summer, if the Cutter *Bear* could not be induced to transport them, they concluded that school teachers were pretty useful after all, and their gratitude knew no bounds. And as this plan and hope unfolded in their minds, the more worthwhile and necessary we became to them."[10]

Strange as it may seem, while these people and their teachers were enthusiastically planning for the speedy realization of their reindeer dream, Dr. Sheldon Jackson, during the same months, was trying to interest Congress and philanthropic people in the eastern states in the same humane cause, although it had never been discussed by Jackson and the teachers in the summer of 1890.

---

[10] Lopp, op. cit.

This reindeer dream, born simultaneously at Wales and Washington, was not realized until the summer of 1892, when a government school and reindeer station was established about fifty miles south of Wales, at Port Clarence. That summer, 171 reindeer and three Siberian deermen were taken aboard the cutter *Bear* and landed at the new station. With the Siberians to look after the herd and instruct the Eskimo apprentices who came from the Wales and Port Clarence villages, the new industry for the natives of Alaska was inaugurated.

Under a reindeer code, approved by Secretary of the Interior Garfield in 1907, this new industry became a vocational part of the school system, a sort of outdoor boarding school so to speak. With meagre appropriations several scores of schoolboys were given four years of reindeer husbandry, rewarded after their apprenticeship with six, eight, ten or more deer, which with their natural increase, averaged about forty-five for each graduate. At the end of his course a graduate is not only a competent herder but has a herd of his own and is able to marry and support a family in native dignity and comfort.

During the next two decades, government schools and a number of missions were established on the islands, rivers, and along the coast, from Point Barrow to the Pacific. As the 1,280 Siberian reindeer, imported from 1892 to 1902, increased, herds were driven from parent herds and established at practically all the schools and missions in western and northwestern Alaska. Under this system of training and distribution the Eskimos became the owners of about two thirds of all the reindeer in Alaska. In 1924 the natives of Wainwright owned about 8,000 deer, apportioned to four herds.

In time Mr. Lopp[11] became Chief of the Alaska Division of the Bureau of Education. "He adapted and supplemented the work of public school teachers to fit the needs of these native peoples in a great variety of ways, sending among them teaching nurses, securing provision of physicians and hospitals, improving their standards and practices as regards housing and industrial habits and methods, furthering the cultivation of little farms and gardens where such things were practicable, and directed the important development of co-operative buying and selling. It is not to be forgotten that his work for many years covered the whole of Alaska, including the Indian and Aleut population, as well as the Eskimo." (Dr. E. Ellsworth Brown.)

Tooruk came in to tell me he was off for the village to get his fox traps. He loaned them to Matulik last winter for one fox skin. This year he made a better bargain. Tingook was to have them for two fox skins. Also he bargained with Aguvalook to help Oyalla with the coal and the ice while he was away. Aguvalook accepted with alacrity. Jam and toast and coffee in my kitchen may have been the consideration.

Aguvalook came in to see me often. He is known in the village as the children's storyteller. He tells his stories accompanied by string games, the kind we used to call cat's cradle. Each pattern has its own peculiar story. He changes from one to the next in the most fascinating manner singing the tale to each as he weaves the string picture. His face is round and jovial, his eyes bright below a fringe of shiny black hair—no less black and shiny than the wolverine trimming of his parka-hood.

---

[11] Mr. Lopp died April 10, 1939.

"Listen to the *Song of Two Puppies* drinking soup,"
he begins. "Some people inside the igloo is call them."

> *Kock! Kock!*
> *Kick mia rua look*
> *Aluck tuck*
> *Kock seek! Ho!*

"Missus Eva, that two boys run out from the igloo and
chase the puppies away." Under the clever manipulation of Aguvalook's nimble fingers, the pattern of the
puppies on the string disappears to magically continue
with the *Song of the Swan*, a bird that was eagerly
sought by a mighty hunter.

> *U moo ni mia mah na*
> *U moo ni mia mah na.*
> *Tinga wunga!*
> *Tinga wunga!*

The swan flies away but leaves a leg after him as the
hunter comes up. Aguvalook laughs heartily, "Ho! Ho!
Ho! that swan he make that good joke on that hunter."
Aguvalook dexterously begins the *Song of the Blackbird*.

> *Cwak! Cwak!*
> *Kit mia rua luan*
> *Ting-ee ka rah!*
> *Ting-ee ka rah!*

The blackbird flies away but the hunter comes home with
an egg in his bag, and with that a small knot is adroitly
crocheted on the string. Aguvalook had a song for
every pattern. There was one about the whale, for the
string picture of which he used the tip of his boot and a

AGUVALOOK.

Eva Louise Richards

longer string. A mighty hunter spears a whale and when he throws the spear, (the string gives a sharp thwang) the mighty whale rolls over. Aguvalook yells, *"Oo-lah! Oo-lah! Oo-lah! Muk-tuk! Muk-tuk! Oo-lah!"* all flushed with excitement over this imaginary prospect of a whale. A sort of one-man Punch-and-Judy show is Aguvalook. And how the children love him!

Storytellers are popular the world over but no raconteur ever held an audience more spellbound than did Tomaichuk, the old man of Wainwright. During the long winter night-days when trapping was not yet taking the men from the village, they would gather together in the native store, men, women, and children, to listen to the tales this grand old stager of the North could tell. Reindeer hides and wide strands of dry sinew, dog harness and bear skins on the walls, made a fitting background for the dark faces turned towards the old patriarch who holds them to strange attentiveness.

All is quiet and the story unfolds. A child whimpers, the mother makes haste to comfort it. After a long time of measured cadence, Tomaichuk pauses. I seize the opportunity to whisper to Tooruk, "What is the story?" "Long time many year—*ipanee*[12] day—big serpent come to land of people." "But Tooruk," I whisper incredulously, "how a serpent in your country where we cannot find the smallest worm?" But Tooruk is firm. "Long ago time come big serpent." Could it be, I thought, for long ago days the Arctic was tropic. The coal veins tell that story—had the tales of jungle monsters been handed down or was it all an inherited dream? The small lamp sputtered. Nasholook takes it out to refill it. The tale continues in the velvet darkness. Tomaichuk's voice

---

[12] Eskimo for long time ago—or ancient time.

now is soft and caressing, the cadence of it dreamy and wishful. I leaned against Tooruk, a gesture of yearning to understand his language, to understand these wonder stories of fantasy, of heroic action and daring. (How long would it take me to learn a little Eskimo, just enough to admit me into this absorbed listening company?) Nasholook returns with the lamp. I look at my watch. 3 A.M. Not a head was nodding. Every face wide eyed and eager for more. And was it any wonder? Did not old Tomaichuk promise in the beginning, "that storytelling do make all old things, old things of beasts, old things of land, old things of men, much young again?" Who would not remain up all the night or many nights to recapture the youth of us which leaves us, white folks or Eskimos, all too soon?

In the evening of the third day the saga was ended and Tooruk told me the story.

THE TIME OF FIRST CARIBOU

as told by Tooruk of Wainwright.

"One time was village near the sea. And the people who lived in the village had never up to this time seen the caribou near the place on the river, which is inland. One day three brothers went out to hunt the seal and they hunt many days but they could not find one seal. So come to the village again and sit down by side of igloo and talk about hunting place. One brother say, I will go that way to the land and in many days I will come to good hunting place for seal. And he started to the eastward.

"Now everyone knows that if you travel eastward from Wainwright you soon come to the sea again, but long ago days was no ships and no one could tell how big the world was. And that brother traveled many days and nights and all he hunted was lemmings. One day he was much tired and he stretched himself on the warm moss of tundra for sleep. Quick he is sleep, my! that brother is much tired. When he sleep he hear noise like water is make on shore, only that noise is come nearer all the time in his sleep. When his eyes open, he see funny land moving like maybe it walk away to the sea. And all that make a noise. On the land was willows growing and the willows was moving on the legs to the sea. That brother he sit up. He rub eyes plenty when he see that ground break like ice is do in the spring—in pieces. And one piece come near and he look that piece and he is see that is living something that have eyes and mouth, and that mouth was eating moss. Now that brother he take arrow and is much afraid. But he is plenty hungry so he shoot arrow and that piece of land is fall down to tundra and is very still and do not move no more. Then that brother he go to see and he find mouth and tongue is hang out that mouth and he cut little piece and that was good meat. He see that have much good skin and he is cut that skin and he find much good meat. That time he is full of crying for hungry villages. He make sled from that skin. He make man harness too. That time he put all that meat on that sled. He take that liver and that heart and he is walk to village and all the people very much hungry and now is have big feast and that brother is now big man in village. And that was first time the people eat caribou meat."

"But Tooruk, where does the serpent come into the story?" "Oh that was other time—that other brother, that young one, (Tooruk pronounced it jung) he go far now and see how big the place is where he is hunting."

THE STORY OF THE BIG HUNTING PLACE

as told by Tooruk.

"Now when that old brother go to the eastward, that young one he have very fine kayak. He paddle many days and soon he see the sun, and the sea was not much waves then, is good like river and plenty ducks swim in that place. But yet he did not see how big the place could be for hunting seal. Now he paddle again and many days. Now all the water is river color and he see much fish, plenty fish. Tomaichuk say is little water—all fish. But is yet not see how big is place for hunting seal. And now he is get much warm and is take off his parka and paddle plenty more time. Now that kayak is begin to get soft so he go to shore, but that was not good place for landing kayak. Every place on that shore was plenty driftwood and no place for kayak—and my! but that was very big place he think, but yet he did not know how big for hunting seal. That time he was much hungry for seal meat and he hunt plenty long time but is not catch seal. But that kayak is get very bad soft, so he paddle to good place and go to that shore. That young brother look around but that sun was not near sea no more. That sun is very high in sky and much warm. That was summer on the land. Long time he did not see seal, so now is think better he go back to village. Now that kayak is very bad and rotten so he go ashore again and walk to village. But now was big river and that was very deep river, so he go inland up river but yet he is not cross that river. Now he have boots is very bad and he say, 'I wish now my wife is here to make good boots and to make new grass in that boots so my feet is good, but that warm sun is dry the boots and make very bad time for my feet.' "

Tooruk.

Eva L. Richards.

"Poor man, it's a sad story, Tooruk."

"Yesh, he many time of days he lose his boots and his shirt and he make shirt from roots and grass."

"But where does he find the serpent, Tooruk?"

"He is find that serpent that time he is find that mastodon. That very big mastodon and is have plenty tusk like walrus tusk. That serpent is kill that mastodon— that serpent is go round and round and round that mastodon's legs—kill him plenty. (Tooruk wound his boot thong around his leg here to demonstrate.) That young brother is run to his kayak. He is run same like Matook he run from polar bear. That kayak is dry fine and is good. That brother he paddle quick for that time sun is come near to sea again. *Ai-yah,* he is much glad when he see driftwood places on shore and he know he is come soon home to his village. He see many ducks flying south that time and he paddle quick for is soon cold days coming. The people is all laugh when they see crazy man with grass shirt and he is now much old man, same like Tomaichuk. But that place for hunting seal is very big."

"Is that the end of the story, Tooruk?"

"*Na-ga,*" replies Tooruk, meaning emphatically NO. "That other brother he have very sorry time."

THE VERY SORRY WHALE-HUNTER

as told by Tooruk.

"That other brother he go all the time whale hunting. He is very good whale man. He have good whale boat and he kill many whale for all people in village have plenty *muk-tuk* that time. One time in open lead he see big whale and that whale he speak words like man talk. He say to that brother, 'You come I tell you where is fine woman. That woman is make very good boots and make seal poke for seal oil. I go now to that woman. You come in whale boat to good igloo and fine woman. I tell you where you find that igloo and that woman is live.'

"So the third brother followed the whale, through open leads in the ice and turned to the eastward many days.

"When man was tired and stop paddle, that whale blow and man is see whale all the time. Now soon ice go out and that whale is come to fine place, plenty open water and on shore is fine igloo. On top of igloo is woman. She is make nice snow shirt. That woman is very nice woman. She is laugh all the time and that brother like that boots she make and that seal poke is much filled with good seal oil. And he is like much that duck soup."

"Did he bring her back to his village, Tooruk?"

"*Na-ga*, that woman tell him now where plenty seal is catched, and walrus is many on ice. That igloo is nice warm igloo."

"What a happy man, Tooruk. A fine wife—a good igloo—plenty seal and walrus—don't you think so?"

"*Na-ga*, he is very sorry man. That woman she say, no more he go hunt whale. He tell that woman he very big whale man in his village. He like hunting whale and he like plenty good *muk-tuk*. But that woman she say, *Na-ga*, no more he go hunt whale. She say *na-ga* all the time. Now that man stay in igloo all the time. Not much good now for hunting whale. That very sorry man, Missus Eva."

From the tone of his lament, there was no doubt as to what Tooruk thought of a tragedy so profound. The forlorn picture of a valiant hunter alone in his igloo, his head in his hands, the open leads and his comrades calling

—no beautiful woman or comfortable igloo could ever
be worth such sorrow. A birthright of whale-hunting
for such a mess of pottage? *Na-ga!*

Contemplation of the moral to this tale was inter-
rupted by the arrival of several Eskimos, one of them
limping badly. So quickly do we turn in sudden kaleido-
scopic manner from one mood to the next. The Arctic
is never dull. The weather may remain in a sullen mood
for days, but the daily happenings in an Eskimo village
are varied enough to keep one on tiptoes.

Esagak hobbled in assisted by her husband and Nasholook. Painfully she moaned that she was much hurt and
began untying the thongs which fastened her boot. The
others smiled and talked and the tale must have been very
amusing, for suddenly they burst out in a great guffaw
of laughter at which Esagak seemed more than a little
chagrined. She had a broad smile for me, however, when
I examined her foot. No bones broken. Thank Heaven
for that! (We thank Heaven for so many things in the
Arctic. "No broken bones," is one of them.) I brought
a basin of hot water. Blessed Saints! what a relief! *"Na-
gooruk—na-gooruk!"* You should have heard her. Off
came the other boot. Esagak's reasoning was sound.
What was good for one foot must be good for two feet.
I could not help but admire her fine firm heels, the supple
ankle muscles and well-shaped toes (civilization's corns
and bunions not present). How she did enjoy the novelty of that hot water! and the big basin to put her feet in!
Little bits of carex grass and reindeer hair floated to the
surface from their lodgment between her toes. I added
more hot water. *"Na-gooruk,"* and then seriously she
began to tell me how she hurt her foot, faithful Nasholook interpreting.

"Esagak and that her husband Anga, they get coal from coal mine. That Esagak she is have sister up to Attanik. That sister is have four good sealskin for boot sole. Esagak she like one skin. She take coal to Keruk. (Attanik people were always glad to get coal.) Anga he thinks maybe he see seal on ice. Esagak is drive that sled. Soon she see big fine goose is flying south. That is much late for goose. All the time she is look on goose. Too bad. That ice is catched her foot and she is fall down. Anga, he say Esagak she is look too much on that goose and is not see trail," and with that they were all merry again. With her pain subsiding under the bandage, Esagak could appreciate the joke, but she couldn't resist the clenching comment that if Anga and Tagarook had been *really* good hunters, she might have had a fat goose to give me. Wasn't a goose in the air worth half a dozen seals under the ice? This gave her the last laugh and the injured foot was forgotten.

Three mornings later she came in to tell me that her foot was well enough to continue the trip to Attanik, and jokingly added, in pantomime, that she would have an eye to the trail. She was sure the last goose had gone south anyway. I walked down with her to where the sled was waiting, captivated by the joyous verve these natives fling over their daily living—meeting life's comedies or tragedies with the same hearty cheerfulness.

How pleasant to stretch one's toes out to the lazy warmth of blankets and down quilts on a Saturday morning—no school bells to ring—only a long fair day for one's own affairs and planning to make the most of it. You pull on a robe and slippers and shake up the banked fires, pile on fresh coal and crawl back into the comfort of pillows. The world of daily papers and traffic of trains and other nuisances has long since ceased to exist. You cuddle up exulting in your aloneness.

Alone to think, to plan, to catch the gleam of a bright dream in the future. And maybe you think that can't be a panorama of rose-colored anticipation in the Arctic? When you begin to multiply a year's salary by two— well, say by three (time flies you know) or maybe four, (four years in the Arctic can't be so long) then you add the interest on the first two or three (confidence in your banker expands at this point) and there it is—your magnificent last year of college and the coveted sheepskin— and after that, a year at that Art School in Florence say, or six months there and maybe six in Paris.

Here the warmth of glowing Wainwright coal coaxes you gently away from these rosy dreams of distant ateliers, while the singing purr of a teakettle heard between the staccato clinks of briskly wielded ice knives outside wakens your practical mind, gets you right up and doing.

There's grapefruit for breakfast, farina, toast and coffee,—the little pottery bowl now holds white paper daisies—the blue linen cloth matches the blue-white world you look out on through a window curtained in yellow gingham. A dog team rushes past. These Eskimos are always going somewhere. The driver waves as he goes by. His sled is loaded with camping gear, almost hid by his numerous children cradled on top, like so many kittens, playful and happy. Tooruk and Oyalla come in with the ice for the water barrels. I give them a plate of toast and prune-apple jam and what's left of the coffee. Wish I could eat frozen fish dipped in seal oil with as much relish as they eat toast and jam.

The village today is all astir. Natives going in and out of igloos. Children stand around the sleds expectantly. Dogs are aware of their own importance, those to the north of the village howling it on high C, those to the south doing a chorus in low G, but all yip-yip the same tune as soon as they are harnessed and on the trail.

I was kneading bread into loaves, stopping every little while to wave a floured hand to the families as they went by on their way to the place where the natives are fashioning a corral for the annual roundup of reindeer. The village council had been discussing this business for days. News was received only yesterday that the herders from Icy Cape had started with their deer for Wainwright. Two other herds from up the river are due to follow.

Around noon I concluded there is nothing more desolate than a deserted Arctic village; the sounds of its happy people fled. I put off the letters I had planned to write and the chocolate cake I was about to bake, finished the bread baking, banked the fires, and moved out with the village to build a reindeer corral. Of all the different types of enclosures used for a roundup and the counting of stock, this was the most unique. Great monoliths of ice were cut from the same tundra lake which had yielded the water supply. Six feet long and two feet wide, varying in thickness from twelve to sixteen inches, they were hauled to a comparatively flat place on the tundra where they were placed on end and side by side to make a U-shaped circular wall of ice, the open ends turning out like wide pasture gates, to admit the herd. As I watched the men, eight to ten of them, tugging along with their burden of ice, I thought of the sturdy Oregon pioneers trekking the logs to build their cabins. These Eskimos were pioneering too—if one may call the slow process of converting a hunter people to a herder people, pioneering.

The last block was no sooner in place than the first of the docile deer were sighted just over the low hills toward the river. On they came, grazing leisurely and Tooruk's word picture of a moving antlered herd, a "land of willows moving on many legs" was a reality.

The men stationed themselves every twenty feet on each side of the wide entrance, closing in like great arms when the deer had entered the corral. Once inside, the deer are docile no longer, but mill round and round, wild eyed and affrighted, their hoofs beating a crepitating tattoo on the hard frozen ground.

The moisture rising from their heated bodies hangs over the corral like a fog.

Suddenly a lasso whings out—far and true! Now another—and another! The natives are roping the deer they have chosen for meat—or it may be their sled deer that is wanted. After the deer have been killed and partially skinned, they are placed belly down on the snow with legs propped under. They are not bled or gutted in the manner we are accustomed to seeing. The natives like the meat filled with blood. This may be a wise provision in this country where meat freezes so solid in storage, drying too, in the process. My year's supply of meat was purchased—fine fat hind quarters, the suet on the rump five inches thick. The natives had removed the precious sinews from these, leaving the meat a bit ragged but that did not spoil the joint for me. My larder was now quite complete. (In 1925 the natives at Wainwright were taught how to butcher the deer in the prescribed manner for shipment outside.) There is no abattoir so clean as the snowy tundra—the vast outdoor ever-serviced refrigerator of the North.

Four herds were counted, two from up the River Kuk, the others from Point Lay and Icy Cape. The enterprising herders with their families happily know how to combine business with pleasure—the men light their pipes to swap village news, enjoying their smokes together—the women visit their cousins, aunts, or uncles—go shopping for bright ginghams or a new kettle, or maybe a package of bright needles. At intervals they come to see the teacher and are served the always-ready biscuit and tea, also receive packets of simple remedies, salves and bandages, also books, tablets and pencils, all making for pleasant diversion before returning to their distant herder camps.

Eight thousand deer are moving on to their winter grazing grounds today and the older schoolboys who were recruited for the roundup are back at their desks. Tooruk says he likes "Better I like that school." Oyalla agrees, but adds "That herd is good."

November 1. Temp. -10°. Powdered snow flying before the wind. The coal bin is full and last evening Tooruk brought in a roast of reindeer from the icehouse. He used a saw to cut through the frozen mass. The suet was hard and smooth as ivory, the flesh looked like pink marble. This morning it does not look so romantic—just a piece of red oozy meat lying in a platter of blood, thawed out and ready for the pan. Mighty good roasted, the meat dredged well with flour and brown sugar—skewered over with strips of salt pork or bacon, browned in a hot oven for twenty minutes, then braised with onions, celery-salt, a dash of black pepper, basting frequently until done, adding salt in the last ten minutes of cooking—a venison and wild duck blend for flavor. And such brown gravy! Yum! Yum! But I forget, it is *Na-gooruk,* very much *Na-gooruk!*

There is nothing more exhilarating than a walk out on the ice after a day in the schoolroom. In November it is like walking in a twilight of gray shadows with white chalky spaces marking the ridges where the wind has had a tussle with the ice, carving great masses of fantastic cubist structure. There is a cozy comfort in fur boots, your toes spreading out easily to grasp a sure footing, a springy lightsomeness to the thick fur of which they are made. (Feet never know this freedom encased in stiff leather pinned to a heel stilt and then given a cement surface to travel on. Poor city folks!)

A mile out on the sea ice I meet Aguvalook. He is bringing home "the bacon" in the shape of a fine fat seal. He drags it along as if he were harnessed to a sledge. This leaves his hands free to carry his spear and a small spoon-like net that he has fastened to the end of a long staff. He uses this net to strain small particles of floating ice from the seal hole he has chopped in the ice. On his back is strapped a small three-legged stool made of driftwood on which he has been sitting beside the hole, waiting with poised spear for the seal to poke its nose up for air.

I return to the village with him. In the distance we can see the skin windows of the igloos glowing, orange-colored lights of home, like so many jack-o-lanterns. His wife comes out to meet him, his two small children like little bear cubs, following after. He gives one the stool to carry, the other the spoon net. His wife deftly twists an extra loop in the thong fastened to the seal and gives an arm to the task. Aguvalook asks me if I "like that seal liver." I most certainly do, I answered, brave in my high resolve to conquer any food prejudices which may be lurking, but I add quickly, "just bring me a very small piece."

What a pleasant welcome my rooms give me as I come in from these blustery walks—my cheeks red, eyes shining and a zestful appetite for a hot-reindeer-with-brown-gravy sandwich and a fragrant cup of coffee.

The days have been full since the opening of school with little time for leisure moments. Tonight with lamplight mellow on the flowered chintz which covers the pillows and chairs, the bright bindings of my few books, the cozy warmth radiating from the huge stove, and deerskin rugs on the floor, it is a lovesome place indeed. A few records on the Victrola, (the music of Edvard Greig, that great Chopin of the North, seems strangely at home in this clime) and I am ready to make out my school reports.

(From my Journal.) November 16. Temp. -18°. Wind N.E. The stars are brilliant tonight, gleaming sequins pricked in a sky of black velvet. Orion marching on with the Dog, Sirius tagging his heels—flaming Aldebaron, Vega and Arcturus—a pageant of constellations mandrelling their bright allegiance to the Polar Star. Will we ever know the meaning of this Pageant? Who knows? Enough tonight to have the companionship of these twinkling eulogies of beauty, to listen to their silence, eloquent with words no language has ever been able to sing, set to the melody of the eternal verities.

November 20. Temp. -22°. Wind N.E. The beautiful

white fox skins are beginning to make a luxurious display
in the native store. Neokok came in with four today.
Anakok has eight. Tagarook came in with a lustrous
silver tonight, a magnificent pelt. Already he plans to
trade it for lumber to build a new igloo. Neokok's wife
accompanied her husband to the store. She did most of
the trading for his skins. I am not sure Neokok got all
the tobacco he wanted, but she did get flour and sugar
and tea. On these trapping expeditions the men are gone
for several weeks at a time. For shelter they construct
small snowhouses, or occupy deserted igloos. The traps
are baited with seal meat, walrus or whale meat. Anakok
says he has only fish on his traps, some he brought down
from the river in late summer.

This morning when the boys came in with the ice for
the water barrels I had them move the cases of milk
around. These are stacked around the kitchen walls but
there is always danger of freezing next to the floor. One
could get on very well with the powdered milk and the
condensed sweet milk, but the creamy richness of evaporated milk is such a luxury up here on cereal and in
coffee, and for creamy sauces and desserts, that it is well
worth this eternal vigilance to keep it from freezing. So
every few days the boxes on the floor are brought to the
top, and the side that has been next to the wall is turned
toward the room. (Remember the winter does not last
forever and the cases grow fewer in number as the
months fly by.) While the boys were making a great
clatter of this business, I brushed the frost off the walls
and swept it up like so much dust. This unique task is
now part of the daily routine. In the early morning it
is a simple job, but if left until noon, the heat of the
room melts the frost, water drips and has to be wiped up,

and if left until evening,—oh what a backache! It means the wretched business of chopping ice off the floor! And I might add that one experience with this is enough. One learns a lesson well in the Arctic, mistakes are not often repeated. Evaporated milk curdles when it freezes and is just no good, and chopping ice off the floor is irksome, but these are nothing to the trouble-making thought that walks in and says, "Now don't you wish you had stayed home," and that isn't good either.

(Journal.) November 24. Day of days! What a day! If my sojourn in this Arctic comes to be remembered for just one day of it, this will be *that* day. The mail is here! Heaped up on the chairs, on the bed, on the table, everywhere, three letters in my bosom. I take them out and lay them next to my cheek, run with strange excitement to the window as though I would call on the Arctic and all the stars in heaven to come in and share my joy.

I became aware of the unusual commotion in the village as soon as I heard the dogs preluding their chorus with thin long whines, when a rush of banging doors brought Nasholook into the room shouting, "Mail come! Mail come!" Panigeo rushing in after him with the great sacks, all of them for Wainwright. Panigeo was in a great hurry to get off to Barrow.

This is the first of our three winter mails. The teams leave Kotzebue the first of November, January, and March. At the same time the mail starts south from Point Barrow with the mail for the outside. The drivers usually meet near Point Lay, exchange loads and get back to their stations about the last of the month. Only first-class mail is carried on the sleds. Package mail, papers, and magazines come once a year on the ship. The schoolteachers, missionaries, or sometimes a trader, are appointed postmasters.

Panigeo met the Kotzebue team two miles south of Point Lay and on his return encountered so severe a storm that he was obliged to make camp where he and his dogs were blizzard-bound several days. "That was much bad wind and my dogs plenty tired." He had faced head winds every mile of the way, and a head wind, traveling north, is a bitter wind. One longs for words, words filled with sufficient praiseful meaning to tell the courage, loyalty, and devotion to duty of these Eskimo mail boys, these couriers of the North, these bearers of letters from faraway loved ones and friends, of medicines and serums for the ailing, books and other literature to make our lives more interesting.

Right after dinner I hunted up Nasholook and to-gether we went down to Anakok's igloo to read them the letter that had come from the hospital at Nome. Their son was well, his arm nearly as good as new again. He was bouncing a ball now, each day for exercise. The superintendent of the native schools at Nome had found a good home for him with an Eskimo family and he was going to school every day. He would return to Wain-wright on the first government ship next summer. At once, his mother said she would begin to make a parka for him in the morning. I left the letter with her. She folded it to a small thick wad and put it away happily in the bag where she kept her sinew thread.

It was after midnight when I finished sorting the mail. From the piles of it I'll be reading letters until January. Sixteen letters came marked, "Do not open before Christmas"—as if I'd have time before. A king's ran-som in first-class postage brought a great stack of maga-

zines all the way from New York City. What was it
Stevenson said about "in this era of postal union we *laugh*
at separation"—not when we read three precious letters
in Wainwright with the "union" stretching across miles
of snows, over rough trails, through bitter winds and
storms—three precious letters come that way—pages
blurred with beloved faces, glowing there in the lamplight of home! No, Stevenson, we do not laugh. We
hang a pillow back of the cannon ball next morning to
dry the tears that wet it in the night.

I was highly entertained this evening when Segavan,
one of Wainwright's most enterprising and progressive
citizens came in. Segavan, you know, of the nice clean
igloo, whose wife carefully wipes the cups before pouring
tea. And a high pride he takes in his well-ordered home,
as any man would who can boast of such a household;
meals well cooked and served when men are hungry—
his woman clean, with a heart in her tasks, busy with
affairs of comfort and warmth and serenity, bearing his
children with joy and inner gladness. A living palpable
pride is Segavan's and he delights in telling of it. Also
he converses well in my language and is pleased to visit
and exercise this talent. Also he is pleased to have a dish
of prune tapioca and a cup of coffee stirred into a syrup
with very much sugar. Sugar, he says, is *na-gooruk,
aiyah na-gooruk!*

When Segavan was a very young boy he lived with
his parents at Point Barrow. "Not much igloos in Wainwright that many time ago, . . . all Eskimo peoples like
that good whale hunting at Nuvuk (Point Barrow)."
It was a memorable day when the lumber for the first
school at Barrow was unloaded. Segavan liked to tell

about it, how the heavy beams were floated ashore; how the window frames and doors, glass, hardware, cement, shingles, felt paper, all such were unloaded in the skin boats; clumsy and unwieldy loads to manage among the ever hazardous floes, and by men unaccustomed to such labor. Segavan told me how the natives had helped. He and some of the other boys had rolled the kegs of nails up from the beach. "All Eskimo peoples help that school. All Eskimo peoples is glad that school and that Dr. Stevenson is come to village. Now I tell you something. Me, Segavan, is first boy walk in that school. That Dr. Stevenson is very fine man. He is very good teacher. He teach many thing. He teach little book to keep diary. I write everything in diary. I write, '*Icepack go out.*' I write, '*Icepack come in.*' That many year I write in my diary. That Captain Cochran on ship *Bear,* he say, 'Segavan, when did the ice go out?' I tell him in my diary."

Segavan liked to talk about Captain Cochran. They were old friends. The captain, as many other white folks have done, was more amused than interested in that an Eskimo should keep a diary, but each summer when the old ship *Bear* anchored at Wainwright and Sevagan's little record of weather and ice conditions was always found to be up to date and accurate, the captain conceived a great liking for this fine native, and they became fast friends. In the summer of 1925, a new captain came up with the *Bear.* This was a great blow to Segavan. For many days he sat in front of his igloo quietly and thoughtfully turning the pages of his many little diaries. Then one day he came in, holding his little book, and wanted to know how to spell Covell, the name of the new commander. For Captain Cochran, the captain

Segavan had known and loved, who had made twenty cruises on the *Bear* and whose name will be forever and inseparably linked with the history of Arctic waters, Segavan had this to say, "I tell you something. Segavan is feel very bad. That Captain Cochran come never back to Eskimo. That Captain Cochran is very good friend to Eskimo. Long time of years, I remember, that captain is take all Eskimos on ship *Bear*. He say, 'I shake hand all the time good Eskimo. Never shake hand bad Eskimo. Bad Eskimo drink whisky. Whalers give whisky, Eskimos say no.' Segavan never drink whisky, always shake hand that Captain Cochran. I am feel very bad here." And "here" was over his heart, for so he placed his hand.

Rev. L. M. Stevenson, you will recall, came to Point Barrow the same year the first teachers came to Point Hope and to Cape Prince of Wales. The influence of this good and wise man who served under the subsidy contract with the Presbyterian Board of National Missions, is still as splendid and alive as the day he opened school under such primitive circumstances. Today, at Wainwright, there are four natives who attended this school and who remember him well. Segavan says Mr. Stevenson first taught them the word "book." He stood before his first class, composed of old and young Eskimos, holding the Bible in his hands and said, "Book, Book, Book." Here Segavan walked over to my table and, grasping a book between his hands, proceeded to demonstrate in what must have been the true Stevensonian manner, then added, "I never forget that book."

Another day Segavan came in with a picture carefully wrapped in a piece of seal skin. He wanted me to tell him about "that picture." Years of igloo smoke and seal oil had mellowed its once chromo brilliance. It represented a woman dressed in white with a robe of red and gold draped in graceful folds about her. Her golden hair fell in a great cascade of curls down her back as she pleadingly clung to a cross in the midst of an ocean tempest—storm-blackened sky with lightning cutting across it in a fierce and menacing zigzag. You have guessed the title, *Rock of Ages*. But Segavan had noticed something, "That is very bad storm and much wind," he said. "That woman is look not much wet. Long time my wife Tegausena is in that big whale boat and is very bad storm and Tegausena is wet like seal. Segavan is much wet. That was time like Rock of Ages."

What did it mean to Segavan? Why had he so carefully cherished this picture which had once faced a religious calendar? I could learn only this, "that Dr. Stevenson he teached that song to sing to God Father, that God who make Segavan, that God who all time help Segavan, that Rock of Ages." And then Segavan moved by the love of his old teacher, sang this beautiful hymn in his own tongue, tremulously and reverently.

Aregakama savunga,
Pitkurapkuakniangitchut,
Pisutipayagmaune,
Kiagaluagumaune,
Pilutiakniangitchunga,
Kissivin anautunga.

Tigumiangitlukmaune,
Angarauraknittunga,
Anugaksrakviurutin,
Naklektuktigigatin,
Anaksakvikmoktunga,
Salumanga anaure.

Anignigiaksiguma,
    Asengiagiagataguma,
Nalurame nuname,
    Tautnukupkin inakne,
Jesus agmautunga,
    Eriklunga ilignun. Amen

There is a naïve simplicity to the wording of Eskimo translations. Take their meaning of the Lord's Prayer for themselves. The words "Heaven" and "Kingdom" they simply translate as God's village, or His many villages. The word "temptation" they ignore. No word in the Eskimo language or nothing of Eskimo living, corresponds to our definition of the word, and I did not choose to enlighten them. Segavan would always say, "God's will be done on village," instead of "Thy will be done on earth." The earth was a bit vague to Segavan. Nasholook interpreted it, "Thy will be done on *tundra*," and Tooruk understood it, "Your will be done in *this place*." So with these three, who could speak English and who did most of the interpreting in this village, there was achieved this translation of the Lord's Prayer.

THE LORD'S PRAYER,

as translated by Nasholook, Segavan and Tooruk, working together under a kerosene lamp in the living room of the schoolhouse at Wainwright.

Appowvut kilyugmittuatin ilwit atkin nakugirauli
Our God Father who is this time in His village, holy is that
    name

Ilwin umeadrigutin kilee. Ilwin pikutin nalautauli. Nunani
Your Kingdom come. Please our Father, you do for this place

Nelaudrusiatitat kilyugmi.
The same like in your village.

Netsikaruptigni ublumini aitkoktigut
Seal-meat this day you give us

Pilutivut kulekotigingerglugit kulekotingernigosipsiktut
   pilugidriptignum.
Our many things we owe to people and village, we give
      the people.

Iglegotunnutta piluksisummon asi pilunmin anaututigut
Send people many things good like that peoples is good
      the same,

Ilwinumeadrugun pipigin kwungudlu maununeglu isuit-
   suamig. Amen.
And from many bad days save every people. Amen.

What a simple and adequate prayer was the last line of
this in the Eskimo tongue! "And from many bad days
save every people."

(From my Journal) November 26. Temp. -20°. The
sky is all gloom and overcast though one has no sure way
of knowing whether these be clouds or no, the days are
now so Stygian dark. A light south wind blows.

The two black brant are thawing in the kitchen. When
I took them down from their frosted peg in the icehouse this morning by the light of a lantern, they looked
as if they had been cut in crystal. It is always with re-
luctance I close the door on this enchantment wrought
by icy fingers. Day after tomorrow we celebrate.

THANKSGIVING DAY AT WAINWRIGHT.

Knowing that home letters would contribute to the
joy of this holiday, I purposely kept Dad's letter to read
today. It was dated July 12, and if that sounds like
reading old news, there was one of its lines that read very
much up to date. "You will get on swimmingly up there

until the holidays. Thanksgiving may bring on an attack of home-sickness—be careful of your diagnosis, it may be only indigestion. If acute write a letter home and tell your old Dad what you are doing while we were carving the Bird."

I lost no time acquainting Dad of "the Diagnosis."

> "Wainwright, Arctic Alaska.
> "Thanksgiving Day, 1924.

"Dear old Dad:

"Your letter of July 12th arrived on the first winter mail, day before yesterday. That's waiting a long time for one of your letters, but I content myself with the thought that considering the distance it travelled by dog sled, it might not have come through at all. Don't deceive yourself, Daddy, into thinking that one can indulge in an acute attack of anything up here—home-sickness or indigestion. It just isn't done. But even if it were, I'm taking the surest cure for both—keeping so busy I haven't had time to be homesick, and being so busy lends scant chance to overstuff on food. (What else brings on indigestion?) You will likely take this last statement with a grain of salt when you read what I had for my dinner. Our festivities really began yesterday, when the boys came to prepare the large schoolroom for the native feast and dance. They moved the desks to one side and took the benches to the adjoining storage room. The two tables were covered with oil cloth and it was here I marshalled my older girls for a Domestic Science lesson. Since they are able to obtain flour and canned milk and dried fruit from the Trading store, and know so little of how to prepare them, this was my golden opportunity. The girls were trim and neat in the gingham aprons they had made in the sewing classes, their hair in thick braids hanging down their backs.

"All day long we brewed and baked and last evening the place looked like a cafeteria. I counted the biscuits. There were 912 large ones. We used some lard, but as this is an expensive commodity here for the natives to use, I taught them to utilize their seal-oil and reindeer fat for shortening. Then there was twelve gallons of dried apples, prunes and figs cooked together, almost like the Norwegian sweet soup, twelve gallons of beans cooked with reindeer joints, and two gallons of boiled rice and raisins for the small children. The natives prepared meat, seal and walrus and reindeer at their igloos, and brought it to the schoolroom. Also a delectable compound (to them) of reindeer tallow beaten with bits of meat and seal flipper until it was a creamy mass, or shall I say mess. Eskimo mincemeat I suppose. And no New England housekeeper ever took more pride in her cookery than did these native women making this particular concoction. I had a taste of that Neokok's wife had made. It was quite fluffy and had the stiff consistency of whipped cream, but alas! never the flavor.

"Last night when everything was finished, I felt like the Queen of Hearts surrounded by all those tarts she had made, only I was glad I did not have to worry about some Knave running off with all the good things. An Eskimo would starve before he would steal.

"This morning, at ten o'clock, the natives came in for a short service of Thanks-giving. From my windows I could see them coming with their lanterns. I had trained my little primary children to recite that short verse, a line of which runs 'We thank Thee for the morning light.' It did not take me long to change it to 'We thank

Thee for the lantern's light.' These days we have no morning light, or afternoon light for that matter. In the evening the natives had their feast and when that was over, they cleared the room for their native dances. And Daddy, how you would have enjoyed looking in on them! Three hundred natives in holiday mood, sitting in the big schoolroom enjoying their own good food.

"But I started to tell you about my own Thanksgiving dinner. I went about the preparation of it as though I were expecting all the family. I would send you my recipe for Roast Brant, but you may have some difficulty in securing the bird. The *Branta Nigricans*, I believe, is not to be found in your part of the world. On second thought I'll send it. You stuff them with Danish dressing, 1 cup of pitted prunes, 1 cup of canned pie apples and 1 large cup of bread crumbs. Of course you chop the fruit, then season with a dash of salt and moisten with prune juice. Pop into a hot oven. The oven of my range is always like that (I wake up in the night with the coal shovel in my hand). Oh, yes, you baste the bird every few minutes, especially if it's the first time you ever roasted one. And then you make that epicurean delight, Sauce Bigarade. (Remember the day we had this at Valiquet's?) I wonder if you could duplicate mine. I doubt it, but it seems a shame to send you directions for roasting an Arctic bird without the sauce. So when your bird is done, beautifully braised and crackly, remove from the pan and pour off all but half a cup of drippings. Blend in a spoon of flour, then add a big cup of reindeer stock. Please stir this until smooth and then dash in some salt, sugar, and pepper and the juice and grated rind of an orange, that is, if you are where an orange can be had. Here we add the same of Dundee marmalade. That's where an Arctic cook makes an improvement on the sauce. Now serve up the rest of the dinner. Currant jelly, candied sweet potatoes, and buttered hominy. Top it off with French coffee and if the evening is still young, go to the Opera. Go to twenty Operas,—one for yourself and all the rest for me. (Flesh Pots of Egypt. Acute Attack.)

"Same day . . . Two hours later.

"All the time I was dining I could hear the rhythmic throbbing of the native drums; I left the dishes to enjoy their entertainment. The schoolroom was crowded and suffocatingly hot. All the natives were sitting on the floor. Up in front, where my desk stands on school days, a native was dancing. Tagarook, Nasholook, Neokok and Tingook were the orchestrists. They were beating drums made of driftwood, a hoop of it, over which had been stretched the dried stomach of a walrus. An ivory handle is attached. From where I sat they looked like palm leaf fans. Held in the drummer's left hand, tapping from beneath with his right, using a light willow withe to drum a series of weird monotonous rhythmic stanzas while the natives accompanied the music with as monotonous a song. A song of sounds mainly, for it hasn't any words. *"Aiyah-e-yah ang-ah aiyah, aiyah-e-yah, aiyah ang-ah."* The dancer poses through various interpretive gestures, keeping time with the drumming. One of these was an interpretation of a hunter hunting seal on the ice. Another hunting a bear. Still another was the dance of the loon. For this the man donned a headdress, a crown of sealskin to which was attached the great yellow beak of this bird. He was certainly a most active loon. It was a popular number, encored again and again.

"The women danced in groups, their arms swaying to and fro in unison, their legs stiff pedestals for the swaying bodies. The effect was dreamy and relaxing. Suddenly Tingook threw down his drum and leaped into the dancing area. Ah-regah! Fresh interest animated the crowd. His quick jerky movements and rapid turning of head and arms, whatever he was interpreting, was adjudged the hit of the evening. The older men reclined against the walls quietly, leisurely smoking their ancient and odorous pipes. The babies went to sleep. Several of the older children did the same, but the women, wide awake, never lagged in their droning accompaniments to the drums. Occasionally an accenting note would thwang out, like a gong to waken those who would sleep or whose interest might be waning.

"The room held a varied strata of odors, ripe seal-oil, the thick pungence of human exertion, and a blue hovering of strong tobacco. I sat beside old Tooklamora, whose rheumy eyes were bright with little lights remembering when she too had known youth and had danced, when Takuluk, now long since dead, had loved her.

"Though the dancers were far from wearied, the school regulations enjoined them to wrap up their drums and seek their igloos at midnight. I waited at the door, to bid them goodnight. The women were happy as they trudged out laden with babies, wooden platters and cups, the children drowsy, as only children can be at midnight. The men were as alive as when the dance first started.

"Long after the last native had crawled into his igloo, I watched the stars and the faintest glow of the Aurora, stretching its long pale fingers westward and wished that I could drink in enough of the peace of an Arctic night to provide my soul with serene bright beauty forever. I send you of this beauty as much as this letter will hold. The mail sled will start southward about January fourth and sometime in April, when your garden is like green lace, you will be reading about my Thanksgiving, and I'll be waiting for the first ship, though I am well aware it cannot possibly get here before the middle of July.

"Postscript.—December 3.

"This is the week for bathing the children. As there are sixty-eight of them, two days are set aside for this phase of an Arctic school teacher's job. In the summer the children are bathed every two weeks, in the winter every month. The parents provide the ice, blocks from the reindeer corral. It is melted and heated on the cannonball, a tedious all-day business. You may be sure there was none of it wasted, mercy no! not in the Arctic. A small basin of hot suds is sufficient for the actual scrubbing of each child, after which he steps into a tub for a rinse-down, poured from a pitcher of warm water. The older children help to bathe the tiny tots, though the darlings are so cunning I can't keep from wrapping them up in the big towels just to feel them wiggle and see them smile. Yesterday the boys had their day. What a pity they cannot know the joys of an 'ol swimming hole.' Today was the girls'. In the afternoon the older girls wash their hair, enjoying the luxury of the warm room, drying and brushing and combing their long black tresses until they shine like lacquer. How prideful they are of their thick braids!

"Considering their mode of living, the Eskimos keep extraordinarily clean. Bathing, however, will never become a fetish with them. Responsive as they are to so many of civilization's ways, you may be sure it will be sometime before the Eskimos indulge in bathrooms of orchid and gold. But I'll challenge any white woman: —Forget about bathing your feet for a month and see if at the end of that time your toes and heels will be as clean as was old Kaivarinyah's, when she came in recently to tell me of the 'Pain in that leg.' Nor had she ever bathed them, for she thought the hot water I was using for hot packs was medicine.

"Oh, I nearly forgot. Yes, the towels are provided by the department, a big bolt of linen crash, hemmed by the girls in the sewing classes. And they are given a practical lesson in laundering when the towels are washed, folded and put away in the schoolroom cupboard ready for the next swim. And just one thing more, the rinsing water in the tubs is used to scrub the schoolroom floor. Don't turn up your noses. We add a dash of lysol to it.

"I've never mentioned a bath, the bathtub kind, for the good reason that we haven't a bathroom. What I do have is a thick bathmat on which I can turn around and around in front of the cannonball, to keep one hip from freezing while the other is being sponged. One morning, however, the happy combination of a warm room and plenty of hot water almost proved my undoing. There I was, turning on the bathmat, lathered to the fluffiness of a birthday cake, when Taliak, one of the herders, walked in. He seemed not at all disturbed by my unusual appearance and sat himself down to casually announce (please believe I was making frantic efforts to reach a towel or a robe or something) that he had just come from Herd No. 2, that he had killed a wolf and a caribou, and 'that chief herder's wife, she like that same kind medicine.' There was no use asking him to wait in the schoolroom. He was leaving at once for the herd, he said. So I bottled a prescription the while a pool of soap-suds trickled down my shins. I finished my bath in the pantry. For my next one—well never mind, I was never so embarrassed again. Why didn't I lock the door? For the best reason in the world. There wasn't any key and no one could remember if there had ever been one—and besides, it was the morning for those (blessed again) coal-bin boys. Thus do we keep clean in the Arctic."

Tingook's mother died this morning. Only yesterday I had taken her some barley broth and she had seemed stronger. A very old woman, ailing since last summer, patient and uncomplaining, grateful for the small comforts I had been able to take to her. She lay on a bed of greasy skins, dressed in an old parka. An old stone oil lamp was beside the bed, where she could reach the moss wick to keep it trimmed. She was often alone in the miserable hole she knew as her igloo. Her two sons, men of the village, took turns caring for her, one at home while the other would trap. Four mangy dogs, ill kept and too thin to bark were tethered near the entrance. It was like entering a reeky grave. Crawling in, one met the stifling air, fever laden and hot with fetid odor, repellent and sickening. For weeks Tingook or Tokomak had been coming to my kitchen every day for the cup of warm milk or soup.

The first time I saw her, Nasholook had taken me. She was propped against a heap of old skins. A band of dirty sealskin was tightly bound about her head, wisps of gray hair escaping over her eyes. Her head ached and the band was to cure it. The native doctor had been there before me. I gave her no medicine that day. One had to proceed slowly for she had protested before against seeing the missionary doctor or having anything to do with his white medicine. The doctor had taken her husband to the hospital at Barrow and he had never returned. Next morning I asked Kittik to take her a nice new comb and to comb her hair. I allowed Kittik enough time to do the hairdresser's job, then I followed with some soup. Just as I thought, they were about to bind the greasy band about her head again. I took the filthy thing promising to send a ribbon, a bright red ribbon (cut it in two lengths so it couldn't be used for a band). It took several visits to gain her confidence and to quiet her fears and then one day, voluntarily she asked for "teacher's medicine." She swallowed the cascara without protest. (Even a doctor is grateful if after nine visits his patient will be good and do as he directs.) And I persuaded Tingook to clean the igloo. It was a wretched place.

Today they came for lumber to make the coffin. You remember the boards of the organ crate we saved? Those, with odds and ends of boxes were used. The schoolroom became a carpenter's shop this morning. By noon it was an undertaker's parlor, and this afternoon a place of worship where the burial service was read. A sled waited outside for the coffin.

It was a strange procession that wended its way to the low rise of ground back of the village. A brilliant moon lighted the way. The hard snow gave back its light as water glistens on white marble. The men of the village led the way, their long black shadows making a path for the women and children who followed. When the place had been selected, (they were careful not to top another grave beneath) the coffin was set on the leveled snow, and the men went off to cut the huge snow blocks to build a mausoleum over it. Their long bright knives glittered in the moonlight as they worked swiftly. The women huddled in groups around Tingook and Tokomak who sat hunched over on the empty sled.

With blocks eight inches thick and three feet square, they soon had a double wall built round with great slabs in two layers for the top. Every chink and crack was filled and tamped with snow—everyone helping to scoop up loose snow—the women and little children running back and forth with handfuls, patting it down, the men smoothing all with their long knives. When all was finished, Nasholook asked me to "sing please and pray." In that still cold, our voices seemed to freeze in midair, the melody rising and falling over the vastness in a sustained twanging as if a bright sword had cut across some silver string. Rest in peace—and silence— the snow blowing across the moon, low on the horizon then.

There is so long a time to wait here for friendly dust to return to friendly dust in this eternally frozen God's acre. In the summer when the surface has thawed, the natives will bury their dead, but even then the tundra must be picked out, frozen clod by clod until a shallow grave is there. One can only associate the white gleaming beauty of frost with the dead in the Arctic. In that moment, remembering the rimed beauty of the plumage of dead birds, I saw myself interred, lying there sheened in silver frost— eyelashes and every strand of hair a shining lovely thing —beautiful at last—and dead—the velvet sky and white stars radiant, my shroud forever.

(From my Journal) December 16. Stars out and clear as a bell all day. Temp. -32°. Saturday, I started out with one of those housewifely programmes that are always a part of the week before Christmas. Mincemeat for one thing. Reindeer meat and suet, dry apples, raisins and sugar and spice. The rooms are sweet-smelly tonight, like mother's kitchen long ago. I could almost be a bit homesick. Suppose Kipling could have had a yearning for home and plum-pudding when he wrote that "Smells are surer than sights or sounds to make your heartstrings crack"? Mine almost did but for another of those penciled paper night messages. Trust some woman in Wainwright to have a baby about the time I'm heading into the bluest of blues. I was never so thankful to start off with my little black bag.

At midnight, Kivik, wife of Negovanna, gave birth to a baby girl. Negovanna is away trapping. A few weeks ago, taking advantage of her husband's absence and the good weather, Kivik decided to visit her people at Attanik, driving a sled and eight dogs and taking her children with her. The igloo was cold, floor and walls white with frost. She had not had time to prepare food for her little family, but the dogs were tethered and the moss wicks were trimmed and burning brightly in the old stone lamps. While the new baby was on the way, the children sat on the bed shelf, chewing on lumps of tallow. I shall be taking soup to them for a few days. Whew! Two hours in that igloo! My rooms were near to Heaven when I returned, sniffing sugar and spice in the first hall.

The beauty of the Arctic quite unfits one for the practical business of life, or at any rate, I was unfitted today. My Sunday dinner was cooked and eaten between rapturous intervals of gazing at the moon. I could trace three luminous halos, shimmering like white flames around it, when frost effulgence obscured its bright disk this afternoon. Tonight the air is diamond clear and the moon is spilling quicksilver over every knoll and ridge as far as eye can see. Flung from the northeast, the Aurora crackles its strange fire overhead—wavering searchlights from another world.

December 22.

This date on the calendar should be a comfort. We *know* the sun is on its way north again, but there is no way of telling midnight from noon as yet. Only the set habit of being up a given number of hours, then in bed for so many hours, makes me feel that when the sun does return, I'll be doing things at the right time of the clock's going-around. I hope I'm not mixed up on this and eating my luncheon at midnight instead of at noon. Winding the clock is very important business these days, religiously attended to.

We had a dress rehearsal this afternoon for the pageant the school children are giving for their parents and their friends from Icy Cape and Attanik. I must confess I had some misgivings as to just what a Christmas entertainment would mean to the Eskimos taking part, but when the Wise Men walked on the improvised stage today, (the native store provided the costumes) I simply exulted. Tooruk, Panick, and Agorak entered into their characters with a dignity quite befitting Three Wise Men from the East. So with the Shepherds! Dressed in their own fur garments, carrying ice staffs for crooks, the younger boys looked and acted the part to perfection. After all, herders of sheep are not so different from herders of reindeer. They could well understand, "While shepherds watched their herds by night." And no chorus of white children ever sang the carols and Christmas hymns so joyously as did these herder Shepherds of the North.

For three days running my children have been painting drawing paper green and cutting it into fringes, and making colored chains and stars and cornucopias. Our tree is unique. It isn't any kind of a tree that ever grew, but when it was decorated and the natives had brought their gifts for each other, it was every bit as Christmasy as any evergreen. For the benefit of those who may be contemplating a sojourn in the Arctic over Christmas, here is the secret of its growing. Take a pole of driftwood eight feet long and about four inches thick. Now bore holes in it where your imaginative eye tells you branches should be growing, insert some old broom handles or pieces of driftwood, wind these with green fringed paper, hang up your kindergarten cornucopias, chains and stars, and behold: the spirit of Christmas in the Arctic!

The day before Christmas the natives decked the tree with their gifts for each other—sealskin for boots in pieces bleached white as vellum, walrus meat and seal liver, a few gun cartridges, a sumptuous gift by the way, skeins of sinew thread and needles, flour and tea, wooden platters made of driftwood, pieces of ivory and whalebone, fur for mittens and braces of frozen birds.

Before the white man came, the Eskimos had no feast to compare with our celebration of Christmas. Gifts, to them, were every day happenings, for all seasons and for all occasions; very especially when visiting relatives or friends in distant places, as when the reindeer herders from their camps inland visit the people of this coast village of Wainwright, they come with presents of deer skins, trays of fish caught in the inland rivers, or bunches of willow withes, sometimes a wolf skin. In return they are presented with pokes of seal oil, seal meat or whale *muktuk,* or household utensils carved from driftwood or bone.

CHRISTMAS EVE

The igloos are deserted tonight. Our pageant went off beautifully and now the schoolroom is a noisy place of fun and laughter, thrumming of drums and natives dancing, with the younger men putting on exhibition feats of strength and skill. Children sit wide eyed and sticky with raisins and candy—old women pleasuring in little bags of tea and lump sugar—old men supremely content with small blocks of pressed tobacco. "*Ah-regah!* presents from Missus Eva!"

CHRISTMAS DAY AT WAINWRIGHT

Merry Christmas, Tooruk!
Merry Christmas, Oyalla!
"Yesh, that fine Krishmush, Missus Eva,—that plenty good Krishmush all the time."
Tooruk and Oyalla were in a gay holiday mood. The ice and coal came in with a bang. The Victrola was pealing out a record of Cathedral bells and college chimes —"the Christmas bells of my homeland, Tooruk." Tooruk was all ears with enthusiasm. "That fine moosik, Missus Eva, I make 'em same in Wainwright," and off he went with Oyalla to clang joy to the world, pulling the bell rope long and vigorously. I must confess it put a strain on my imagination to see the sameness, audition-

ally speaking, but I swear, no bell or set of bells was ever
rung more joyously for the glad tidings.

Our weather was the woolpack variety, with snow
as thick as that flying before the wind. The natives
ploughed through it gaily for the services, stamping the
snow from their *mukluks,* jolly as Christmas, in the
halls. We sang the Christmas carols and read the story
from the Gospel of Matthew. Old Kunoodluk prayed
long and fervently.

After my dinner of roasted wild swan, currant jelly,
and apricot soufflé—imagine such a feast within eleven
hundred miles of the Pole!—I sat me down in the cush-
ions of a fawnskin robe to while away the time with
coffee and music until the clinic hour. Little Kavik
would be coming in for her daily spoon of cod-liver oil
and Similuk to have his shoulder dressed, a stubborn
wound he had suffered during the reindeer roundup.

Heaped high on my table was the strangest collection
of Christmas gifts I had ever received; everything from
a small bunch of walrus whiskers (looking like dirty
porcupine quills), given to me by one of my schoolboys,
to an old caribou skin bag that Anakok's wife was careful to explain had been used by many generations for
women's clothing. The herders from Icy Cape presented me with three frozen reindeer tongues, shining
with frost on a wooden platter. There was fur and
sealskin, enough for several pairs of boots, to say nothing
of pairs all made and ready to wear. One, trimmed with
white fox is luxurious enough for a queen's carriage
boots. Another of dyed sealskin, embroidered with
white reindeer hair in an intricate and beautiful design.
There are tassels of glistening ermine skins, and little
bags of walrus teeth, an ivory handle for "a woman's

KAVIK.

Eva Louise Richards
1928

knife," and an igloo window of bearded seal intestine.
Come to think of it, they had given me everything but
an igloo.

These gifts did not come wrapped in bright tissue and
tinsel ribbons. They came with happy faces, with quaint
holiday greetings, and many many *Tank-oo's* and *Kwayanna's* from hearts overflowing with affection and
genuine gratitude. A teacher's biggest job up here is to
be worthy of so much.

The lamplight glittered on the frosted windows when
Tooruk and Oyalla came in to fill the coal buckets for
the night. They were in a hurry to be off. "Yesh, Missus
Eva, the peoples have Krishmush singing to Segavan's
igloo, same you teach 'em, Silent Night."

Vacation lasts until January 3 when the mail sled is
due from Barrow. The days are filled with writing
letters, making out reports and getting requisitions
ready. It does not seem possible that I have come to the
time when I must think of next year's supplies. I scarcely know what I will need, with half a year's supplies still
on the shelves and yet the orders *must* be sent. It will
be April before these requisitions can reach the outside.
Orders must be in Seattle at least a month before ships
sail for the far North. The coast guard cutter patrol for
the Arctic leaves San Francisco about May 15, calling
in at Seattle for supplies and mail. Our *Boxer* sails for
the far North about July 15. These are the two ships
we are certain to see this summer—certain? Well we
never know. The ice may go out, and again it may stay
in. An Arctic uncertainty, thrilling to contemplate,
somewhat expensive if the worst happens. The supplies
would have to be landed south of here somewhere, Icy

Cape probably, and the natives would sled it up next winter at something like six dollars per ton per day. More than once has this happened to the teachers at Point Barrow, when their coal supplies were landed here at Wainwright. As you may surmise, the supplies were sledded, but the coal—well, no one cares to burn money. The teachers had to resort to blubber as fuel for their kitchen ranges and the school heaters all winter—nasty smoky stuff to burn, the stench worse than the smoke. It was several years before the chimneys were free of the greasy smelly soot.

January 1.

Happy New Year! The bag of mail is ready for the sled—letters, reports, requisitions, everything—cause enough to be happy!

To stretch my legs after such housed concentration at my desk, as well as to celebrate the day, I singled out a great ridge on the sea ice as the objective for a walk this afternoon. I never got there. A southwest wind was blowing, the wind that plays havoc with the ice pack, heaving and shifting and crushing it in weird detonations. I had scarcely left the bank when I froze in my tracks, hearing the unearthly thunder of it beyond the shore. I hurried home through the strange muffled silence that followed and had no sooner reached the door when the rumbling started creeping up again, the increasing terrorous booming reverberating all through the night. The dogs of the village were in a panic, their wolfish howls adding to the uproar. The sound of it was nerve-racking. I fidgeted around with a number of tasks to turn my mind from it, arranging medical cabinets, emptying ashes, cleaning drawers, when I chanced

upon my pocket volume of Milton, only to make matters worse. Trust Milton to make vivid some terrific
disturbance like this!

> I heard the wrack as Earth and Sky would mingle; but myself
> was distant; and these flaws, though Mortals fear them, As danger-
> ous to the pillar'd frame of Heaven, Or to Earth's dark basis under-
> neath, Are to the main as inconsiderable, and harmless, if not whole-
> some, As a sneeze to Man.

Well, a cannonading ice pack might be as harmless as
a sneeze but I was mighty thankful to have three halls
to shut out the tumult. When I went to bed the snow
was doing its best to silence it, packing its felted layers
against the south windows. Through the dismal gloom
I could just make out the lighted window of Kayalluk's
igloo, my nearest neighbor, and what a cheering sight
it was!

But I could not sleep. At two o'clock I was up again.
The storm was doing its lashing best to blow Wainwright smack to the Pole—a storm that would surely
delay the mail team from Barrow I thought. Dear me!
There seems to be nothing certain about the Arctic except its presence. I chucked Milton, (what a book to
bring to the Arctic!) made a cup of chocolate and sat
down to adventure (in the dead of the night) with
Captain Frederick William Beechey. The story of his
voyage along this coast made me feel as if I were reading
the morning paper—only fancy coming to these shores
in a ship named the *Blossom!*

Truth is stranger than fiction on lonely nights like these
Turning the pages of historic scenes
Hearing the wind drive ghost sails through the seas.
The Arctic wind that drives white smoke today.

Ghost sails! Beechey's little ship, the *Blossom*, drifting

along this coast with a current which was repeatedly tried and found to be always setting to the northeast, the crew keeping a vigilant eye for signs of the Franklin expedition; landing frequently to inspect the shores and question the natives; to place landmarks and signposts along the coast; to do all the things required of expeditions in those long ago days. It is when Beechey tells of the Eskimos in his narrative that one is immediately scudded into the present, for progress in its onward march has not been so mindful of the little polar people.

He recounts that upon landing the natives would at once proceed to offer articles to trade with him, or to entertain him. At one place an old native perched himself on top of an igloo and began a song accompanied by his "skin tambourine," and Beechey says the old fellow "seemed as happy as if fortune had placed him in one of the most favoured spots on earth." Presently two old women joined in the singing and "it was," he says, "a sight on the whole, which clearly proves that happiness itself is but a relative idea, for it was here witnessed amongst a people, who may be truly said to be without a comfort on earth."

The good-natured disposition of these people, and indeed of all the natives along this coast, was a source of highest gratification to Captain Beechey, "as it was," he says, "in some measure a guarantee for the safety and protection of the Franklin party." He tells of their honesty in their dealings and of their generous hospitality and kindliness. It was hard to believe that all this was written one hundred years ago. For the Eskimos are much the same today. Education has greatly fostered their well-being but this prosperity has not robbed them of their old-time virtues.

Nearly forty years since the first school was established. Much has been done. They have been trained to care for their herds of reindeer, affording them a better mode of living with many comforts. Co-operative native trading stores have been established in nearly all the villages, so that the pious fraudulent traders must go elsewhere to practice their oily methods of procuring furs, whalebone and ivory. In every village today there are a number of natives who intelligently study the fur markets and the prices of the goods for which these are traded. The time has gone when a few bottles of cheap whisky can be traded for bales of fine furs, leaving a village and its people destitute.

On the other hand, Dr. Knud Rasmussen believed that education for the Eskimos on this coast was being pushed with too much vigour. He deplored the fact that many fine old hunters had become herders of reindeer and that the old traditions and customs were speedily being lost forever. He could not see that the white man had depleted the waters and that the fine old hunters had little left to hunt. What's more, he did not see the comfortable camps at the herds. It is to be regretted that Rasmussen did not visit Wainwright in the winter months, for tonight he would have felt that all was well on this northwest coast. With the temperature registering -42° the old traditions and customs seem very near.

The wind has gone so we may look for the mail sled to sleek in at most any hour now. To reach the satisfied certainty that I have not forgotten something I am checking over my list of supplies for the nth time.

FOOD SUPPLIES FOR ONE YEAR IN THE ARCTIC

2 bbls. White Flour
½ bbl. Graham Flour

```
 10 lbs. Yellow Corn Meal
 30 lbs. Rolled Oats
 10 lbs. Steel Cut Oatmeal
 50 lbs. Rice
 10 lbs. Bayo Beans
 30 lbs. Small White Beans
100 lbs. Cane Sugar
 10 lbs. Elbo Macaroni
  5 lbs. Spagetti
 75 lbs. Butter in Brine
 10 lbs. Coffee
 10 lbs. Tea
  5 lbs. Cocoa (in 1 lb. tins)
 10 lbs. Sweet Bar Chocolate
  3 lbs. Tapioca (in ½ lb. Packages)
 16 Cases Evap. Milk (Tall Tins)
  2 Cases Condensed Milk
 15 lbs. Powdered Milk
  5 lbs. Malted Milk (In 1 lb. Bottles)
  1 Crate Potatoes (For immediate use)
 10 lbs. Dehydrated Potatoes
 10 lbs. Dehydrated Onions
 25 lbs. Dehydrated Soup Vegetables
  2 Cases Sweet Potatoes (canned No. 2½ tins)
  1 Case Peas (No. 2 tins)
  1 Case Corn (No. 2 tins)
  1 Case Midget Peas (No. 2 tins)
  2 Dozen Whole Small Beets (No. 2 tins)
  2 Dozen Spinach (No. 2½ tins)
  1 Case Hominy (No. 2½ tins)
  1 Case Tomatoes (No. 2½ tins)
  1 Case Peaches (No. 2½ tins)
  1 Case Sliced Pineapple (No. 2½ tins)
  1 Case Raspberries (No. 2 tins)
  1 Case Pears (No. 2½ tins)
  2 Dozen Strawberries (No. 2 tins)
  1 Dozen Dundee Marmalade
  1 Case White Figs (No. 2½ tins)
  1 Case Assorted Jams (Jelly Glass Size)
  1 Case Pie Apples
  1 Case Pie Loganberries
  1 Case Alaska Red Salmon (No. 1 tins)
```

1 Dozen Boned Chicken (No. 1 tins)
2 Dozen Minced Clams (No. ½ Size)
1 Dozen Oysters (No. 1 tins)
2 Dozen Sardines (Flat tins)
1 Dozen Glasses Dried Beef
20 lbs. Bacon (Alaska sealed)
3 Hams (Alaska sealed)
20 lbs. Leaf Lard (5 lb. pails)
25 lbs. Dehydrated Apples
25 lbs. Italian Prunes
10 lbs. Seeded Raisins
5 lbs. Seedless Raisins
1 Dozen Grape Juice (pints)
1 Dozen Orange Juice (pints)
1 only Lime Juice (quart)
6 Bottles Maple Syrup (pints)
1 Vanilla Extract (8 oz.)
1 Lemon Extract (6 oz.)
6 Glasses Peanut Butter
6 Small Bottles Pickles
3 lbs. Walnut meats (Vacuum packed)
2 lbs. Mixed nut meats (Vacuum packed)
6 Royal Baking Powder (12 oz. tins)
6 Spices (Ginger, Nutmeg, Curry, Celery Salt,
    Mustard, Cinnamon)
2 Pkgs. Corn Starch
3 lbs. Popcorn
10 lbs. Iodized Salt (1 lb. tins)
1 only 2 oz. Pepper
1 only Paprika
6 Pkgs. Yeast
2 Instant Postum (8 oz. tins)
1 Pkg. Soda
2 Pkgs. Bran
3 lbs. Cheese (Edam)
5 lbs. American Cheese (Arctic sealed)
6 Bottles Catsup (pints)
3 lbs. Pearl Barley
5 lbs. XXXX Powdered Sugar
1 Case Carrots (No. 2½ tins)
1 Case Asparagus (No. 2 tins California green)
6 only Brussels Sprouts (No. 2½ tins)

6 only Pumpkin (No. 2 ½ tins)
2 only Lobster (Flat tins)
5 lbs. Honey
2 Jugs Molasses (quarts)
½ Case Eggs (Wax sealed) 16 dozen
2 Tins Evaporated Eggs (2 ½ lbs. each)
6 Pkgs. Crackers (Wax seal)
6 Pkgs. Rye Crisp (Wax seal)
2 Gallons Salad Oil (½ gal. tins)
1 small Jar preserved Ginger
12 Pkgs. Knox Gelatine
12 Pkgs. Assorted Jello
1 Tin Marshmallows
2 Bottles Maraschino Cherries
1 Jug Vinegar (2 quarts)
2 Tins Beef Cubes
3 Tubes Vegetable Color Paste (Red, Yellow, Green)

FOR THE CHRISTMAS TREE

12 lbs. French Mixed Candy
12 lbs. Satin Mixed Candy
10 lbs. Cube Sugar
20 lbs. Pipe Tobacco (½ lb. tins)

Nothing like good food to square up with an Arctic assortment of wind and weather. These supplies plus reindeer roasts and steaks and tongue, brant, goose, and ptarmigan made for variety in meals, a year's breakfasts, luncheons and dinners for myself, about five hundred bowls of soup for my patients, a number of treats for the coal boys and plenty of extra milk for the babies.

These babies! My babies! They were always on my mind. It's no small job teaching Eskimo mothers to feed the little ones reindeer broth with rice or duck soup, when it is so easy to give them a bit of blubber or frozen fish, and so much trouble to cook rice or make soup, the trouble due to their mode of living, not indifference. I have heard enlightened white mothers make flimsy excuses when a certain formula was advised for their infants, and they with all modern conveniences. If you could see the meagre cooking accommodations in these igloos! The older natives with stone lamps and moss wicks burning blubber, the next generation with stoves, makeshift affairs made of oil tins, but so ingeniously constructed that coal may be burned in them. There are only two igloos in Wainwright with small cookstoves. So you see, cooking broth and rice for babies is not only a trouble, it's a problem.

January 6. Panigeo and the mail have started south. He stopped one hour in Wainwright, just long enough to adjust his load (the mail from here and Barrow consists largely of furs this trip), augment his team with two fine young dogs from Otoiyuk's team, eat a hot lunch, and he was off. He hopes to make Point Lay in record time.

January 10. How long and dark this day has been! The white glare of the gas lights in the schoolroom is trying. All day they burn. Today it was necessary to pump up the pressure (40 lbs.) in the gasoline tank twice. It is so cold that the gasoline is milky thick in the drums outside. Attendance at school is perfect—darkness or storm, nothing keeps the children away. After school when the girls had finished sweeping the schoolroom, we all went out to sweep the snow off the south windows. Just to see the light of Kayalluk's igloo is a comfort. The ground around the building booms like a cannon tonight, cracking in the intense cold.

Temperature -48°. Thus it stands, noon or midnight, 48 below. Bitter and desolate country, and yet how snug and warm the Eskimos have made it their own.

How they have adapted themselves, in comfort, to its cruel circumstances! If one could find the words to make an epic poem of their lives, born, begotten, and buried in this land of bleakness!

With this mood coming on, I went to visit Kayalluk and his wife Kittik. I nearly didn't get over the high drift which has piled up at the south corner of the school-house. It was like trying to climb a pyramid of polished marble. In the steep slope on the other side, Kayalluk had cut small caverns for his dogs where they lay all curled up out of the wind. The entrance to the ice tunnel was covered with a walrus hide, thick and so stiff and heavy that it was with difficulty I lifted it away to crawl into the dark passage. But such a welcome, such a chorus of *Ah-regahs! Ah-regah! Ah-regah!* as greeted me! their happy faces blurred through the frost on my eyelashes.

At once a place was made for me on the floor. Old Tooklamora, who lives with them, dragged her bearskin from her corner to sit beside me. She was busy splitting sinew for thread, rolling it against the palm of her hand, twisting the needle ends firmly, tying them in skeins of equal length. Kittik was sewing a pair of boots. A few days after Christmas she had asked me for the pieces of red crepe paper which had served as decorations. She had used it to dye some white sealskin, and now the red stripes around the crimped soles were very attractive as was the trimming of tiny red squares she had sewed at the top. Her husband smiled his approval of all this fancy work. Presently he reached into the dim recess behind him for a wooden box made of driftwood, brown and smooth with the oily patina of age. The cover was hinged with walrus thong. In it were his treasures, pieces of ivory,

Kittik feeding her dogs

Eva Louise Richards.
1925.

a sack needle, buttons, and a small fishing kit consisting
of an ivory hook attached to a stiff black cord. This
cord, he told me, was whalebone split very fine. Both
hook and line were wrapped in a strip of breast of loon,
the oily feathers matted to the skin. It was a neat little
roll, easily carried in a boot top with no danger of injury
from the sharp hook. Also he was proud of some shuttle
sticks he had made of bone, for weaving fishing nets of
braided sinew thread. Next, he produced eight heavy
walrus teeth all smoothed with a hole bored in one end.
To these he had fastened strands of sinew, all of a length,
the ends caught together under a little tuft of feathers.
He whirled them rapidly, the weighted strings flying out
like the spokes of a wheel, to demonstrate what could
happen to a flock of ducks in the spring, a flying trap to
bind and entangle their wings and legs, bringing the birds
down quickly.

And then Tooklamora pulled out a large bag made of
caribou skin. It was almost as big as herself. From this
she took some old fur clothing, two pairs of boots, an old
sewing bag made of eider duck heads in which she kept
her neat rolls of sinew thread, some in skeins all braided
and of proper length for boots. Also some large skeins
for sewing the canoe skins of *oogooruk*. The canoes
would be recovered in the spring. She showed me a
curious old needle case, a hollow tube of ivory through
which was run a strip of sealskin, thrust with some ancient bone needles. On an ivory hook at one end she had
strung her thimbles, queer little circles of tough walrus
hide with a small flap cut to fit the index finger, the
Eskimo woman's thimble finger. It was trimmed with
some old blue beads, once the coin of the Russian naviga-
tors who had traded along this coast. She had another

bag made of dried walrus stomach in which she kept pieces of fur, her piece bag I gathered, with bits of light and dark reindeer fur, some ermine both white and brown, winter and summer skins, and a short length of intricately pieced border for trimming, beautifully checkered, light squares and dark together. Kittik explained that she herself would finish it. Tooklamora was now too old and much too sick. She could not sew any more at which Tooklamora beat her chest and wailed, *"Muck-ee—muck-ee,"* and again, *"muck-ee"*—"soon I will be dead."

Then Kittik made tea and wiped my cup carefully with a swatch of old underwear. We had a jolly time. I told them how comforting it was to see their light to which they replied that the schoolhouse lights "was plenty glad." Kayalluk could see by them, he said, to cut walrus hide up on the cache for his new dog harness.

When I returned to the schoolhouse Kittik came with me, to get some syrup of wild cherry for old Tooklamora. Next morning, to my surprise Tooklamora herself hobbled in to thank me and to return the empty bottle. This was not required but she felt very responsible for "that teacher's bottle." Also she wanted to visit. Nasholook came in to interpret.

Tooklamora had long claimed some happy kinship who had come from afar. It was her sister Kayunah and Kayunah's husband Tigik, who had accompanied Captain Fred Tilton on his adventurous sled journey from Point Barrow, when he sought relief for the stranded crews of the whaling ships that were wrecked there in 1898. Many months later, when Kayunah and Tigik were returned to their village on a Liebes Company trading ship from San Francisco, they had much to tell of their travels and sight-seeing. Tooklamora was tremendously impressed and from then on lived all her days in the reflected glory of her sister's high adventure.

February 10. Where shall I begin? So much has happened since the last entry was made in this chronicle!

The long dark days are over and the illness and despair which were so desperate a part of them, have been marked down as a full share of an Arctic winter. One ought to possess a heart full of faith and song and sunshine to go through with it—an ever-flowing well of these in a heart to keep one's body going day and night —to ease the beating throb against one's fevered eyes— to strike new strength down weary arms and legs. One could pass through three halls then, or it might be three hundred halls, to get to Nowlik's igloo, or to Musinginga's, say, and never need the wall to steady one, or door to lean against in anguished need; a heart gone begging, "Oh God, lend a hand this night—." So do we go on caring for a village of sick Eskimos with our last shred of energy sustained by prayer—but let that pass.

Early on the morning of January twenty-third, Otoiyuk awakened to a strange unrest among his dogs. Tumbling out of his shelf bed to investigate, he found the mail sled had arrived with Panigeo in a heap between the bags, too sick to utter a word. Otoiyuk's two dogs had found their way home, dragging the rest of the team and the sled with them.

Panigeo had taken sick after leaving Icy Cape and soon was too ill to handle the team. Knowing the dogs would fetch up at Wainwright, he tumbled on the sled and knew no more until he was roused from his delirium. Someone brought the mail sacks in, but to this day I cannot remember when they were opened. Letters were forgotten in the anxious concern over this illness of Panigeo's, his body so tortured with fever and pain he could scarcely move. His temperature was 106.08.

Influenza! Among Eskimos in crowded igloos! Like a meteor straight down it struck, this epidemic! In three days there was ushered into this village such an overwhelming fever of inflamed throats and morbid headaches, with contagion leaping and gaining in virulence, as to shake the courage of the stoutest heart. It spread with flame-like swiftness into every igloo.

School was closed. Instructions given to stay in their own igloos,—to remain *in* the village,—to keep warm, and at the first symptoms to send someone to the schoolhouse to tell the teacher.

With the children it took the form of a mild rhinitis with sore throats. The day I closed school I marshalled the children, sprayed small noses and throats, rubbed their little chests with hot camphorated oil, and gave each a dose of castor oil. They were the first to recover. The older natives suffered pitiably—endless nights of moaning delirium and racking cough—and the cold creeping stealthily into their igloos—too weak, they were, to attend to the seal-oil lamps—no fire, not a swallow of hot food or drink to restore their ebbing warmth of body or strength. Such a feeling of utter helplessness assailed me, as I went in and out of the fever-laden dwellings. And the fear that would grip me!—the self-paralyzing fear for one's own safety—as I thought of the one hundred and eighty seven under my care—my Tooruk and Oyalla among them. And then came the storm, lashing down like a demon from the north, sending the glass down to fifty-four degrees below zero!

The aloneness of the hours was more terrible than all these! Formulate what you will of a sound philosophy of life, some cherished theory you believe will tide you, equip you with strength of heart and good courage for the difficulties of this world, and then meet up, face to face with a crisis like this. It's like floundering in a fog around an ice ridge that has suddenly blocked the trail of your smooth sledding. Old spectacled Philosophy tiptoes out of the picture and leaves you in the fog; and as for your theories, they are like dogs with frozen feet, helpless. So you make the rounds of the village dispensing quinine and camphorated oil and enemas and hot-water bags and pneumonia jackets, salts and castor oil and cough syrups—all these, trying in every way to find surcease for the kindly people who had never harmed a soul, lying in their igloos helpless and suffering looking to you for relief. And you sleep in a chair with your clothes on, and keep up the fires, and after awhile you get very tired and you kneel down and ask God to do something about it, and there comes only the dismal moaning of the storm for an answer, or the shuffling of *mukluks* in the hall—some feverish one after medicine again.

This time it was Kayalluk, (his own body burning with fever) come to tell me that Tooklamora was "much bad." Into the furs again and out into the night! Dear old Tooklamora! Smiling her gratitude as I rubbed the oils on her sunken chest. Yet she could smile and mumble her dying *"muck-eee."* She knew no fear of death. Her body was too old, too weak to combat this ravaging malady. She died in the night. Next morning Kayalluk carried her small body to the schoolroom, where it lay until the men were well enough to make a box. (Somehow, I can't call these boxes that were made of old crates and packing cases, coffins.) I held the lamp for Kayalluk as he laid the small stiff corpse on one of the school benches, our breaths blowing white in the cold room. The effort cost him much. He was one of the last to recover.

Then there was old and feeble Outanaruk who rebelled at taking "white man's medicine." Nasholook, suffering himself, came to tell me of her. Musingahna had just come in with her sick baby, so I sent the remedies by Nasholook. She died an hour later, and we laid another corpse in the schoolroom beside Tooklamora's. Every time I went to the dispensary, I saw them there, on the other side of the wall, starkly dead and frozen, we three beneath the same roof together.

Then Samaruna was carried to my rooms. Her husband braved the storm that I might help her. They were the lovers in this village, always together. She could not speak, only moan in her delirium, *"muck-ee, muck-ee."* Quickly I decided to keep her with me. There was an old cot in the storeroom. Her husband helped. With hot oil on her chest, pneumonia jacket, one of my flannel gowns, hot-water bags, (thank heaven the government sent ten) quinine, hot drinks, I told her man she would be all right, to come back in the morning. I went out to get coal later, and stumbled against her husband in the hall. He was planning to spend the night there. It did not take much coaxing to persuade him to lie down beside his beloved Samaruna. How grateful I was for the comfort these two Eskimos were to me! The company of two living was a great relief after spending three nights with the dead.

(From my Journal) February 26. Samaruna is gain-

SAMARUNA.

Eva Louise Richards.
1921

ing strength and today was very cheerful. Talks to me in Eskimo quite as if I could understand every word. Tingook and Panikpuk came to build the coffins today. What a strange assortment of lumber they carried in! Two shelves from the Trading Store and several boxes. Saws and hammers pounded out a weird rhythm. Why should the sound of these strike one so strangely today? Not so when they made the Christmas tree. The children came to the school in curious groups this afternoon, some of them with their cups and pails for soup. Samaruna's husband is quietly helpful. He has been getting the ice for me. Today he brought a large piece of caribou meat for the soup I make each day for our convalescents. He tries in many little ways to repay my care of Samaruna.[13]

Taliak came in this morning. I scarcely recognized him, so thin he was. Then I remembered that I had not seen him in my daily rounds of the igloos. He had gone to his traps the day before I closed school. Now I've always regarded warmth and rest in bed as essentials in combating influenza. Hear what a bomb Taliak placed under that pet theory. He was taken ill far from the village. He built a small snow igloo, large enough for himself and his dogs, propped his sled against it, and crawled in with his team. The dogs whimpered and crept close. After some time he divided some seal meat with them. He said "that storm was much bad and very cold. I like to come back to village," but he thought best to stay until his headache was better. He tousled his hair as he told me how it affected his head. "That igloo go round and round and I see many dogs—just

---

[13]Samaruna's true name was Kittik. I did not wish my reader to identify her as the Kittik who came in to help me occasionally.

I got six dogs." Except for the loss of weight he is quite recovered. Eight days in a snow cave, and he is better, in every way, than our natives here who have had medication and care. He ate nine slices of bread with three bowls of soup and then took a kettle of it to Akadrigak's igloo, and to Tagarook's. Gallons of soup I made of reindeer meat, caribou, dried onions, dried vegetables, rice and barley; rolled oats and warm milk for the wee ones. Every day a wash boiler full, until everyone was well again.

Taliak was one of those who took the boxes to the hill. There are now three glistening frozen mausoleums on the knoll to catch the last rays of the setting sun. From the school playground they seem but part of the landscape, quiet and cold. Death imparts a certain dignity to this strangest of burial grounds, in cold blue sky, white shroud of earth with the silent dead between, mantled in a shimmering frost—the "white radiance of Eternity."

"Last rose rays of the setting sun." To be sure, I have yet to tell you of the return of the sun, our brighter days. You could never dream "such darkness lay concealed" within an Arctic day—not an exact quotation but let it fit, since it is impossible, (if you've never been in the far North) to imagine days as dark as the many we have had this winter. I had formed the queerest notions about Arctic winter days, based on my one No-Sun experience —an eclipse of the sun one summer, when a dusky shadowless twilight crept over green fields and flowers, their brilliance of color and beauty stricken as with a strange jaundice. So I had pictured a No-Sun winter in a land of almost perpetual snows. It would be colorless, I thought—leaden—dead. And so it appeared when the

PHOTOGRAPHS

One of "these babies"

U.S. Bureau of Education ship *Boxer* smothered in cargo

The forty families of Wainwright

Tigalook

Kivik's little daughter playing mother

Snow smoking before the wind

Knitting class

Building the ice corral

Blue shadows on the sea ice

A bearded seal—the *oogooruk*

Photo courtesy Van Ness Studios

Mementos of the *Maud* Expedition

"the tongue a great lolling lumpish mass"

" . . . the walrus skin was lowered"

Pacific and King eiders

". . . when two meeting fields of ice are jammed"

Midsummer night

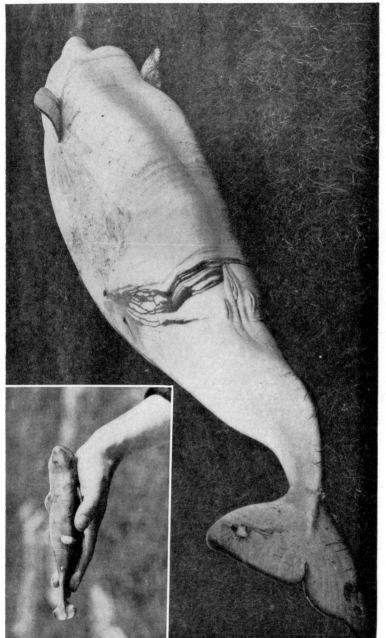

White whale and embryo

Three of the thirty-three Belugas

The bed of an ancient tundra lake

The author at Wainwright, Arctic Alaska

The Eskimo artifacts pictured on the following pages were, for the most part, fashioned in the village of Wainwright. Among them the reader will recognize the gifts which are mentioned in my Christmas at Wainwright. Here too, are some of the hunting and household articles which Kayalluk and Kittik and old Tooklamora were pleased to give me from their old igloo chest made of driftwood. Indeed, with few exceptions, the artifacts represent gifts—appreciations rare and unique—from a little people whose hearts must ever have been the generous giving kind.

Through the kindly and interested offices of Dr. George Miksch Sutton, these artifacts may now be viewed and studied in the beautiful little Cranbrook Institute of Science in Bloomfield Hills, Michigan, where, arranged beside other and more notable collections from Greenland, Baffin Land, Southampton Island and Hudson Bay, they constitute an unusual and comprehensive display of Eskimo culture, open evidence of the ingenuity and artistic traits of this primitive race.

The photographs were made by the late Mr. L. B. Linkletter of Seattle, Washington, during a private showing of the artifacts, one arranged especially for school and mission groups then engaged in the study of Eskimo life and culture.

The author regrets the distracting inclusion of the exhibit labels.

The Author.

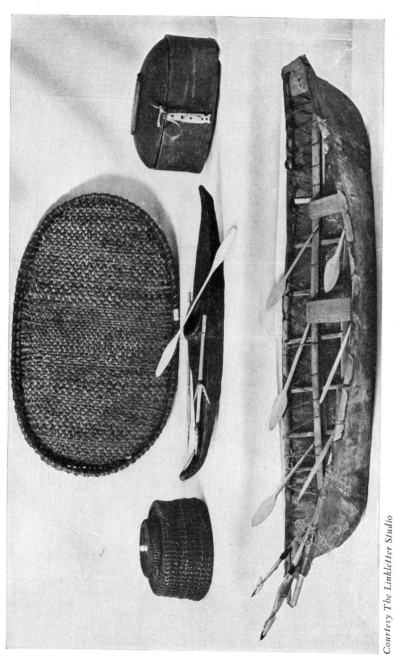

Models of oomiak and kayak. Harpoons in oomiak with paddles. Bird dart and spear in kayak with double paddle. Whalebone basket. Ivory knob in cover. Willow tray. Driftwood box with ivory handle.

Courtesy The Linkletter Studio

Balls made of colored sealskin—stuffed with reindeer hair. Sitting mat made of bird skins. Dolls of wood dressed in reindeer fawn skins. Boots embroidered in reindeer hair.

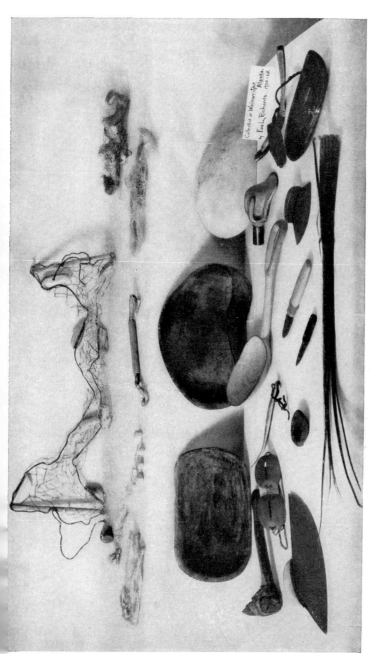

Collected at Wainwright
Alaska
by Emil Richards, 1924-25

Above: model of fish net. Sinew, bolos, flying traps for birds. Sewing case of ivory. Sinew thread, fishing line and hook with skin case. Lower: household utensils made of wood—two woman's knives with ivory handles (look like chopping knives), snow glasses (wood). Skin scraper with wooden handle with piece of gun barrel sharpened. Men's knives—one of flint point. Bundle of whalebone partly split for making baskets. Small round dish of ancient pottery. Left: jade adze with bone handle. *Courtesy The Linkletter Studio*

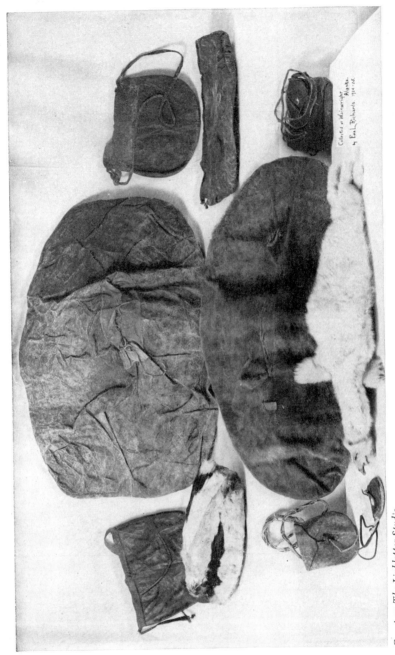

Two large bags for women's clothing.   Other bags for fish and gun cartridges

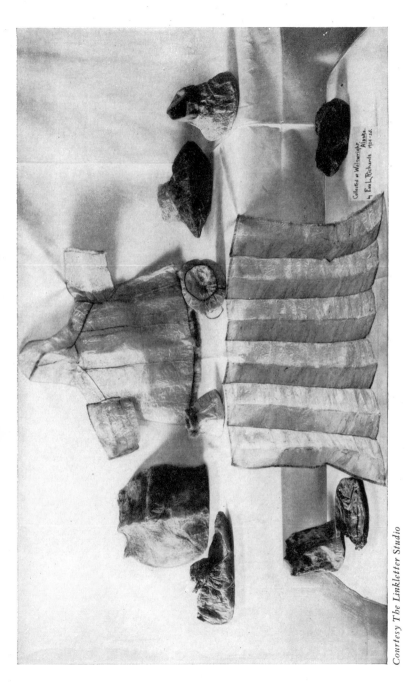

Courtesy The Linkletter Studio

Below: Igloo window. Thread bags made of walrus heart and kidney membrane.
Above: Bags and parka made of seal intestine

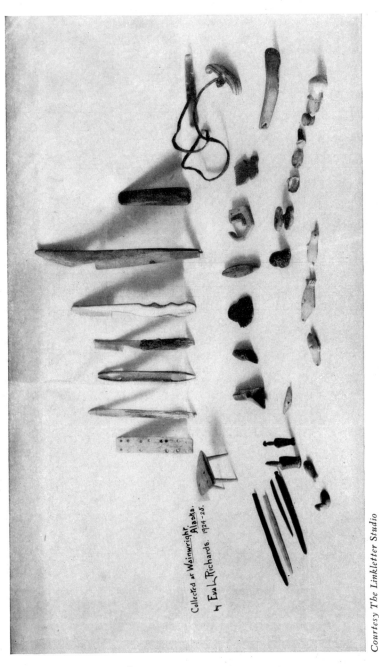

Collected at Wainwright,
Alaska.
by Earl Richards. 1924-25.

Courtesy The Linkletter Studio

Model of sealing stool (left). Model of throwing arm for bird darts (right). Shuttles and gauges for making fish nets. Handles for drums. Drum sticks (left). Amulets for whaling. Ivory whales, seals and duck. Labrets (right). Woman's comb of ivory; spear heads; hook for use in braiding sinew thread. Two ancient ivory figures (left)

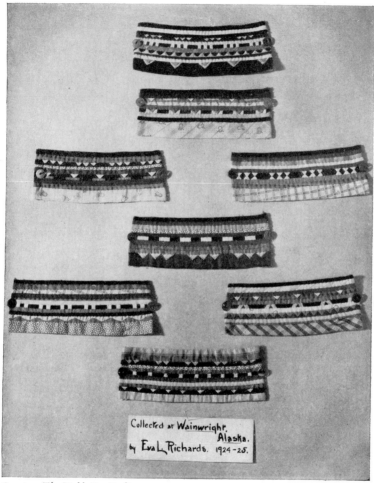

Collected at Wainwright,
Alaska.
by Eva L. Richards. 1924-25.

Samples of borders on denim parkas. Made of small bits of calico and
braid. Note fine hand stitchery

snow was blowing, but on clear dark days, when the stars spangled the heavens like jewels, the rolling tundra and roughened sea ice threw back exquisite tints of blues and lavenders, gossamer eerie shadows that began no-where and ended everywhere—and always an unfa-miliar violet-gray twilight at noon, with never a hint as to where the horizon might be. Towards the end of January, the sky and earth in the south parted in the faintest thread of light at noonday and as the days lengthened this ribbon of light widened to a brighter and ruddier glow, as if the sun was slowly prying a lid off the earth. Every ridge of ice and snow was crested in rose, deepening to purple, then darkly blue as evening came on.

And then at last, *the day* when we cheered and saluted the golden ellipse. It came up at noon as silently as a dream to lazily stretch its golden refraction of light to every corner of our blue-cold world—stirring our hearts to wonder—gone in an hour but leaving us com-forted and glad that spring was on its way again. The next day it stayed with us a little longer as with a tender lingering, and the next day and the next, until today the sun itself is spilling its brightness over the walls and furnishings in a gay reckless manner, quite transforming the art of Jack Frost upon the windowpanes into dream visions of pink loveliness, like enchanted scenes of fairy-land glittering in their own fantastic light.

(From my Journal) February 28. Sled team down from Point Barrow today. Letter from one of the nurses at the Hospital. "Epidemic has struck the village," with an SOS from doctor for "Quinine Caps. gr. II, Lysol, whatever you can spare, Infant's Corrective 100, and Camphorated Oil, all you can let us have. Must postpone visit to Wainwright until later. Hospital full."

I sent all I could spare, packing the stuff while Otoo-luk had a sandwich and coffee. In an hour he was on his way back to Barrow. Then I sat down to make out an emergency requisition for more drugs. It goes with the Medical Report. Goodness knows when the mail team will leave now! In the meantime I'll get another off to Dad.

Temp. today -26°.

"March 1

"Daddy Dear:

"March came in like a growling Polar Bear. The barometer is falling—looks as if Höder might be on the way in one of his tantrums again. In the gray twilight flurries are flying before a northwest wind. It's good to have normal days again, going on without stop-gaps of filling lamps, trimming wicks, or washing lamp chim-neys, the night too, in its proper place.

"I wish you could have been here the day of the sun's returning. The children ran excitedly to the top of every knoll and drift, the big boys clamouring on the ridge of the schoolhouse roof, all shouting exultantly, the most ardent little Sun-worshippers you could ever imagine! And what a strange looking orb we saluted! Refraction of light rays produced an exaggerated ellipse, flattened like a sausage balloon on the horizon, and glow-ing with an orange-colored incandescence. Since then, the days have been lovely, luring us out for many walks on the sea ice and tundra, both still ridged and hum-mocked in the grip of winter.

"The children are a bit listless these days, writing and number work forgotten as they gaze wistfully out of the windows. Eskimo spring fever, likely. For a tonic I have prolonged the recess period, knowing how good it is for them to be out of doors. They have been playing with some very unusual toys—sliding down the drifts on frozen seal embryos. These unborn seal babies, about twenty to thirty inches long, are tossed aside when the seals are butchered and in no time, of course, are frozen solid. They become a sled as soon as father or mother can take time to strip off the spongy placenta and fasten a thong to the tiny cat-like nose. Then up and down the village the children drag these 'sleds', pulling younger brothers or sisters around on them; straddling them to glide down every little incline, or slide belly-buster down their favorite drift, the high one on the east side of the schoolhouse. Their fun lasts until thawing time—June or July—when the women will rescue these silvery white furry dead 'cats' from the drifts or wherever the children have abandoned them, to skin them for boot linings or mittens, or, cut in narrow strips, this glistening fringe may adorn the kamlikas they make of intestine, garments for wear in wet or foggy weather.

"I am enclosing a copy of my report on the epidemic. Do not take seriously the reference to my own illness. I am tiptop again, smiling over the days when I was sure my temperature was running too close to Eternity, and the one night when I could have sworn Death was waiting in the second hall. I believe when *he* saw me dispensing medicines wrapped in a down quilt, and this with my head afire and the rest of me diddering with chills, *he* decided I was too busy to join him. I moved my bed near the stove that night— (I think it was Kayalluk helped me—it made for fewer steps to keep up fires) —and thrust some needed remedies under my pillow, beef cubes and crackers among them. Once or twice during that long night I caught myself longing (Heaven

knows how helplessly) for a dear kindly country doctor. I could not picture a white smocked M.D. walking in and anyway, had one come in, he would have
cleared the room at once of all the old women, Sosorlik
and Elenaua and the others, who came in that night by
twos and threes to pray for me. I was grateful for their
presence, their comforting soft Eskimo prayers, mur-
muring me on to Heaven's protection and to deep
health-restoring slumber. After all, it isn't medicines
we need so much when we are ill.

"Now, I am eagerly awaiting the spring visit of the
Missionary Doctor from Barrow. A few of my natives
are still under the weather for whom his coming may
mean relief. Then too, three of our fine young men have
declared their intentions to the parents of three of our
finest girls—means at least one marriage ceremony for
him—and there are several new babies he will want to
baptize, besides the special services he will arrange as
part of his missionary duties.

"A missionary's work is a happy one among these
Eskimos. No fire-and-brimstone revivals; no soul-stir-
ring adjurations are necessary to christianize these people,
for they come nearer to being true followers of the
Master than any other peoples of the earth. Deep in the
permeations of their own ancient beliefs is something
akin to what every Missionary who has come among
them believes and teaches, that God is governing the
world. His laws are their laws and they observe them
as intuitively as do the whale and the walrus, the reindeer and the birds, and like the birds, manifest an unper-
turbed maintainance of the spirit of gladness in all the
conflicts of life, a simple faith, as natural to Eskimos as
sleeping or breathing.

"March 10. Whaling time is in the air! The men are repairing the oomiaks and rounding up their gear. There will be four crews this year. Two of the boats are to be recovered. Kootook removed the old coverings this morning, slitting the dark stiff hides off the slender latticed frames with his hunting knife, saving suitable pieces for igloo doors, ice tunnel covers, and such things. From my window the frames look like the skeletons of some prehistoric dinosaur. The women, a dozen or more, are working on the new covers in the native store, sprawled on the floor, scraping hair from the large hides of the bearded seal, their *oogooruk*. Last summer, after the hunt and its attendant butchering, these skins were rolled in tight bundles, a peculiar curing process, which serves to preserve the oil in the hide and keeps them pliant as wet chamois. Seven to eight skins are needed for each oomiak, ingeniously hand stitched together with a double felled seam done with sinew dipped in seal oil. The skeins were lying in wooden bowls filled with the rancid mess in Kootook's igloo yesterday.

"And what do you think they are using for a boat-house? The men have scooped out a great cave or snow-shed in the side of the great drift, the high one near the schoolhouse. Already they have six stone oil lamps heating the place, the entrance closed with a huge polar bear hide. You see, the skins must be kept pliant, so are not allowed to freeze. When the cover is ready it is quickly stretched over the frame and made fast over the gunwales with a stout lacing of walrus thong. When new, an oomiak presents a pretty sight—a pale ochre in color, the paddles and driftwood thwarts stained a bright crimson or blue—the whole weathering in a season to a dirty brown.

"School closes about the last of April when 'whaling' should be on in earnest. After that the walrus hunts begin, then the flights of strange birds to note, their nests to find and sketch. When the snows have melted, there will be the brave little flowers, that somehow unfold their fragile petals on this Arctic air, to gather and press and paint, and when the sun begins its annual spree of insomnia, tipsy with continuous daylight, when we never know just when it's time to go to bed, there is no telling what may be accomplished.

"Daddy, do you know I am forgetting what cement walks feel like, with the traffic of civilization, its bells and shrill whistles, auto horns and such? Memory can play us queer tricks sometimes. What is crisp lettuce; and strawberries; and the small matter of whipped cream and a bona fide porcelain bath? 'There,' you are saying, 'she is yearning for the "flesh pots" at last.' Don't be too sure, Daddikins. Do you sniff the mince pie? I am leaving shortly for that long promised sled trip down to the Inlet, to Amundsen's station *Maudheim*. It is three miles south of here over a rough trail, winding from tundra to sea ice all the way. I am taking baked beans and mince pie and the thermos full of hot coffee for the picnic when we get there. My dearest native friend Elenaua is going with me. The sled is heaped with luxury, furs, and fawnskin robes, and polar bear rugs. No Russian Archduke on the frozen Neva ever leaned back in his troika in so warm and rich an equipage. Bye-bye. The fifteen huskies are outside and howling to go."

One needs to take a chapter from the life of Roald Amundsen, the less generally known one covered by the years 1922 to 1924, space the lines a fraction or so to

read in between, something of the interest one finds at
Maudheim—for it is the story of Amundsen's vision,
his dream of exploring the vast and uncharted areas of
the nebular polar regions—searching out their geo-
graphic and meteorologic import by a means as yet then
untried for polar work—the airplane.

Ice conditions in the summer of 1922 determined the
locating of the base for these flights at Wainwright.
Here the Junker was tried and found wanting. Ice-
landing gear had yet to be perfected—but in the tiny
winged Oriole, Amundsen and Omdal, his able lieutenant, glimpsed the possibilities: there was no doubt now,
the next crossing of the Pole would be by air. This little
scouting plane was a gift from the president of the
Curtis Company whose enthusiasm for studying the
Arctic by air was a great boost to the expedition. All
this, and more, this little depot here on the inlet could
tell us, its walls still eloquent of the Viking personality
they once sheltered; mindful of the high hopes, and the
disappointments perhaps, of the years preceding its
building when Amundsen attempted the polar crossing
in a stout ship of his own designing, his own ship, the
Maud, only to suffer the crushing mishaps that could
possibly befall an Arctic explorer.

Planned with that care and attention which Amundsen devoted to every undertaking, this little Arctic home
named for the queen of Norway, was a model of neat
compactness, a deal of snug comfort in its twenty-by-
twenty-foot space. One entered through a hall to stretch
fingers out at once to the welcome warmth of a combination heating and cooking stove which centered the
place like a hub, and around which were arranged the
two sleeping rooms, a dining alcove with its table and

benches, a room for supplies, a machine shop and a dark room for photographic work. The table was of a size to spread maps upon, for drafting and calculating observations. Back of the benches, along the wall, was a row of small bins, the country-store type with sloping lids, labeled for rice, beans, soup vegetables, and other dried eatables. There were shelves for the pewter dishes and utensils, fine pewter from Norway, there was a shelf for books, the binoculars, aneroid and sextant in their cases on another, and a well-stocked first aid cabinet. There was a place for fur clothing, boots and caps and great bearskin mittens long enough to cover elbows, some wooden shoes which Amundsen so loved to wear indoors, and warm woolen knits of all kinds—a place for everything an expedition could possibly need—all so shipshape and conveniently arranged with not a foot of space wasted, nor, I venture to say, one degree of heat from that stove all winter. Small wonder, when we consider how efficiently Amundsen stowed away the three years' supplies for seven men aboard the tiny sloop *Gjoa,* that staunch little ship only seventy-two feet long and eleven-foot beam in which he safely navigated the Northwest Passage—(1903 to 1906).

Amundsen liked kitchens. He was always at home in them. One morning, when he sat in a rocker beside the stove[14] while I kneaded bread into loaves, we spoke of the lure of the Arctic and the grip it takes upon our heart strings—something the explorer Fiala had written had set us on the subject—"So," he mused, "does it draw one—like a chilled man seeking warmth of an open fire, as alcoholic spirits attract a man who would

---

[14] This incident occurred at Nome (August 1923) in the pleasant kitchen of the Maynard-Columbus Hospital where I served as nurse for a year.

forget his enemies, but more as a man, long separated from the homeland, approaches the bountiful board spread in his honor, laden with the many dainties he has not tasted since his youth—so I think it draws one"— and even as he spoke his voice held the brave and high resolve—the lure—to cross the Pole by plane, and his steady eyes of blue had that light within their depths such as is only vouchsafed to those who have looked long and far over vast and frozen silences.

Swift gusts of snow swirled about us as we settled ourselves on the sled for the return to Wainwright. The dogs were restless, eager to be off. We drew the drawstrings of our tee-gee hoods close, for the wind was freshening strong from the north, a wind packed with snow. Indeed, we had no sooner gotten under way when we were plunged into the flying woolpack of it, our noses stung by the whirling frost needles. Elenaua shared the sled with me. We were hunched together on it like two sleepy owls, our faces buried deep in the fur ruffs of our hoods.

I was beginning to feel the cramp of one position when Elenaua reached back, fumbled around until she found my face, to quickly pass her fingers over my nose and cheeks. I wondered what she wanted but before I could ask, she was settled down comfy in a hunch again. The wind prevented any attempt at conversation and besides my Eskimo vocabulary was not up to such a situation. I could scarcely hear Nasholook as he called "Gee!" or "Haw!" to the dogs. I wondered how he managed to direct them at all, with dogs and trail swallowed up in the snow fog. All I could see was the backs of the wheel dogs, white in their blankets of snow. I ventured a peek at Nasholook. It was like seeing a ghost, he, too, was blanketed in snow.

Again and again, as we sped on through the thickening storm, Elenaua reached back, always for that instant's spreading of her fingers over my nose and cheeks. Was she fearful of my tumbling off the sled? Wedged in, as we were, between furs, there was little danger of that, though once or twice the sled did career at a perilous angle. The cold had made me drowsy and I rocked like a sack on every movement of the sled. I longed to know the time but my wrist watch lay under four layers of mittens and fur, and—suddenly Elenaua's hand awakened me! Had I really been asleep? I could feel we were traveling on smooth trail again. What a miracle of intelligence these dogs display in ferreting out the trail— through a woolpack of snow and over the humpety hummocks of the tundra—and on to smooth sea ice! Faintly in the distance came the familiar howl of the village dogs. We must be nearing home. I stretched out a foot. Gracious, how stiff I was! But then I hadn't moved a toe since leaving Maudheim. Elenaua slapped my legs vigorously, rubbing and flexing them. How did she know, and yet, in a few moments I was more comfortable.

I was almost asleep again when we were jolted back, the team pulling up and up, Nasholook pushing and shouting and every dog straining in the harness. At the top of the bank the village chorused a welcome, all the dogs howling. The children, coming out of the thick atmosphere like small gray apparitions, ran along the sled, some of them piling on for a ride. Here and there I could make out the dim orange glow of an igloo window, and the next instant we were halted before the

ELENAUA.

Eva Louise Richards.
1925.

Children at Entrance to Igloo.

Eva Louise Richards
1925.

lighted schoolhouse. I tumbled off, feeling for the first time that peculiar tightening browache caused by extreme cold. Tooruk and Oyalla had kept the fires burning. The kettle was singing, but I was too weary to make tea. Nasholook came in with Elenaua. "Elenaua is much glad you have no freeze of noses and not much cold for the body. Elenaua say, now she is much happy you not much cold." So that was her tender anxiety! In my first stormy experience of sledding in a wind I had not dreamed of frostbite. Elenaua had divined my ignorance and was watching over me. Blessed native woman! (Some day I must write a book about Elenaua. Ever since the epidemic I had come to know and love her as a sister—a cheerful little woman going her way quietly and neatly about the village—a dear companion!)

March 12. The storm through which we tussled a week ago is over, but a light northeast blow keeps the snow flying and the drifts grow higher. The shining sun penetrates this flying mist with a strange turquoise light. The children are jumping rope on the south side of the building, protected there from the wind and happy. The rope swings hammocklike between two youngsters; the others take turns leaping over and back. They do not employ the full turn of the rope such as I knew in my jumping days. Sure footed little creatures, they seldom miss, and what fun they do have!

March 20. Changed from fur boots to lighter ones made with denim tops today. It was a great comfort to put by heavy woolen hose and the tall fur boots I had worn all winter. My feet have wings today. So has the temperature. It is warmer—only 4° below.

March 25. The missionary doctor arrived today from Point Barrow. He travels well padded in lustrous parkas and fine boots, comfortably quilted in thick furs on the sled, quite befitting an able physician and surgeon in this country. His native driver, who serves also as his valet and cook, faithfully and efficiently attends his every want. They made the trip down in little less than three days, considered good time, counting the stop at Attanik for services.

He held a clinic the first afternoon. I had sent word to my chronic patients to come to the schoolroom where the doctor set up his office to examine and prescribe. Aveanna's wife, who had been ailing off and on for over a year was ordered to the hospital at Barrow for surgical treatment. The others, Ahmaulik, his little daughter Kavik, and my lovely Musinginga, had been on my sick list ever since the epidemic—tardy recoveries which had given me much concern. I feared some deep-seated phthisical trouble might be at the bottom of it. My apprehensions were soon dispelled. "Give 'em plenty of cod-liver oil," came the cheerful and reassuring prescription.

Musinginga is the daughter of a whaling captain, as fair of skin as any princess of legend. With her dark liquid blue eyes, there is little to indicate her Eskimo mother, save her lustrous straight black hair, perhaps. There is about her an air of quiet repose, a gentle refinement of expression and demeanor clothing her, as did her well-made garments of fur, becomingly. The doctor saw at once she was of mixed blood. He had been making an extensive study of mixed blood cases, and was always keenly interested whenever he could add to his researches—"Dental caries—enlarged tonsils—adenoids

—all symptomatic of mixed bloods," he would say. So it
was, he asked me to mark *mixed blood* on Musinginga's
chart for his records. She lifted her head as if frightened
at the words, but the doctor was putting away his stetho-
scope and took no notice. I had read a troubled question
in her startled eyes.

At the preaching service in the evening, Nasholook
interpreted the doctor's story of the Prodigal Son. The
whole village was in the schoolroom. I had to step over
the crowd to get to the organ. There I could watch
brown faces brighten when the "Prodigal arose" to go
to his father's house. A father's igloo was something to
understand—as was the joy of a father at seeing his son.
*"Peoples has parents sometimes—they gets very lone-
some for happy talk to parents"*—How the words came
back to me! Nasholook's words on my first day in
Wainwright. Every native was listening, absorbed in
the missionary's story of a father and his son. But *husks*
and *swine?* What were they? as every face grew sober.
How was Nasholook interpreting these? What in the
life of his people could parallel husks and swine? Abso-
lutely nothing, and what's more, no son of an Eskimo
father would choose to leave his home, save to move
to one of his own, or to go hunting and trapping. The
story must have been all mixed up for them—but no
congregation was ever more seriously attentive. I was
hard put trying to explain Biblical husks and swine for
many weeks after. It was their questioning in this regard that suggested the going over their favorite hymns
with them—so little did they understand about "the
land of corn and wine," and "out of the ivory palaces,"
and "marching as to war,"—but they could sing them
to high heaven, so that always, their singing was the
best part of the services.

Of course there was a company dinner for the doctor. For it I had saved my last can of chicken. This, creamed in ramekins with candied sweet potatoes and a raspberry compote, was well to his liking. I could not eat. It was all too exciting having someone of my own race to converse with again. My tongue ran around like a loose puppy. The doctor had traveled around a lot—his periodical furloughs had taken him all over the country, lecturing in the churches and to the various missionary societies. I was hoping the conversation would lead to the homeland cities—to a discussion of books, or good music—the operas, maybe. I had been told the doctor was fond of good music. I mentioned that I had heard the golden voice of Lucrezia Bori in Manon Lescaut at the Metropolitan before leaving New York and that I had brought a set of the opera records with me. But the doctor had been a long time in the Arctic. He was all for enjoying his cigar in a reverie—the kind of a reverie that is induced by a warm fire after miles of dog-sledding on a cold trail—stretched out comfy—dreamily meditating his Arctic footwear. "No, I do not own a pair of muskrat boots. You say you left yours in New York?" I quietly closed the Victrola. Beautiful Lucrezia could sing her "Sweet Manon" for my solitary evenings. After all, Arctic clothing was more important and I had much to learn about it. The doctor talked on, extolling the virtues of muskrat skins for northern clothing—"the black skins, now, are as beautiful as sealskin—and like them can be worn in all weather. Kotzebue is the place to get the skins—reindeer parkas have to be protected with outer parkas of denim or sailcloth—those cold cotton things are a nuisance—but one never dares get reindeer fur wet—lose all the hair if it does. Still, you

can't beat it—nothing like it for winter travel. Take—
these—boots now—" his voice trailed off into silence.
I tiptoed out to the kitchen to set some rolls for breakfast. You don't know how easy it is to drop into a
drowsy reverie after three days of sled travel.

The next day our three young couples were married.
Right after breakfast I was off to the native store for
the wedding presents—three bright aluminum kettles.
There was no stir of "Lohengrin"—filmy bridesmaids or
candle glow. The doctor wore his trail clothing. The
girls wore the gingham dresses they had made in the
sewing classes, (somewhat rumpled from being worn
under fur garments, but neat for all that) and the boys
looked very fine in their snow shirts of white drilling.
Koosik's was trimmed with a border of bright red calico.
They stood in a row in front of the long blackboard,
quite as if they were there for a spelling class, wide-
awake and ready for the first word from the missionary.

When the ceremony was over (and one did for all
three), while the doctor was writing their names in the
marriage register, I slipped away to my kitchen to get
a tray of doughnuts and the tea I had prepared for the
occasion. Passing the cups, I missed one of the brides.
Oh, she had gone home to finish flaying a seal her new
husband had killed that very morning. "She is cook
that seal for our parents"—her wifely duties begun,
very pleasing to a young husband.

The doctor had presented each couple with a Bible.
Koosik and his bride sat down at once, squeezing together in one of the small desks to read the story of the
marriage of Cana—a chapter the doctor had marked
for them. Incidentally, I was asked to explain the water
and wine miracle later—but for this I was not so hard

put. It was so like the way they had of stuffing seal poke
with lardaceous lumps of seal blubber to draw off the
rich seal oil a few days later. *Ah-regah!* it was wonderful
as any miracle the way big blobs of blubber could change
to seal oil—change to a golden liquid there in a seal poke
stored on top of a cache—Vitamin D's beneficent sunshine for the long dark winters.

Our third couple, bursting with smiles and many
"Kwayannas," went off to haul coal, swinging their new
kettle, like happy children, between them.

Koosik and his bride were still laboriously spelling out
Bible words when the group of fond parents brought
their babies in for baptism—and not a child visible until
the doctor set down his bowl of water and was ready to
begin. Then each mother hurried to loosen her waist
strap, her right arm under her parka supporting her
baby as it slid down and into her arms. Four little latent
Christians! Sleepy as puppies, sucking softly on tiny
closed fists, their tiny bodies warm and moist and
gummed up with reindeer hair. How cruel, it seemed,
to awaken them so rudely with this drenching ceremo-
nial—their little fists clutching at the air—their baby
lungs gasping in fluttering terror—so they could be
called Esther and Daniel and Rachel and Lazarus.

There was a great to-do about baby Lazarus. His
father, Tuzroak, was one of the new elders, solemnly
impressed with this rite of naming his infant son. More-
over, he was one of Wainwright's most industrious
natives, one of the few who think of saving something
for the rainy day. For some reason his wife fancied the
name Lazarus, but could only point to it in the Bible.
Tuzroak pronounced it "lazy." "Lazy! Why you mean
Lizzie," exclaimed the doctor. "I thought this baby was

a boy. Lizzie's no name for a boy." Tuzroak and his
wife were confused—but only for a moment. Tuzroak
knew what he wanted. Very slowly he removed the
sealskin cover from his Bible, turned the pages carefully
to find his place, and went to the blackboard, where in
large letters he chalked the name for the doctor. "Oh,
the name is to be Lazarus! Splendid name! Splendid!"

Years ago, the captains of the old whalers found it
rather boggling business to remember the native names
of the Eskimos whom they recruited to accompany the
ships and to lend dexterous hands to whaling operations.
It was easier to dub them John, or Hooligan, whichever
the captain happened to think of first. When they were
returned to their villages, these Eskimos were very prideful of these by-names, retaining them as part of their
native appellation.

The early school reports record only the Eskimo
names, until about 1900, when teachers and missionaries
found it more expedient, indeed almost necessary, to
bestow upon the natives names more easily pronounced
and remembered. Later a man's native name became his
children's surname,[15] thus: Tuzroak's children are now
called Elizabeth Tuzroak, Mary Tuzroak, and now I
have just recorded the wee young Lazarus.

Bible names are the most frequently chosen. In Wainwright we have most of the Apostles, a Samuel, a Noah,
and a Mark. Also there is a sprinkling of former popular
missionaries and teachers.

This system of nomenclature is still so new among
them, that one day when I inquired the names on meeting a family of Eskimos I did not know, the native
names were given in every instance save one, a young

---

[15] Mr. William T. Lopp inaugurated the system in 1900.

man who had been employed for two years on the government ship. My enthusiasm to learn and remember the Eskimo names and their meanings, received a sharp prick when he promptly extended his hand saying, "My name is Robert—Robert James."

"Your father then, is a white man?"

"No, my father is of Wainwright people. His name is called Angashuk, only I calls him James." It was like meeting someone in a downtown office. However, much as I have come to admire the poetry of the old names, the newer system has its advantages, best appreciated in the schoolroom. It is somewhat disconcerting to ask Kunaginga to go to the board and have two Kunagingas respond. When an Eskimo dies who has been highly esteemed for his or her courage, industry, charity, or other outstanding virtue, the child, first born after his or her death usually receives the name, an endowment as it were, of the spirit virtues of the dead. When the news of the death of one so reputed reaches another village or camp, the endowment is likely to be unwittingly shared by another new born, as was the case with our two Kunagingas.

Next morning the missionary doctor left Wainwright for home, in a fanfare of farewells and uproar of dogs howling. The village is now happily restored to the business of its preparation for the whaling. And increasingly difficult does it become, in the face of it, to hold the attention of the children in these final days of school. All this activity out of doors is so much more enticing than dog-eared books or short pencils could ever be.

Musinginga came in looking rather wistful after the

doctor had gone. She sat down while I put away a number of bottles and labeled others. "Now I say to you something," she began. "That doctor he say mix blood. What that mean, mix blood?" So the subject had troubled her. Her sweet face and the naïve manner in which she put the question was most appealing. I told her that when a white captain marries an Eskimo woman, their children are said to be of mixed blood. "White Captain marry! *Naga!*" How quickly and emphatically she answered, eager to clear up the matter once and for all about this half-blood question! "Oh that my fadder, that captain he *never* marry that my mudder, just he give her things, that's all."

Kootook climbed to the ridgepole today and carefully scanned the horizon with and without his telescope. He was looking for signs of open water. The temperature had risen to 10 degrees, the air almost balmy. In the night I heard the thumping clump-clump of his soft boots going up the ladder again.

On the last day of March the wind blew mildly from the north, sending the temperature down to 10° below. Whether this portends a lamb or lion abroad we little care. There are beautiful blue shadows on the sea ice. Tooruk and Oyalla took me out there today to see the great tracks of the polar bear. *Great* puts it mildly. They measured fifteen inches across. The men are all excited and have gone out with guns and telescopes to reconnoitre. The women watch from the village; the children from the tops of the igloos.

Kittik and Esegak have been sewing on my new parka. It is made of fawn skins spotted brown and white, soft as rabbitskin. Kittik designed the borders for skirt and cuffs, of tiny patchwork of fur done most exquisitely.

The sleeves and shoulders are trimmed with tassels of mink tails. Wolf and wolverine make the ruff around the hood, very fluffy and warm.

Some costume designer should see what an Eskimo woman can do with tiny scraps of fur by way of decorating her garments. She achieves the same effect that a Chippewa woman does with bright beads and silk threads—a brightness and gaiety. Many of these designs are very elaborate, demonstrating a truth that "the first spiritual want of primitive man is decoration." This yearning finds expression also in fanciful patterns on the cuffs of their boots—and in many and varied styles of their thread and sewing bags.

I invited them to stay for dinner. They were exceedingly praiseful when I worded it in Eskimo: *Uvunga muktuk—suak igloovut,* Kittik, Esegak? I helped out my Eskimo with the sign language of placing three plates on the table. *"Aiya, eeeyah!"* they accepted jubilantly. Wishing to serve something they would relish I brought out several cans of food for their selection. Salmon— *"aiyah ahregah!"* Tomatoes—*"aiyah aiyah!"* Their enthusiasm rose. Corn—doubtful. They examined the can, looked at each other. I put it back on the shelf. Raspberries—*"Ahregah-Nagooruk,"* with many nods and smiles. They were interested in every operation of preparation. Cream sauce for the salmon; hot biscuits; squares of toast for the stewed tomatoes; cutting the cake and setting the table. Esegak was joyously excited and talked continuously. Kittik was quietly happy and at once went out to the bin for a bucket of coal. She found the broom and swept the hall. She picked up the empty tins and carried them out to the gunny sack and made herself useful in many little ways.

At last all was ready and we sat down. It was easy to see they had never sat at a white person's table before, that this must be the high light event of their lives, for they were as happy as it is possible for human beings to be. We pampered white folk, dining at Pierre's or the Waldorf, what do we know about the keen zest for food? Or the full enjoyment of it, or the satisfaction it brings? Esegak had three helpings of salmon, four of tomatoes, (I did not count the biscuits), two bowls of berries and three pieces of cake. She mounded the butter on the biscuits with a spoon. Kittik whispered to her, "Look the teacher." Kittik was observing. She struggled with her fork, bent on imitating my way of managing one. The berries were smacked over; the cake was eaten between gurgles and soupings of tea, many cups of tea, and much, much sugar, oh, very much sugar. It was all very *na-guruk!* They yielded themselves completely to the delightful comfort of satisfied healthy appetites, and sat with hands folded over their stomachs, their eyes half closed, serene and at peace with the world. Out beyond the frozen vastness, a golden sunset was yielding its glory to a rose-mauve sky. Arctic solemnic!

Suddenly all was pandemonium! Clumpety-thump! Kootook passed the window on the run, waving his telescope high in the air. Before we could reach the door, the mail team was here. Off flew the mail sacks, and, turning his team, Panigeo wheeled off again with all speed to the south, shouting back to us, "polar bear, polar bear!" Some hours later we learned how his dogs had frightened the bear; the animal, turned back on its tracks, fell an easy prey to the waiting Wainwright hunters. Three sleds brought in the meat. The pelt was soon flapping in the wind, high on Otoiyuk's rack.

I had occasion to examine the seemingly clumsy feet of this solitary animal.[16] The hair growing well under and between the toes affords a safe foothold on the ice, where most of the year, the natives hunt them. Last year Anakok killed one near his favorite seal hole down at the inlet and the next day got the hungry cubs. Kootook takes great pride in showing the big notch on his spear for the one he killed far out at sea and towed home with his kayak. The natives usually hunt them in groups, three or four men surrounding the quarry.

April 3. I wakened this morning to the twittering of birds, and sure enough, huddled on the south window ledges were seventeen puffed balls. The snow buntings had come! The children were all eagerness to report them when they came to their English exercise in school this morning. But where in all this white wilderness do these tiny creatures find shelter and food? The sun is bright enough and we can feel its warmth now through the windowpanes, but nowhere out of doors is there the slightest drip of thawing as yet. The dry snow still whirls like smoke with every gust of wind. At recess time we fastened a big piece of suet and part of a loaf of bread to the sash. I walked around the building but saw no buntings. At noon a cold fog drifted in from the sea, smothering the village in a blanket of white mist. I wondered where the buntings were then. Temp. at noon 12° above. At 5 P.M. 8° below.

I have finally, after very much talk, persuaded Aveanna to take his wife to the hospital at Barrow. The natives are inclined to accept illness as they do bad weather: when it blows over all will be well again. But Aveanna's

---

[16] Polar bears travel in pairs only during the mating season.

wife had been ailing for over a year, since the birth of
her last baby, an illness that wasn't going to blow over
without surgical assistance. So when Aveanna said,
"Yesh, I go today," I lost no time getting him started.
I gave him coal oil and alcohol for his primus stove, tea
and beef cubes and cans of milk, and he went off to pack.
In a little while I went down to see how things were
going. Dear me! if we had to move all our possessions
we would take our time going to hospitals, too.

A few weeks before, Aveanna had moved into his
summer "tupek," a tent made of bent willows covered
with pieces of old canvas and reindeer skins. Aveanna
needed these skins and canvas to wrap his wife in, so he
kicked away the snow and ice that were heaped about
the base and soon had the stiff unwieldy things on his
sled. His wife, who lay in a sleeping bag, smiled up at us
through the framework of willows. At this point Aveanna remembered that he had loaned one of his dogs to
Matoo for hauling coal. Matoo lived at the other end of
the village. This made for a pleasant interlude. The
women of the village had gathered round and were in a
neighborly mood. Did she have food enough? Was she
going to be warm? Practical Kittik thought not, so
off she went to get a good thick parka. It was accepted
gratefully. By and by, Aveanna returned with the dog,
but now he must needs cut a strip of sealskin to mend
the harness, and after that was done it was his fur mittens that were missing. A search among oddments of
clothing in a bag brought two pairs to light. The extra
pair Aveanna pulled over his wife's thin hands. At last
the dismantled tupek was on the sled with grub box and
dog food and wife, and in a great to-do of dog howlings
and a shower of snow, Aveanna was off for Barrow.

Where the tupek had been, there was nothing to show for a human habitation—nothing but the few scraps of old sealskin and these a famished dog was fast gulping into his ribs. Okilyuk and his industrious wife were to care for the three children—two of them attend school. When I reached the schoolhouse there they were, a pathetic little trio sitting on the steps already lonely without father and mother. I gathered them in where soap and water and bread and milk speedily restored their forlorn little faces to smiles again.

April 12. Spring comes on apace in the Arctic. Bare brown patches are making their appearance on the tundra. The halls are dripping. The coating of frost which collected on the ceiling and walls during the long dark winter is now coming down like a gentle rain. Puddles mixed with coal dust lie in the halls, in the path of every one who comes in. The natives are not concerned about hitting the high dry places. It tracks in but there's a mop handy. I wiped down the walls of the bedroom today. No more will the deep pile of frost, so like sparkling velvet by lamp light, work its chilly annoyance on my peaceful slumbers.

To celebrate the spring I put on my "city shoes" this afternoon. They felt like clodhoppers, stiff and clumsy and cold: Still I learned something. Wearing the soft native boots does not weaken the arches nor tend to spread metatarsal structure as has been erroneously believed. Rather does it tend to strengthen the foot and ankle. My oxfords were actually a size too big, and glory be, the noise they made as I clumped around in them! In fifteen minutes I had them off and back in the trunk.

Tooruk has just breezed in to tell me that Otoiyuk's whaling boat is ready. The dark fog bank for which Kootook has been on the lookout for days—the starting signal for the crews—made its appearance over the ice this afternoon and is lengthening rapidly along the western horizon. Also Tooruk wanted to use the ice picks. "Please, Missus Eva, I go now to make grave on hill. Eskimo mans all go now." I went to the east window. On the low rise beyond the village the men of Wainwright were burying their dead. I walked with Tooruk to the place. The snow, never very deep on the windswept tundra, was almost gone. Through the sodden grass of yesteryear spring was thrusting tiny points of green. The sun was so bright it blared in golden tones over our world. I have come to believe the legend that a northern god's trumpet awakens spring in these vastnesses. I heard it today.

"Easter Day at Wainwright

"Dearest Ones:

The beauty of stained glass windows, divine music, and the fragrance of stately lilies! I see you all (Visions in sweet spring bonnets!) walking on the Avenue; nothing in all that spring glory to remind you of the North, yet your thought of me has reached me here on Easter Day.

"I'm only now beginning to find the bottom of the March mail, so mixed up was its arrival with polar bears and whaling crews. Do you know of anything finer in this world than a good correspondent? I don't. God bless you for the dear ones you are—not one mail did you miss this winter.

"It has been an exciting week. Twenty-five miles out

from the village on the sea-ice four whaling crews have made their camps along the open lead of water. They are widely separated but each crew seems to feel that its own position is the strategic one. Otoiyuk and Anakak, with their boats and crews left last Tuesday sometime during the night (it is daylight all night now) so I missed them. I wanted above everything to see a whaling crew start out. Someway, the news got around. So on Thursday, Angashuk, the grand old *Oo-malik* of Wainwright, and of a faithful crew who have whaled with him for years, sent for me just before they were ready to leave the village. He is our most industrious native, a devout old soul too, and wanted me to say a prayer for his camp. For such a momentous occasion I wore my new parka and my Christmas boots, the ones embroidered with the long white hair of the reindeer.

"There at the edge of the bank over which the north wind had banked the snows, modeling them to a smooth and perfect ramp, stood Angashuk's beautiful skin boat, the new one on which he has worked all of one year. The driftwood frame and paddles were stained a bright vermilion. Some whaling captain had given him a small can of paint. Mixed with seal oil and coal oil it had been enough and Angashuk's heart was filled with pride. Every paddle bore his mark I II neatly carved on the loom. At the bow were the guns and whale harpoons, laid carefully over a coiled roll of thong. An inflated seal skin for a floater, bundles of clothing and seal boots, and wooden boxes for food completed the outfit. The boat was lashed stoutly onto a long sledge and to this the excited dogs were now being harnessed. Everyone was in high spirits. Prospects of a *muktuk* feast was something to look forward to and lend every effort toward its success.

"The men chosen for the crew looked as if they might accomplish whatever they set out to do. Angashuk with his two sons, Segavan and his daughter, Aguvaluk, Okilyuk, Neokok, and Shoudlak and his son, and Akadrigak and his adopted daughter. The girls will cook for the crew. Both are skilful and neat and lovely to look at withal.

"The scene reminded me of the launching of a ship: the sled and boat waiting for the signal to glide down its icy way. At the bow I said the prayer which I had come to say, and Nasholook to interpret. 'Oh, Thou God Father, Bless this whaling crew. Bless this fine boat. Grant to all fair weather, that they may be successful in this hunt for whale, the meat, the good *muktuk* for themselves and their children, the blubber, for heat and comfort in their igloos, the whalebone, which they may trade for flour and sugar, for tobacco and cloth. May we never forget Thy goodness and ever remember Thy blessings to all Eskimo people. Amen.' With a handshake all around they were off, the men supporting the canoe as the dogs started on the run, tails high. Swoosh! how swiftly the sled glided down the smooth snow runway! Soon they were following the sled tracks of the crews who had gone before, around the high hummocks, a moment lost to our view, then in sight on the smooth ice again. We passed around the telescope until there was only a string of black dots to be seen moving north on the hazy horizon.

"Kootook who leads the fourth whaling crew came in to say goodbye this morning. It was very early morning for me, three-thirty A.M. I was awake, wondering what I was going to do about the window shades to keep out this all night light—fashion a dark screen or curtains—for sleep was fast becoming too negative in quantity. I tried a black silk stocking, but the discomfort of that binding my eyes was less conducive to slumber than all the light the glare of which seems to penetrate the very walls.

"So when Kootook came in and said, '*Oomiak electa*,' I donned my furs and went with him. Kootook is our fine hunter, you know, of fine physique. His strong face is somewhat disfigured by two labret or orifices, flesh button holes on each side of his lower lip holding huge ivory disks, giving his mouth a rather uncouth expression. These orifices were cut in Kootook's early boyhood when small bone labrets about the size and shape of a shirt stud were inserted. As he grew older these were replaced by larger labrets, then again larger, until today and on other special occasions, great ivory or jade discs ornament each side of his mouth. Several of the ipanee men here wear these lip adornments. I am glad to say that this ancient custom is no longer practised at Wainwright.

"It was a rugged crew that started off in the frosty morning. They followed the trail of the earlier crews until they were well out on the ice, then turned to the northwest and were soon lost among the ice hummocks and in the light fog which hovered over them. I walked beyond the village watching them. The sun in the northeast, clinging to the horizon as though loath to rise to the heavens, was slowly stretching long rosy feelers across the boundless wastes. It gave me the unearthly feeling of being one in the fantastic scene of Flammarion's *Last Days of the World*, I shivered. Why choose such an hour to go whaling? I laughed aloud. Why choose it for a stroll over the tundra when at such an hour it could only present the strangest of scenes. It was as if I were following a receding canvas—a flat scene of gray white ridges and chalky blue shadows leaning into mauve depths—for one cannot distinguish any horizon distance—or middle distance for that matter—and what seems near is far and the far near. A dark smudge might be the black tail tip of a frightened ermine, or it might be Oyalla with his sled and dogs returning from his traps, for the tundra in winter reveals no perspective and one becomes confused—lost indeed. I gingerly retraced my footsteps to the schoolhouse. A steaming fragrant cup of chocolate, three hours of restful sleep, and I was back in the schoolroom again.

"There are three rows of empty desks now. My primary Department will continue to attend until the end of the school term. The older children have lost interest. They spend their time drawing pictures of whales, or gazing with long long thoughts out to sea, or reminding me that maybe 'catch whale tomorrow.' In that case school would close tomorrow."

EASTER DAY

The women and children and the few old men made up the small congregation this evening. Elaborate Easter Programmes depend on the ice and weather conditions. The wise teacher will ever keep in mind the needs of the people. Hunting for their food must take precedence over every schoolhouse activity or programme. A few years ago, a zealous missionary insisted on the natives keeping the Sabbath in his orthodox way and forbade them to hunt on Sunday. They came in obediently but sadly from the whaling camps, leaving one man to watch the camp gear. Even the dogs were doleful dragging the meatless sleds. The second Sunday three whales were sighted, swimming leisurely up the open lead, and not a hunter there to harpoon them. There was great suffering in that village the following winter, for a late season coupled with adverse winds closed the leads and no more whales showed up that spring. Present rules have made it optional with us government teachers whether we take up this Sunday church work or not. What we do not have to do, is usually the pleasant thing we like to do. It affords an excellent opportunity to teach the older natives who never fail to attend these services.

Wainwright has been assigned to the Point Barrow Presbyterian Mission territory. Three natives are appointed Elders by the medical missionary there, to serve this village.[17] These three, Kunoodluk, Nasholook and Neokok, faithfully assisted at all religious services. I wish you could hear old Kunoodluk pray. You wouldn't need to know the language to understand the genuine love he holds for his God Father. He would come in just before "church" time to ask me what I was going to "preach" about. Nasholook told me that he always included the subject of the "sermon" in his prayer. These "sermons" were very simple—mostly an attempt on my part at explaining various and sundry passages of the Bible, which the natives themselves would select for me. The Elders would often come in together, greatly puzzled about some chapter or verse, confounding me with most profound questions. I believe Nasholook spent all of his spare time reading and interpreting the Book to Kunoodluk and Neokok. The missionary doctor's visits

---

17 In 1925 five elders and two deaconesses were serving. In 1936 a small chapel was erected.

always inspired a revival. In between I chose my own subjects.

One Sunday, during trapping time, I told them about two Eskimo families; one, an energetic and industrious father and mother; pictured in vigorous terms what their chances for prosperity would be, together with the advantages their children might enjoy. The other, shiftless and lazy, (yes, we have some lazy Eskimos, just like white folks) forever visiting their relatives whenever they were hungry, complaining of lost traps, or the foxes so big the traps were too small, or a "pain on his ear," or "my wife she make boots and have no sinew," or "my dog he have broken harness," and all the rest of the niggling excuses forever on the tip of the lazy man's tongue. Now for most of these sermon talks, the interpreter would merely translate without any attempt at expression, but on this Sunday Nasholook grew magnificently elocutional. I actually could see as well as feel through his Eskimo tongue, the degradation and misery the lazy man's family was certain to come to. I must tell you the guilty ones were in the audience. One was thoughtfully picking reindeer hairs off his little son's artiga, the other naïvely attentive, his expression one of profound indifference to this type of sermon.

Next day I learned the reason for Nasholook's outburst of eloquence. One of the lazy ones owed the native store several fox skins. Nasholook did not like to see the natives piling up debts on their company books. The other one had long owed Nasholook's wife one fox skin for two bleached seal skins. That afternoon I casually strolled by their igloos and found one of these men earnestly engaged in mending his dogs' harness with a pathetic equipment of broken needle and spool thread.

I returned to the schoolhouse for a canvas needle and linen thread. The smile he gave me almost melted my determination to see him off to his traps. He left next morning. The other was off to his traps two days later. There were only industrious families to preach about after that.

The Eskimos are fond of the old Book. I have come to believe they know the commandments even better than did the Israelites of old. They not only know them; they live them without a finger pointing to "Thou shalt not" to order their behavior. Every Bible in this village is covered with a beautiful jacket of white seal-skin—most of them decorated with cutwork of dyed skin, the women expending their most exquisite needle-work skill on them.

Anashugak, the chief herder at No. 2 herd has just come in. "How you, Missus Eva," he greets me, "fawn come plenty good now." I had told him I expected to visit the herds at fawning time. He had not forgotten to let me know when. Here was a dilemma! Baby rein-deer versus whales! A silly jingle popped into my head that minute.

> With fawning time on the tundra, and whaling time at sea,
> I'm surely twixt the devil and the deep blue sea.

How funny the last line sounds up here! The devil much prefers to employ his nefarious trade in crowded marts of civilization, and the sea is not blue at all. Just at this minute it is all sparkling white with rose and mauve shadows in the frost mist, scintillating stuff hovering between the sun and where I happen to be writing.

Now to decide whether to wait on the whalers, or to go inland about thirty-five miles to see the baby reindeer.

May 22. Here I am, snug as a feather on a goose, in a little white tent set down at the edge of Herd No. 2 now at its fawning. Swift and exciting transportation this sledding, following on the heels of swift-footed reindeer, glossing over the smooth frozen river Kuk—broad winter boulevard leading from Wainwright to the beautiful shining inland country. My neck is stiff from dodging the clods of hard snow hurtled back from reindeer hoofs as we sped along.

The undulating white tundra spread outward to the boundless horizon. Anashugak pointed to the first coal vein, a black smudge on the banks of our highway. When we reached the second coal vein, Takomuk was there loading his sled with the sacks he had filled last summer. We could hear his dogs howling miles before we could see them. Our wary reindeer raised its head, the sled lurched, and Anashugak had reined away to the opposite bank where the only sound to break the silence was the Pluck-pluck—Pluck-pluck, of the steady hoofs. The Eskimos, who for generations have been accustomed to discerning objects at great distances, have truly remarkable eyesight. When Anashugak pointed and said, "Herd!" the landscape appeared to me no different than the hour before. The binoculars disclosed only a faint gray line on the horizon. Our sled deer plodded on. Anashugak was stolid and unconcerned about his passenger's enthusiasms. How could he know that I was revelling in the midst of wonder and unrevealed beauty and knowledge? How could he understand my interest in the many species of delicately formed lichens, that grow in wild profusion over these trackless wastes and upon which the reindeer grow fat, live, and bear their fawns? True, these lichens are covered now with frost and thin crusty snow, but here and there where the contour of the land sloped to the south, brown patches were to be seen, first signs of the spring thaw, but the wind and temperature precluded any sign of thawing today.

Soon we were slithering up the left bank with the crackle of dried and frozen tawny grasses and ground willow under the runners as the sled lumbered over the niggerheads. And how the clods did fly! It was a glad relief to see the herder boys running towards us as we reached the camp. Thirty-five miles from my Arctic home, and come to a place of hot tea and ship biscuit, and to a little white tent facing a munching herd of reindeer—contented as cows in a sunlit valley.

The two herders and their families live in small skin tents, which are easily moved as the herd moves on to fresh grazing grounds. Anashugak's apprentice boys were down near the riverside with their faithful Lapp dog, rounding a few strays towards the main herd. His wife was busy with the tea. And if you are the kind of guest who enjoys matching a host's hospitality, you have plenty of cube sugar and raisins in your grub box.

The children crowded near my tent (they are too polite to enter without invitation). They could hardly wait to recite their school lessons, or ·to exhibit their number work. We agreed to hold school after tea. Now it is here I would tell you of the educational extension work inaugurated this year for the children of the herder camps established near Wainwright. School material and lessons are sent out to the camps about once a

month by the herder boys who usually come to the village that often for supplies. At the same time they return the work assigned on the previous trip.

This extension work follows the regular school
courses, and tests are given whenever the children themselves happen in the village. For the herder boys, the
apprentices, emphasis is placed on problems covering
their training in reindeer husbandry and the growing
importance of this industry in the economy of Eskimo
life. It will be remembered that these boys serve an
apprenticeship of four years under an experienced chief
herder, and are rewarded after this service with six to
ten deer, which with the natural increase, average about
forty-five for each graduate. Many of the chief herders
along the coast have had the benefit of meeting with an
experienced stockman and so improved their own methods of caring for their herds. Anashugak was one of
these and his herd is one of the best in the North.

While I was hearing the school lessons, Anashugak
came to take me out to the herd. Pupils were dismissed
for the time being, consolingly, on treats of cube sugar
and raisins. Dear little Eskimos! How their eyes can
shine!

Anashugak was very proud to have "Missus Eva" visit
his camp. His sled deer was now unharnessed and free
to mingle with the herd until the next trip to the village,
when a lasso flying true will single it out for sled work
again. Soon we were skirting the fringes of the herd,
to come upon little long-legged awkward coltlike creatures, the first baby fawns. Softly spotted brown and
white they were, with mild brown eyes strangely startled—bewildered in their new world, my guess. A
mother deer near us lowered her beautifully antlered

head over her newborn. Anashugak told me this fawn was about two hours old.

We walked around slowly—scarcely noticed by the deer—and enjoyed watching several females whose small young bucks trotted boldly beside them. It is amazing what strength these newly born youngsters derive from their first warm milk meals and still more amazing how fast they grow. Anashugak explained how the males lose their antlers before the fawning season, while the females retain theirs until after fawning, assurance for their own protection, also the means for defending their young.

But for the deer, the scene with its saucer-shaped valley and warm southern exposure, might have been a Minnesota meadow in early spring. Anashugak declared that "this place good for fawning time—warm, fine."

The fawning season is a busy one for the herders and in these latitudes, takes place about the first of May lasting well into the first week of June. The yearlings, however, bear their fawns a few weeks later, but these often prove to be capricious mothers and usually desert their young. The herder boys collect the dead fawns, the pelts of which are saved, carefully dressed and used for lining heavier fur garments or for children's clothing.

The sun was low on the northwest horizon when Anashugak and I returned to the skin huts for the evening meal, bean soup, (my own make) biscuit and tea. The wind was blowing cool when I retired to my small white tent where my sleeping bag looked out on the resting herd. Lying thus, on the tundra ground, I could hear the muffled thudding of hoofs, and somewhere very near, the cheerful cry, invitingly sweet, "Come-

ere, Come-ere" of the mating ptarmigan. And far off
as a dream might be, the plaintive whistling of the Arctic swan, most poignant of all the tundra love calls—
minor in key and hauntingly beautiful.

Next morning I found that my sleeping bag had been
unrolled on a soft bed of creamy lichen. I gathered
some, pressing the succulent corallike sprays between
the pages of my notebook, much as we gather four-
leaved clovers at home and for the same wistful reason.

The pell-mell rush to get back to Wainwright when
the news came with Kooluruk that Otoiyuk's crew had
killed a whale, reminded me of a crowd of small boys
starting out after the fire reels at home. Such a rounding
up of sled deer! The air was alive with thwangs from
the lassos. And dog teams—it seemed as though suddenly the herders were going to leave the reindeer to
their own whims. How strong the urge for the hunt
in these people! The excitement of the chase, the zest
for the kill, the appetite for whale flesh! *Muk-tuk!*
Magical word to populate the village again! But chief
herder Anashugak was not excited. He knew the waters
of the Arctic were fast being depleted of whale and
walrus and the big seal, that the time was soon coming
when his people would no longer find their food there.
He remained with the herd contentedly certain of his
own well-being. (Certain that he would soon receive
a present of *muktuk* too.)

I returned to the village with Kooluruk. His dogs
must have anticipated the feast. Nothing so hotfoots
these animals as the prospect of fresh meat. Whether
they understand this from Kooluruk or due to their un-
canny dog sense I couldn't say, but there was no lagging

on the trail. A frozen river highway has no red or green light signals to full tilt us forward or fetch us up to a burning-rubber jolt; no startling klaxons or screeching brakes; no constant nervous tension of threatening disaster, but only exhilarating smoothness of wind lightness with dogs trotting briskly, their tails high and jaunty.

Lucky for me! Tooruk was just leaving for the whale camps. I had just an hour in the village, long enough to see to things at the schoolhouse. Then off to the whaling, over the icy hummocks and far away! With the village far behind, I settled into the sled to have a look around. How could I believe I was out on the sea ice? The trail going on before us as tho' it were on land, the ice of the Arctic Ocean firm as the terrain. With unhesitating surety the dogs threaded their way between and around the great ice ridges thrown up as by some titan wind upheaval, as if mountainous waves had frozen instantly at the climax of their fury.

The sun was shining; every hummock sustained a melody of blue, every subtle hue of this ethereal color deeply beautiful in the shadows. At last we reached the tattered flag with its white "W," with which the natives had marked the limits of safe shore ice. Beyond lay the new ice (an open lead newly frozen), covered with a recent fall of snow which immediately slushed upon sled and dogs as we traveled through it. Here we changed our course to the northward, heading into a wind that whipped the color to our faces and made of breathing an exultant joy. Such air! How can one describe air that is forever being filtered through infinitesimal frost crystals, filtered to a fineness so rare that one wonders if here could be the source of earth's life-giving oxygen? I can only say this—such is the air of the Arctic!

Twenty miles now, out on the sea ice—the landscape appears as rolling hills with great white rocks at their base, like a carved in ice coast of Maine stilled in winter. Sledding was impossible. I left it to stumble and climb over the icy rockland as best I could, while Tooruk made it easier for the dogs by pushing and lifting the sled. Sometimes I waited for the plucky little beasts, more often they waited for me, as down in the gullies of the piled up masses I would stop to inspect huge cracks between enormous blocks of ice, almost fearful lest the waters of the Arctic would suddenly appear and engulf us.

On top of the next arduous climb we glimpsed the dark lane of open water, like an inky black river, threading and widening far to the southward—far as eye could see. It reflected none of the blue of the smiling sky overhead. Perhaps because above it hovered the gray-blue fog, that quavering smoky barometer registering open water. Along here there was smooth trail again with Tooruk and I once more happy and riding easy on the sled. The dogs too, trotted along with awakened interest and here and there a sniff in the air, which Tooruk interpreted as "whale not much far now."

And for certain it wasn't. Around another ice dune and we came upon the excited populace of Wainwright village—twenty-five miles from their igloos. Whether seeing them grouped about a whale created the illusion of numbers, I will never know, but I could have taken an oath there were a thousand Eskimos sharing the joyous enthusiasm of the prize.

The dark hulk of the giant cetacean they had killed was being drawn up with an ingenious block-and-tackle contrivance onto the ice. Already the great head lay out of the water and the natives were cutting new gashes in the huge jaws, giving a fresh grappling hold on the rest of the carcass. From the upper jaw of the yawning mouth a forest of whalebone spread apart like black palm leaves, the tongue a great lolling lumpish mass as big as a cow. With gustatory glee a few men were hurriedly flensing, tossing the big chunks of pink blubber and black skin down to the women, who, with a thrust or two of their women's knives, divided it for the eager and happy children. Again and again the men, old and young, toiled at the tackles, its blocks firmly anchored in the ice, and slowly the oily hulk moved forward.

The excitement was tense. Twenty-two men strained at the gear. Flensing was in operation full tilt. Sleds were sleeked alongside the mountain of whale where the women and children heaped the greasy, pinkish chunks of *muk-tuk* on them. When the sleds were full the dogs were harnessed to the loads and the sledding trek to the village began. There was need for this strenuous haste. At any hour might come the change of wind, crushing and shifting the ice, with the probable loss of precious meat and whaling equipment. And no native relishes the thought of losing his meat of meats, or of being marooned on an ice pan to be buffeted about in open sea and wind.

Tireless Eskimos! Hour after hour they worked; hour after hour in sunlight—night and day the same— only the shadows changing round the diminishing carcass. Soon the sleds returned for more meat. I would have liked to have been in two places at once; in the village to watch the caravan of sleds arriving, see the meat piled up on the tundra near the schoolhouse, to see the light in the eyes of the old men and women as they enjoyed the fresh kill of the meat they loved above all other; and the whalebone piled up like so much ebony lumber near the shore. But I could only watch the more interesting picture: the sleds drawing alongside the whale to load up and then away.

Hour after hour, each process contributing its own peculiar note to the cheery shoutings and gay laughter of the Eskimos; the clup-clup of the flensing, the soft, thuddy "squash" of the meat falling on the sleds, the decided and wrenching crunch of the whalebone being extracted from the huge jaws. It was only when the men sat down for a bite of *muk-tuk* and cups of hot tea brought by the busy women, that I ventured to inquire of Nasholook what manner of whale this might be. "Whalers say plenty long time Arctic Right Whale,[18] this whale same kind. That is female whale. Maybe seventy feet big, maybe half on ice now. Maybe small whale in belly now."

Nasholook's "thinks" were right. It was a female whale and measured sixty-seven feet. The embryo, perfectly formed, and but for its pale gray skin, an exact miniature of its mother, was seventeen feet long. Piteous tragedy of the Arctic! So soon would it have known birth. And while I waxed foolishly sentimental about dead baby whales, Tooruk came up all smiles, his white teeth shining, to tell me he had counted the layers of bone "on that one jaw." There were 276 of them. And "that long bone in middle he is nine feet and" so much, holding up two greasy fingers. We had talked about taking these measurements while on the trail.

Tooruk would have made a first-rate naturalist. He felt very important mushing up and down that whale

---

[18] *Balaena mysticetus.*

with my six-foot rule. I say mushing. There isn't anything on this earth that I can compare with the experience of walking on a whale. You might try walking
on a wet rubber mattress with very pliant springs hidden
within. Perhaps piling up three mattresses would be
better, then walk about on the top one. This would only
give you the sensation of sinking in as if presently you
might step straight through to the ground mattress. But
the slick, greasy uncertainty of each step you wouldn't
get at all, to say nothing about losing your balance and
coasting oilily down to the tail flippers, if you were lucky
enough to be headed that way. I should say "tail flukes."
The flippers are what may be called a whale's forelimbs,
smooth paddlelike appendages, which come in where the
body begins. The head measures one fourth of the length
and is mostly taken up with the mouth. The eyes are
where you look for the ears. And you can't see the ears
unless you search for them. They are tiny whorls just
back of the eyes, as if some one had tried to punch holes
with the tip of a cane. If you punched deep enough you
would strike the ear bone, shaped like a conch shell and
about the size of your fist. From the ear there is a perfect streamline down to the flukes which take a sudden
turn laterally to a wide tail spread. It must afford him
excellent whacking power in any direction. Here Tooruk emphasized the proceedings by telling me a story
of a wounded whale and of how it struck his father's
uncle's skin boat. "That skin boat is on edge of ice, and
is not have people paddle, not yet."

"What happened to the oomiak, Tooruk?"

Tooruk is always amused by my questions. "He *pee-
chook* quickly time." (*Pee-chook* is the good Eskimo
word meaning *all gone*. If a man has gone trapping he

is *pee-chook* from the village. If he is tired, his strength
is *pee-chook*. If a trap has been sprung, the fox is *pee-
chook*. The language is as simple as that.)

When the blubber, meat and whalebone had been removed from the great jaws and head, the tackles were
once again grappled with and the tail end of the carcass
brought up to a safe shelving on the ice. The dogs were
showing signs of fatigue, their tails hanging wet and
wilted. The weather continued the favored whaling
variety. By this time the hummocks must be completely
worn off the trail, thought I, and since I had been whaling (?) for thirty-six hours without sleep I was beginning to feel the meaning of *pee-chook*. The whale was
fast settling down to a skeleton. Shreds of dark flesh
hung—fanning a strange odor among the great ribs.
Let all this be food for polar bears and the foxes—I was
going home and Tooruk was not sorry.

The whaling crews went back to their camps along
the lead. One whale was not enough and watchful waiting was again the accepted mood. A faded bandanna—
flying pennon of hunting prowess—was fastened to the
peak of Otoiyuk's ice windbreak, in front of which
his crew rested—resting but never closing their eyes on
the lead. I wondered whose crew would be next to fly
a tattered pennant.

We sledded back over the same trail and found the
hummocks higher and rougher than before and oh, how
tough was the going! But how good the return to home
again! Home to a hot bath, to milk and toast, and to the
softest bed in all the world.

I do not know how long I had enjoyed the comfort of
that bed before I awakened. I lay there drowsily think-

ing of these Eskimos, who could keep on toiling throughout the light "night-days" without rest and without food, when suddenly there seemed something strange about the room. An appalling silence filled the place and then I panicly discovered the clock had stopped. I made a frantic reach for my watch. It too, had quit. You know how you will shake a watch that isn't running? Might as well shake a fox skin. That, at least, would show up a poor or a fine pelt. But this—this shaking a watch! What slaves we white folks are to a little gold case filled with wheels! But I had records to keep and one *must* know whether it is the first or the last of the month. Was it Friday? Or Saturday? And what day did I go whaling? The sun was in the west when we started on Tuesday. It had made one round, that was Wednesday, then one more, and that was Thursday. Now how long had I been sleeping? I had wound the clock to its last notch. I could do so again and count the hours of its running. Thus the wheels of my mind spun around in a panic worrying about what day it could be. The sun low in the north brightly and colorfully chimed forth it was nearly the midnight hour. I set the clock, and my watch, and a fresh batch of bread. Then noted on the margin of my journal, "Lost a day or two, maybe three. Mere bagatelles."

You see the Arctic isn't run by a wrist watch. It is run by the seasons. Anyway the Eskimos have it that way and seventeen jewels doesn't enter into it. How could you miss knowing it was the season of the whaling? The very air informs your nose, let alone the sight of many women cutting the *muk-tuk* into pie-shaped pieces and stuffing seal pokes with them. And the heaps of red meat and the whalebone piled up like a lot of old teakwood, and the children with greasy little fists and small mouths dripping oil. They do look dirty, but oil and blood, after all, are not dirt. Some day, when there is time for such things, their garments will be clean again.

(From my Journal) May (?) I believe it to be the twenty-eighth. Another whale has been caught, a small humpback, and the sleds are hauling again. The landscape around the schoolhouse has changed. Snow is about all gone. This morning old Kaivakinga told me the natives will soon be opening up their igloos and moving into the summer tupeks.

Great clouds of eider ducks darken the sky every little while. While returning from the whale camp the other day I saw them, winging their way northward, but I was too tired to notice them. Today the migration seems to have caught up to its seasonal meridian and a spectacular sky pageant is in progress. A dark stippled streak appears on the southern horizon, spreading fanlike upward and onward; presently it passes overhead with strange noises and a swift wind to disappear on the northern horizon as mysteriously as it came. Like a moving sky shadow are the eider ducks in flight.

And the ducks themselves! One pridefully struts an orange-colored protuberance over his bill, soft green featherage on his head, set off by a striking black band of satiny sheen and a fawn-colored waistcoat. A beautiful bird, the King eider—exotic as the tropics. Then the Pacific eider, with brilliant red-orange bill, black satin on his shapely head and the same soft green finishing off, looking more like the mental picture you may have of eiders. The females of both these are very much protected on the brown June tundra, with their softly mottled brownish-red tones, a perfect blend for the little creeping brown stems and tiny red leaflets of the tundra willow, the only plant that pretends to be a tree up here. Then the Steller's eider—the first naturalist to ever set foot in Alaska remembered in its beauty—and the Spectacled eider, gray-green puffs circling his eyes, a wise owl gesture of nature and the reason for his name. Today I noted the flight of eight swan, the great sweep of their wings supporting long eager necks and legs, flying on like a song and the grace of heaven in their flying.

(From my Journal) June 1. (?) Temp. 26°. The air is filled with snow crystals through which the sun is shining. The landscape is a study in brown and white. And I am running about in a circle not knowing what to do first. Summer seems about to burst in any moment, flowers, green grass, everything. Out on the tundra there is a heavenly din of love calls and tender coaxings. I want to be out there listening to it all. Kittik is making the seal boots necessary for this swampish hiking.

I may as well make up my mind not to wax too enthusiastic over summer. It is rather far away today. The landscape is a wintry gray, overtones and undertones. Last night's snowfall was the artist, but the temperature may undo his work. At noon it registered 36° and I've opened all the doors again. I found Tigalook and Mayuenna leaning wistfully against the wall in the outer hall. How they danced when I beckoned them in. Bread and butter and jam tasted better for their bright eyes across the table. Then we went to the schoolroom and gathered up the books, cleaned the shelves and washed the blackboards, setting to rights the aftermath of a hasty departure and dismissal of school when we moved out to the whaling.

This evening I mended books. The soiled or torn pages were surprisingly few, remembering the many chunks of blubber in tight little fists and small mouths and chins glistening with the goodness of it. I mused over the tiny scraps of paper tucked here and there among the pages— mute fragments of great efforts in number work or spelling! One of them was a drawing, Panick's impression of his teacher dressed in her parka. He had titled it, "School my teacher good," and signed his name in the neat Spencerian copybook-perfect handwriting which he has gained after much practice.

Seems only yesterday that Panick came to Wainwright with his parents for the Christmas festivities. What a fascinating time he had with chalk in the schoolroom that day, covering the blackboards with pictures of whales and birds while the other boys and girls were feasting and dancing. When his parents returned to their home at Icy Cape, Panick was left with relatives in Wainwright, (you know about those accommodating cousins Eskimos have in every village) where he could enjoy the advantages of the larger village and its school. Certainly no boy ever worked harder than did Panick to gain the advantages Wainwright had to offer. The canons of his simple native faith did not embrace the doctrine of getting something for nothing. He put in hours of painstaking effort and practice learning to write, and a double score more learning to read. His industry and zeal were contagious. The entire school caught it with enthusiasm. There ensued a pleasant rivalry among the boys during spelling and arithmetic classes. They appealed to Panick with shy glances when stumped on a word or problem. His attitude towards them was one of grand propriety, as though he had said,

"Why ask me when it's all in the book." Was it an urge to end his schoolroom confinement, or a bit of home-sickness, which led him to inquire of Nasholook how long would he have to go to school? Nasholook answered there was so much to learn that it must take a long time. Panick thought it out. Next morning he confided his mind to Nasholook, "I learn many books quick. Teacher say 8 times 8? Panick say 64, quick like is in book. Same all books. Then all the time hunting and whaling and living." And that is why in the late hours of the evening, or early before breakfast, (all hours were the same to Panick) he could be seen running to the schoolhouse, his assignment in problems all worked and his reading lesson word perfect. His was a confident assurance that, *learning is learning. How can one confine it to time? You are teacher in Wainwright. I am Eskimo boy from Icy Cape. Here are my lessons. Suppose we get them over with, and I get back to my village.*

Many weeks now since he left school to join his father's whaling crew. And I muse tonight over his little drawing, Panick's idea of his teacher dressed in a beautiful parka. Not many teachers are so flattered. How skillful your pencil, Panick! How very lovely you have pictured me to be! While you were drawing, Panick, could you, by any chance, have been dreaming of lovely Taporak, Taporak down at Icy Cape?

June 4 (?)

I've been turning over the pages of my Journal. But for this record I should indeed be wondering, where under the Arctic sun, the days had flown to. I recall the croaking prophesies of well-meaning friends, that I would be lonely unto death, and the teacher down at

Kotzebue who warned me of the foot-dragging hours I would experience between the close of school and the arrival of the first ship. Said she had kept some scarlet wool to work with during this time and had found great comfort knitting a garment of this bright color. Knitting! The very thought sent me out into the cold sunshine to find a sled, a harness full of dogs, and my good Tooruk. Together we would go to Point Barrow. Time I was calling on my Arctic neighbors.

Off for Point Barrow!

No mild affair, this making ready for a three-day sled journey of 110 miles—a mere nothing to you who travel by auto. And that distance is reckoned as the bird flies. What mileage will be added by the time we sled around one ice jam and another, together with all the various impediments to sea-ice navigation, no one knows.

Tooruk has been to no end of difficulties bringing his dogs together. Some of them were at the reindeer herd, but now all is ready and we make a start tomorrow. His part of the preparation was most important. You can't travel far in this country without a good sled, strong dogs and an Eskimo. "The peoples has to have good lead dogs"—you know. After these consider food, the preparation of which I've been at all of this sparkling cold day.

When a dog team and driver are hired, it is quite taken for granted that food will be provided for the driver since he provides food for the dogs. And an Eskimo adapts himself so graciously or gratefully (perhaps the word is eagerly) to white man's fare. This is as it should be. I can't imagine adapting myself to, let alone trying, Tooruk's food specialties. And Tooruk loves my biscuits better than his good *muk-tuk*. That is what he tells me and I have always found him truthful. So I have made biscuits, rich ones full of butter such as we make in this country for the trail. You do not carry bread unless you want to hack at it with an ax all the way.

Food for the trail is unique. Yesterday I made thick bean soup with onions in it—dehydrated onions have a bouquet the same as fresh ones—and poured it into large cups to freeze out of doors. Presently I was thumping out the brown blobs and putting them into a sack labelled *Lunch*. I did the same with rolled oats and raisins, and rice and tomato with bits of crispy fried bacon mixed with it. The three sacks hang in the first hall ready to be packed in the grub box. No cooking on the trail since the big objective is to reach our destination without delays. Then we take tea and lump sugar and squares of sweet chocolate. And I slipped in two cans of sardines. (They ought not to freeze packed in oil, thought I.) So much for the food. There are two tin cups, two silver spoons, two enamel plates. Paper napkins, a primus stove, spirits for fuel, matches, snow glasses, cold cream and vaseline, (wash my face with either) the kit of first aid stuff, a small sewing outfit, needles, thimble and sinew thread, a sketchbook and pencil, a small penknife and compass.

Kittik is to come into my apartments and make a fire every day and Nasholook is to take off the outside storm windows if weather permits. Everyone has promised to keep well until I return. Ahlulak laughingly whispered she would have her baby when I came home.

Tooruk has just brought the sled to the schoolhouse. He has a small bundle on it and a huge polar bearskin. These he has taken to the schoolroom where the rest of our baggage waits till morning. He is as excited about the trip as I am, and during supper he tells me something of Koosik's igloo across Peard Bay and "that place that name is Sinaru."

Next morning: I feel like a stuffed owl, look as if I weighed four hundred pounds, but due to the lightness of reindeer clothing, I can skip about as sprightly as the Follies girls do in their fans. The three pairs of boots do not weigh as much as my oxfords. I believe I am going to be warm enough. A suit of forest-green light wool shirt and knickers, over silk and wool undergarments. Over the knickers, a clumsy pair of bearskin pants which come over the knee and allow the long third and outside pair of boots to be drawn up over. Then a parka with the fur turned in under another with the fur turned out. Over these a brown denim water-proofed parka. The latter is provided with a large pocket in front into which I can thrust both hands, and when I filled it with all the articles I wanted to carry there, I took on the semblance of a giant pouter pigeon. In the meantime Tooruk folded the polar bearskin on the sled, then the two sleeping bags—mine has a blanket lining—the grub box, the stove and a can of fuel, and down at the foot of the sled, (perish the smell of it) some very ripe walrus meat done up in a coal sack, Tooruk's food for the dogs.

I shall always cherish the thought, that at some time or other, Tooruk must have been instructed in the art of upholstering, for after he had adjusted the canvas cover over the load, I was as comfortable as on a chesterfield.

One of the pleasant things about travel in the north is the absence of hidebound schedules. We depart when we are ready. No rushing frantically to catch a train or miss a boat. We had hoped to get away by nine in the

morning. Plans of mice and men! It wasn't until afternoon, two o'clock to be exact, that we were ready. And
then last minute I dashed in to get a box of beef cubes
and Tooruk went back to his igloo for a last minute
something while Nasholook held the restless dogs. Soon
he was back with his shotgun which he placed carefully
beside me. It was covered with a sealskin case. Yes, we
might need it on our way to Barrow. Polar bears were
numerous around Attanik. In any event we intended
to shoot ducks for dog food on our way home. Tooruk
took the handle bars. A rush and whirl of snow, a
smothered "Good-bye, good-bye," and the dogs and
sled and I, Tooruk guiding, pell-melled down the bank
trail in one grand glissade out to the sea ice. We were
indeed, head over heels off for Point Barrow.

For some time the trail was hard and a good start was
made. Nine dogs trotted in fine mettle, their tails a
parade of plumes. There was Mug-wa, the leader, a
shaggy unkempt coat covering his determined soul to
be about his business of the trail. Red and Ivuk were
harnessed in place just behind him. Nigger and Puppy,
two young dogs in training, worked with a will followed
by Tow-shek and Ki-kik, and the wheel dogs, Spot and
Blackie. And each, according to Tooruk, possessed a
peculiar cussedness of its own. Blackie now, was lazy.
You had to watch him. And Red was always hungry.
(What Eskimo dog isn't?) And a book could be written
about Mug-wa, faithful leader. Once Tooruk had re-
fused three fox skins for him. And "fox skins that time
is plenty money you get, like maybe forty dollar."
Three times forty dollars—priceless Mug-wa!

Late in the afternoon the trail became soft. Sledding
through soft sticky snow was slow and tiresome travel-

ing for the dogs. Mile after mile, the wide brown-patched tundra on our right, the purple-shadowed ice on our left. Sometimes we hugged the shore, more often the trail took us far out on the ice, but always we followed the smooth places wherever they happened to be.

We reached Attanik at six forty-five and considered we had made good time when the mushy trail was remembered. The village population was out to welcome us, their dogs howling in on the din. The igloos were buried under snow and but for the high racks of flapping skins, we should hardly have guessed there was a village about. Our dogs were tired, curled up right where we stopped, pushed their noses under their tails and were quiet.

And could any travel bureau equal Tooruk's efficient booking of accommodations on such short notice? For here I was, housed for the night, a guest in Keruk's igloo, a clean and well-ordered primitive home. She put my parkas and mittens up on a willow tray swung from the low ceiling, and examined my boots. They were not wet so she hung them on the wall near the door. A small tea-kettle was soon steaming on the tiny black stove. Tooruk brought in the frozen rice and tomato balls which were soon thawed and bubbling hot. Tea was made and together we shared the supper, all of us on the floor around a square board covered with yellow oilcloth. And what a feast when I passed the lump sugar! As fast as the tea was poured from the pot, hot water was poured on the tea leaves. Eskimos use tea leaves until they disappear. Keruk fed the small fire with short sticks of driftwood.

It was a comfy place, warm and friendly. Old Matu-lik and his gray-haired wife Kay-yuk came in, their faces wreathed in smiles. More shaking of hands. More glad greetings. We sat in a circle, our backs against the wall, our feet touching in the center, exchanging news of Wainwright and Icy Cape, of up the river and down. Tooruk was proud, gladly serving as interpreter and feeling very important, which he was. Walook had killed five polars. Samaruna had taken a fine silver fox in his traps. Kungoona came in with her daughter Kumachuk and little son Aklongak. More handshaking, and a moving over to make room for them. Old Matulik filled his pipe from a sealskin bag, crossed his feet and said something to Tooruk, to which remark everyone seemed in accord. Tooruk passed it on to me. "People is like hear story you tell maybe place you come." What would they like to hear of my faraway home? Old Kayyuk reached back under the bed shelf and pulled out a box. She took out a can (an empty can of Pet milk), pointed to the picture of a cow on it and indicated she would like to hear about "that caribou." So it was I told them of our dairy herds; of fragrant green meadows of grass and clover where our cattle were herded; the great barns where they were housed at night, and of the milk and how it was canned; of the tons of hay for winter food, of the summers it rained when the hay was cut, and how it rotted in the fields to give the farmer who owned the cows no end of trouble. Questions volleyed back at me. Did the man who owned the cows have his home in the barn? Did he have a wife? Did he have children? Did the herds get mixed up and did they mark the cows? Like the Eskimos mark their deer? Did they butcher them sometimes and was the meat good? Was it as good as reindeer meat? Did they have male and female cows? And was the fawning time in the barn, or where the clover was?

Tooruk saved me from sitting up all night. It was after midnight and the company as eager to hear more— as eager as I was to get some sleep. Our plans called for two extra sled dogs to quicken the longer trek of the morrow, and Tooruk went out to attend to this business. So again we were handshaking, *"Nagooruk Oonak-puk!"* "Good night, Good night!" The fresh cool air flowed into the igloo every time the small door was opened. When the guests were gone Keruk pulled my sleeping bag into place. I'd better have Tooruk beside me, I thought, as I placed his bag beside mine. Without hesitation old Matulik and his wife Kay-yuk pulled their reindeer beds into place under the bed shelf, stripped off their parkas and lay down, the pungent aroma of their bodies blowing around. The little girls, Talorak and Elusina bounced up on the shelf, heads over the edge, wide eyed with curiosity, ready to shyly tuck their heads under the minute I looked at them.

The light of morning was lighting the igloo when Tooruk returned. I was trying to soothe my wind-burned face with cold cream.

Matulik and Kay-yuk were already sonorously deep in sleep. The two grey heads were sharing one pillow, a bag of feathers tied in dark red calico. I was grateful for that dark covering. It had the effect of a dark curtain as I closed my eyes.

I was dropping off again when someone came in. I was grateful for the breath of cold air, when with it came a sniff of—whew!—that sack of ancient walrus meat. Stinking most awfully! Sleep now was out of the question. I began to recall all the other places where my nose had set up a similiar rebellion; that little farmhouse, now, on the Riviere des Neiges where I once spent a night—the pigs just outside the window; oh yes, and that bed of sea kelp on the rocks above the tide, rotting in the sun; after all, the inside of an igloo wasn't so bad even if there was a bag of old meat near the door. Someone began to snore. Matulik turned over and the floor puncheons teetered under me. Tooruk flung out an arm and barely missed my ear. Driving dogs in his dream, no doubt.

Did I ever get to sleep? Sure, for truth—after I quit counting the boots that hung from the overhead trays and quit contemplating the short lengths of driftwood and how they came to be fitted in so neatly to make these walls, and wondering from whence the driftwood had come. From the great rivers of China and Russia perhaps, flooding out their riff-raff into the currents of the oceans, blown by the northeast trades, flotsam of forest varied in color and grain, joined up with willows and stunted spruce from the near Arctic rivers; all combined to make this effective shelter, an igloo.

And in the morning, did I envy these Eskimos? They can slip a parka over their heads and boots on their feet with one fell gesture and the day and its adventure is theirs. With another gesture they have helped themselves to breakfast from a pan of seal meat or a kettle of duck stew. Practice makes perfect. I may get around to this yet. In the meantime, I hoped that most of the occupants would leave before I reached the more intimate details of my toilet. I marked time by brushing the reindeer hair from my clothes, picking it out of my hair, out of my ears and nose, (precious little do I worry about reindeer hairs habitually speaking) trying to coax a bit of courage into my legs to get up and step boldly into a pair of woolen tights so that I could adjust

them comfortably for the long day ahead. Silly to feel
embarrassed before folks who did not know the meaning
of the word. Matulik calmly smoked his pipe. Tooruk
went in and out; brought in the frozen rolled oats;
rolled up the skins and sleeping bags; sat down to talk
about our table arrangements with Keruk. Snatches of
their conversation punctuated my toilet. It seems that
Keruk had some misgivings as to whether I would care
to use one side of her tiny stove to prepare our share of
the breakfast. Would I? I straightway sat me down to
stir cereal and brew chocolate (it was like sitting at a
waffle iron) while Keruk occupied herself with a great
kettle of cooked ducks which had been stewing on the
stove all night.

'Twas a strange mingling of breakfast smells. Keruk
brought the yellow oilcloth-covered board to place it
on the floor, and a great shuffling there was, the two
children tumbling over each other to get out of her way.
Everyone was around it again as soon as it was down
with the kettle in the center. Tooruk said, "Please,
Missus Eva, I feel much I like that cook duck." So I
shared the rolled oats and raisins with small shy Talorak
and little Elusina, which for them was nothing less than
ambrosia. From the open kettle every Eskimo helped
himself. I saw my Tooruk pull out the breast of some
bird, the wings still attached, dripping with sodden
feathers. Cooked feathers! Stewed feathers! Funny
how I immediately thought of packing some small articles in the pocket of my parka. And I was glad there
were so many to pack. Then I adjusted my boots. Anything to keep my eyes off of Tooruk. But the sight and
thought of those feathers persisted. Just one of the many
delicacies, no doubt, which Beechey mentions in telling

of his appreciation of Eskimo hospitality—"entrails of seal, bowls of coagulated blood," which neither he nor his men could be moved to eat. And back in London, I'll wager, they couldn't be held from stuffing on caviar, calves' brains, blood sausages, or those fungi or tubers they must hunt with pigs, truffles. Squeamish white stomachs! Tooruk smacked his lips. Succulent sweetness, but he had enjoyed his duck! Wiping his mouth with the back of his hand, with a twinkle in his eye, he went out to harness the dogs. We said our thank yous and good-byes to the yipping and howling accompaniment of the village canines. Our faithful Mug-wa again led us northward.

A thin frost fog stirred in the air as we struck out over the Attanik whaling crew's well-marked trail, which led to the smooth sea ice well out from shore. This trail crossed the one used by the mail team, and although it was now obliterated by the action of wind and snow, the dogs sniffed, turning their heads this way and that. It was amusing to see Mug-wa slacken his pace here, prick up his ears, look back at us with a where-do-we-go-from-here expression. Tooruk gave the familiar command and away he flew, the sled almost upsetting on the curve as we turned. This trail was soft, growing more tedious as we approached the long sandspit before crossing Peard Bay. (Another name reminiscent of Beechey's expedition, honoring another lieutenant.) The sandspit was bare. The winds had swept it clean. Here we had to walk quite some distance, Tooruk helping the dogs with the load over the rough places. Driftwood lay about everywhere, some of it piled so neatly I was curious and asked Tooruk about it. "Sure the peoples finds many good wood here; they piles wood many places." We inspected one of these places and found it belonged to Okreesuk. He had cut his mark in the largest piece, a crooked tree trunk about six inches in diameter. Tooruk explained about the bow piece in the frame of a canoe. A native is lucky indeed when he finds the right shaped piece of wood for this. Another pile was marked Walook. And Tagarook of Wainwright had a fine heap of it. Beaches like this are the lumber yards of Eskimo villages. Each collects for himself and no Eskimo risks a good reputation by taking a piece that does not belong to him. He would never have a baby named for him if he did. As I looked down that long sandspit I knew there could be no reason for his doing so. There was so much driftwood. We passed the stark ribs of two old ships, crushed in the ice and wrecked here long ago. Old oaken ribs grayed and weathered to a silver sheen with bent copper bolts sticking out here and there, the metal polished bright on the windward side where the wind-driven sand had burnished and worn the dark oxide away. But oh, the stark bleakness of these forgotten hulls!

How beautiful was the vast table expanse of Peard Bay as we approached it! The atmosphere shone with scintillating mother-of-pearl, as rime from some frozen rainbow! The dogs seemed to sense the easy going ahead, lifted their tails and were off to a brisk trot.

For me, Peard Bay was something new in the way of Arctic landscape. The sea had not fretted itself to rough furrows of ice here; only vast frozen surface, smooth as a bowling green, its icy edge crimped against the shore line, as though the gods of winter had been making a huge pie. Across our path, from southeast to northwest, lay a shining effulgence, a swathe of light, the sun's rays making a little headway melting their way through the frost dust. Tooruk and I rejoiced that our route lay east by northeast, thus avoiding the uncomfortable glare of sunlight reflected from these myriads of frost crystals. There was nothing now to do but to give the dogs the head and enjoy this fine stretch of trail.

Tooruk proves a delightful companion. He sits at the edge of the sled, swinging his legs and munching chocolate, and tells me about the country, the people—everything. I love the introduction to his stories. Just as our familiar nursery tales begin with, "Once upon a time," so do his begin with, "Now many long times the people," and so forth. With that first word "Now," he brings the past into the living present, and the story moves forward as though it were this morning's news. "Now, I tells you about that sandspit. The peoples calls that place Ping-a-shoo-gooruk. Now many long times the people is not find many seal, and have not much for eating. That time is three mens go hunting, and they hunt with kayak. And they is now much tired. Soon they is sleep in kayak. And is dream about many birds. Now is wake up at that dream and is plenty sorry about is no birds at all. So is paddle again. Now they is very happy. All mens is see islands and on islands is plenty big seal. Now the mens is very happy and is sing, 'Oo-la, oola, oo-oo-la.' That very much noise and plenty seal is swim away. Now they is kill three big seal. In this place they is fill kayak with plenty seal meat, and go back to people, that very hungry people. Now that very hungry people is all dead, and the mens is see many, oh, maybe 'undred birds. Now that place is calls by all the peoples Ping-a-shoo-gooruk. And the peoples is name Ping-a-shoog-muits."

Towards noon the frost fog lifted. To the northeast there was as yet no sign of land. To our left and aback of us, the Seahorse Islands and the long flat spit of Pingashoogooruk loomed in mirage, glittering and fantastic, pictures for me like those idyllic castles in Spain, or lofty rose marbled towers shining from a Maxfield Parrish canvas. The sun shone aslant of us, but its light flooded the heavens. We protected our faces from sunburn by tucking bandannas across our noses and around our snow glasses. We passed the time pleasantly, interpreting words for each other. Tooruk was happy when he learned to use a new word, or a sentence of English. And double over in merriment when I'd try my luck on Eskimo.

Sometimes finding the word from the small number of English words in Tooruk's vocabulary was like working out a crossword puzzle. The name of his leader dog, now, Mugwa. It must mean something. I wanted to know what. Tooruk pulled the shock of shining black hair hanging over his forehead. "That word now," he begins, and then after some thought, resorts to the sign language, draws his hand down around his chin. Too much for me. He repeats the performance and almost succeeds in getting that shock of hair down around his chin. Ah! I have it, whiskers. "*Na-ga,*" says Tooruk, with an expression of what-shall-I-do-next. "Do you mean a beard, Tooruk?" His face broadens to his best smile. "Yesh, yesh, you understans good, Missus Eva." So we learn that Mug-wa is the Eskimo word for "beard," in other words, whiskers. You can readily see that not much of a start could be made on acquiring an extensive vocabulary in either language when it had to be worked out in this way. But who could forget a word after staging all this byplay around it?

I had taken a hand at driving the dogs when Tooruk pointed to the dark shore line ahead, dimly seen through the frost mist which was beginning to gather again now that we were nearing land. The trail was soft, too. Apparently the frost mist and soft trail was a combination that prevailed all along the coast of the bay, and we had escaped much of it by the direct crossing, as well as saving considerable time.

One may grow enthusiastic over frost fog, and the play of sunlight filtering through it, but when it comes to floundering in it, groping through a woolpack in search of some old deserted igloo, it ceases to be a thing of beauty, or anything to be gay about. We had made a flying crossing of Peard Bay, had maintained a good nine miles an hour since leaving Attanik; but at the moment we were not concerned with speed records. I was cold and hungry, and my one and only thought was for Tooruk to locate an Eskimo domicile wherein I might crawl and rest my trail-weary body. I am speaking for myself. Tooruk could have traveled on to the North Pole. Yes, I remember saying that the sled was as comfortable as a chesterfield—some twenty-four hours ago. Well now all my muscles, and a few I never knew I possessed, were crying a protest against a statement made in a moment of feather-pillowed ease. Enthusiasm can bound one off as from a springboard, only to give one a pretty bad bump. The same thing can happen to one on a sled; a run up to a sudden halt on a sandy stretch of beach, the dogs all askew in their harness, a fracas of flying fur in straps and toggles, snapping and chewing at each other; your surprised self lands in a slush pond and Tooruk does his best to straighten out the tangle.

I did not like the head of Peard Bay. A cold and penetrating fog enveloped us, wetting our garments, cloud-
ing my eye glasses, mushing the soft trail to a sloppy
slush. The loaded sled skidded along, Tooruk walked
ahead alert for signs which would point the way to the
igloo. Mugwa sniffed at the trail, then trotted briskly for
a team length or two, then more sniffing, here, there,
when bang! we ran into an old boat, bottom side up and
half buried in snow. *Ai-yah!* the igloo at last! Tooruk
disappeared in the fog. The team bounded after him. I
believe we all landed on the top of that igloo together.

Imagine, if you can, my excitement at making camp
for the first time. The dogs tethered, the stove lighted—
oh, but wait a minute. We had first to clean out the
place, and it wasn't so easy clearing away the snow from
the entrance. Some Eskimos had stopped here, storm-
bound perhaps, and from the many frozen carcasses we
found, we knew they had spent their time skinning
foxes. Back of the contraption made of walrus hide and
wood that served for a door, I found a wing from some
huge bird, an Eskimo woman's broom methinks, left
here for her fastidious white sister to sweep down frost
from the wall and an assortment of debris off the floor.
The dogs ate all of it. However, when the polar bearskin
was spread, and the clean snow was melted and steaming
ready for tea, the rice and tomatoes rising like a Spanish
feast to our noses, the biscuits spread with sardines, our
weariness was forgotten and we fell to, like the pair of
hungry folks we were.

Eating in an igloo is such fun. No standing on ceremony. You just eat and grin, make signs—(your
mouth's too full to say anything), pour tea, eat and grin
and pour more tea—and pass the sugar, and pour the

last of the tea, then pass the sugar again. And if passing the sugar sounds like ceremony, please be mindful of Tooruk's shyness. Why I had to make this trip to discover how many lumps of sugar a cup of tea could dissolve. Tooruk made a saturated solution of it and found it very good. And we both agreed that on the next trip we would take a whole case of sardines with us. And dozens and dozens of biscuits. And sugar, no end. "And many this kind," added Tooruk, holding up a piece of chocolate. And what about an extra team and sled to carry the stuff, and a third sled for the smelly walrus meat, and we would wear soft lustrous muskrat parkas—oh, halcyon paradise of full stomachs! And lying back on the thick fur, empty plates and cups licked clean, we planned the ultra in extravagance for another trip, when seventy miles of this one still lay before us. A delicious drowsiness crept over us, emanating from the pleasant warmth of the igloo, the so complete sheltering this tiny tavern of the tundra gave us and the thick luxury of fur beds. We succumbed to eons of deep and perfect slumber.

Eight hours later I awakened with a yawning stretch, my toes touching one wall, my arms over my head touching the other, by which calisthenics I discerned muscles were functioning agreeably again. It was 1 o'clock A.M. Do not be surprised. One hour is as good as another, you know, when daylight is continuous. And trail conditions are better during the "night" hours at this season of the year. Less slush than at noon; less needling of ice; affords greater foot comfort for the dogs as well as for ourselves. And for this particular divine morning, it meant facing the beauty of the midnight sky. While Tooruk was gathering clean snow, I made an attempt to match the color of this glorious panorama by sketching it in pastels. A broad band of orchid-rose circled the horizon like a wide ribbon, flanged with lemon-gold fringy flutings, shading to a deep violet-carmine and red-gold around to the east, the color flowing on to the south in undiminishing banded splendor. Small ice pools threw back the color like fire-opals set about in lapis lazuli, and here and there an amethyst lay purple in the shadows. I worked slowly, thrusting my hands into mittens between strokes, mighty glad I did not carry water paints. What a frost for color they would have been! Between the primus stove melting snow, and my picture, Tooruk shuttled in and out, fascinated with the work. Searching the far horizon quizzically, then a glance back at the sketchbook, he remarks, "Now you makes him fine, Missus Eva," and in a question, "You see plenty lemmings on ice? *Na-ga*. Plenty lemmings is on tundra all the time." So, my little patches of brown tundra in the scene looked like so many tiny brown mice to Tooruk. And not so tiny either, considering the scale of the picture. I would try again. I must paint pictures in which Tooruk can see what I see, or else—

At two forty-five we were ready to sled on to "that place called Sinaru." The early morning air was crisp; the snow crunched as we walked over it. We closed the entrance to the igloo to make it snow tight, and with a broken oar, set up the old boat in a manner not to be missed by other fog-bound travelers. Tooruk pointed out another igloo in the distance, Keowuk's well off the regular trail. "Now that igloo is not much good." Well, Koosik's had been a cozy place. Our pleasant domestic

arrangements lacked nothing of comfort, even though
the entrance had been a tight squeeze and Tooruk had
had to push our sleeping bags in, first taking the precaution—and how careful he was—of rolling mine in
the old piece of canvas. The same piece he carried the
snow in—and the walrus meat to the dogs. Insignificant
details of the trail to which we pay little attention when
we are cold to the marrow, but just let us warm up a bit,
and we take a second look at the stuff—a piece of canvas
so dirty it looked like an old walrus hide. Of course I
know you have never seen old walrus hide. I've a mind
to send you a postcard-size piece of it. And you will
speedily write and tell me I can stay in the Arctic forever. Hurrah! *Ah-regah!*

Light thoughts to be having on an early June morning
as we left our little tavern to go on to Sinaru. The sun
had skirted the horizon and had at last made up its mind
that it was time to rise and shine. The brown patches
on the tundra lost their frosty appearance. The shadows were not so deeply violet, nor did they creep along
the earth so far. The low tundra stretched on and on,
undulating imperceptibly as it met the frozen sea. We
had been following the coast line and found the season
here was not so far advanced as at Wainwright. The
whistling calls of love-making swans and happy staccato
of ptarmigan reached us, serving to speed up the dogs
every time they heard a bird or two. Tooruk remarked
that the trail must have been plenty wet yesterday, and
indeed as the sun rose higher it looked like a plenty wet
one today.

We had been traveling about an hour, when we sighted
a team approaching. Tooruk was all eyes and in a few
moments recognized Negovanna with his team. The

same Negovanna whose wife gave birth to our Christmas baby last December. Tooruk halted his team while Negovanna swung far out with his, thus avoiding a grand tangle of snarling dogs. Our good Mugwa set a good example by immediately lying down. The puppies were up to all their tricks trying to free themselves from harness. What were other dogs doing on this trail anyway? There ought to be something done about these trespassing mongrels. The world should know what a self-respecting dog thought about such. So they tugged and snapped and pulled to free themselves until Tooruk put a stop to it. One smart whang from his whip sent the shrieking duet of wounded feelings down groveling, nursing their imagined hurt, for Tooruk hadn't touched them at all, merely weighted the whang with a yell that meant business. The older dogs which were lying down offered a whimpering sympathy, though their bristling attention was all for Negovanna's dogs who were acting up in the same manner.

Negovanna soon had his team leashed to the ice and walked over to our sled. "Ah-lo Missus Eva, how you?" "Fine, Negovanna, where have you been?" It seems that when trapping season closed, he was far to the eastward, in territory he had chosen for his traps this year. Making his way along the coast to Barrow, he had visited with friends and was now on his way home. Barrow had enticed him with its large catch of whale, he had hauled bone for his brother's crew, thus earning a share. "They catches many whales to Barrow and peoples is much happy." So holding up his hands, fingers outstretched, doubling up his fists, then counting his fingers again, he told us they had killed fourteen whales and the crews were still watching. "You come back to Wainwright, Missus Eva?"

"Yes, I'll be back in two weeks, maybe sooner."

"That trail is much wet." He told Tooruk the rivers near Barrow were melting rapidly, overflowing the sea ice, and unless we had a change of weather, the ice would soon be too rotten for travel. "Peoples ish many glad to sees you, Missus Eva."

And with this parting gallantry Negovanna was on his way. Personally I thought the ice could never melt. But a little later, with the sun cooking our backs, I decided it must be having the same effect on the tundra and the ice of the sea, and the rivers, and that we might enjoy some summer after all—swimming maybe. Soon we were detouring around the overflow of some small stream not large enough to be called a river but certainly large enough to make a mess of the trail. When we had navigated this without getting our boots very wet and had found smooth hard going again, Tooruk rested the dogs, looked well to their harness while I stretched my legs, and then we talked. It was pleasant we agreed, meeting Negovanna, to hear all the news of Barrow. Like a telephone or telegraph, or radio message, a town crier or what have you. Call it what you will, it was news as it is published in the Arctic. We were posted now on what was going on in Barrow and to the eastward as far as Point Halkett. Tooruk went off with our cups and brought them back filled with cold water. We had suffered some from thirst and had envied the dogs as they lapped up mouthfuls of snow now and again. We did not try snow to allay thirst, since it serves only to increase it. Our way of drinking many cups of tea, or hot water and milk with our meals served us best. But this fresh cold water tasted like all heaven. Blessed be water, most especially in the Arctic.

The better trail quite cheered us. In the far distance to our right, we soon sighted the low bluffs, the first of what are called the Barrow Headlands. Tooruk and I fairly shouted. It was like sighting the hills of home, perhaps the very roof itself where presently we would be held in the arms of our beloved families. In all this vast and flat sameness of landscape, these great headlands are surely a milestone to reach. And besides, I had been told that it was beautiful at Sinaru, but at what time of the year, my Tooruk did not say. Sinaru is the site of one of the very ancient villages of the Eskimos, a people known as the Sinarumuits. I was glad that this was to be one of our best of camping places.

Mushy trail again—the worst so far. Instead of a sled trip, it was fast becoming a boat trip. "Half-boot deep that trail," said Tooruk. Again and again we were forced off the trail, to avoid the swift flow of waters poured over the ice by some fast melting inland stream. Deep crevasses yawned menacingly, but always the dogs and sled got around and then came the fun of finding the trail again. The brown bluffs were nearer now. At their base could be seen the half-melted remnants of the great winter drifts which must have been level with the tundra grass now hanging in danky fringes over the edge of the bluffs. Here and there the bank had broken away, sliding to the snow beneath, the dark mass melting over the clean snow like chocolate over ice cream.

The dogs floundered belly deep in water. It splashed and rippled against the sled and Tooruk's boots as we swished along. Mugwa, seeming to realize we were going to Sinaru, would prick up his ears and look up at the banks, as if searching for the old familiar landing. The puppies were tired. Sometimes their feet did not step at all, as they hung in their harness limp to be dragged along. It was certainly true, "puppies gets very tired." It was soon an effort to enthuse over the glorious color in the sky, with water surrounding us on all sides. Too much of that glory was reflected in what was contributing to our weariness and discomfort. I say *our*. Truly, Tooruk had had experience enough with this sort of trail, but I felt keenly my own trail inadequacy and Tooruk's tender concern for me. Time after time we recalled the beautiful crossing of Peard Bay. We were really not suffering at all. Our feet were dry, we were warm, and Tooruk seemed to be enjoying himself at the handle bars. It was this submerged trail and the circumnavigating of wide crevasses which proved so tiresome. Just when we thought it clear ahead, we would be halted by one of these, up or down which we would seek a narrow and safe crossing. The headlands were higher now, and once we traveled in the shadow of them for a short distance. This was a welcome change and we removed our snow glasses for the time. How cheerful were our faces without the brown goggles! "You happy, Missus Eva, all the time happy."

"Same to you, Tooruk."

"Bye and bye Sinaru, is plenty soon now. Nice place Sinaru, nice place." Tooruk was comforting.

No use looking at my watch. I preferred to regard time as I did the wind or the sunlight. Besides, what misery would be avoided, or what satisfaction gained, by knowing the number of hours I had been sitting on this sled, turning and shifting, sitting one way and trying another, and anyway the sun told me all I wanted to know about time. It was nearing noon. Out on the glittering sea ice, a brisk wind was gathering up smoke again. Eddies of snow, curling hither and yon, playing a game among the pressure ice ridges. We came to another stream. Or, I should say, the waters of a stream compelling another right angle turn to our left. Off to Siberia! We joked about it. Then back to the trail, Mugwa turning true as a compass needle, when we reached it. "So far, so good!" he seemed to say, as he trotted along. But what about the barrier of ice that seemed to block our path just ahead? It loomed up as an impassable mass. The sunlight played a glittering and fantastic crescendo across it, a beautiful display of light on many prisms. And when we reached this great pressure ridge, the trail skirted it to the right. Over a flat place, somewhat sluicy with mud, we went around a low bank to begin climbing the bank of a deep gully; up— up—Tooruk shouting to the dogs, hurling with his voice some motivating power to their legs (poor dogs, they were nearly spent), for the long pull to the top of the south bank of the Sinaru River, the place where the sun comes quickly and winter was no more. The gully with its oozy brown banks was half filled with the debris of drifted snows—under which the river gurgled—slushy in the sunny places, blue ice in the shade, but on the flat summit of the bluff, summer had come in all its shining beauty.

Was Sinaru as beautiful as Tooruk had pictured? Depends much on your idea of beauty. What is it anyway? Royal bougainvillea festooned over some pinkish wall in Florida—the Sistine Chapel—a field of lilies in Bermuda—the Vale of Kashmir—or a day in June at Sinaru? Gather it in with your other scenes of beauty, only take heed to wait until months of bitter cold and smoking snow—blowing on and on before the wind—

and crackling frost and biting rime and dark days and epidemics have passed over your head. Then suddenly be "dog-teamed" to this place, this high sunny bluff gently sloping toward the east and warm south. Overlooking the vast field of frozen ocean to the west and north was a wideness of mottled brown and white tundra rolling to the eastward, and in the south the dark crooked line of coast marking our sorely traveled trail. Sinaru was a high dry area, green with tender new grass starred with brave pale yellow calthas—the wee buttercups of the north country—opening their fragile petals to the blessed warmth of an Arctic sun. It was a place to embrace the earth, to refresh oneself in its own good fragrance, to abandon self to the intense joy and gladness of seeing green things growing again; one place to fling one's sled-weary body down and rest it forever.

Tooruk was everywhere. He fed the dogs, examined their feet, rubbing them with reindeer tallow (the dogs heal their own feet by licking it off), brought the sled up to higher ground, found an old pole which with the gun supported a canvas windbreak for the primus stove where our midday meal was soon bubbling. We made a picnic of it, eating bean sandwiches near the edge of the bluff, where we could watch great flocks of eiders flying low, now between pressure ridges, now skimming the smooth ice, disappearing into the noonday mist in the north. Pert and curious little ptarmigan called their "Come-ere, Come-ere," all around us, and twice several snow buntings twittered from the sled. The sun bathed us in its warmth. We shed our outer parkas and talked of sleeping in the open. We only talked of it, for how could we give ourselves up to the full measure of a night's rest at Sinaru with Barrow only twenty-five

miles away? Barrow, with a comfortable igloo for
Tooruk, his own people to visit, three hundred of them,
to say nothing of eleven white mortals as my share; a
veritable metropolis was Point Barrow.

And so it was decided that we rest for an hour or two,
and go on. It was then four o'clock. We would lighten
the sled of excess baggage, the primus, the provision
box, (now almost empty) the tin of oil, Tooruk's bed
bag and leave these here at Sinaru well covered with
canvas. Tooruk said he would watch the puppies. With
the first sign of fatigue, he would take them out of harness and let them ride on the sled. The other dogs could
make it, and with that we lay down side by side in the
shade of the windbreak, our feet in the sun. A tussock
of grass in the sun was like a pillow of duck down—a
place for good sleeping.

At eight o'clock we were walking on buttercups down
the south slope of the bluff to inspect the ruins of two
igloos, dugouts with roofs that had once been supported
by great whale jaws, now sunken in and rotted away.
Nothing more tangible than these ruins to tell the story
of an ancient people, this and the traditions which the
Eskimos now living cherished. The weathering bones
must still contain some source of fertilizer for I gathered
the largest buttercups here, and while the flowers were
of an unusual size, the plant itself was most diminutive.
No flower of the Arctic dares to postpone the time of
its fruitage with the wasteful business of adding a long
stem to its stature, or a leaf of the right size for its
adornment—so short is the summer.

An hour later we were well on our way, our heads
bowed before a wind blowing up smoky weather. The
slush of the warm hours had frozen hard, making for

rough trail at times. The puppies kept up well and Tooruk did not urge the team, content with the pace Mugwa was setting. It was colder. Near midnight we passed the wreck of the four-masted schooner, the *Arctic*, the same that was crushed in the ice here last August, her masts still erect with the wind crying a dirge through the frozen rigging, a desolate picture. The ice had certainly piled up at this point with a vengeance, high and jagged in strange fantastic ridges, a most laborious trail job for Tooruk who managed the sled and dogs. I would see him poised for a second on the top of one of these ridges, guiding the sled, and the next see him disappear on the other side as if he had dropped into the earth. I climbed and slipped and fell, picked myself up only to slip and fall again. It was the toughest piece of trail we had encountered anywhere. And a pitiful mark on the trail we were following now. The dogs' feet were bleeding. I wondered if Tooruk had noticed it and what he was doing about it. Nothing, for I caught sight of him just then, several ridges ahead. He had apparently been waiting for me. I waved a hand to reassure him and he was out of sight. It was then I went down to a head-over-heels fall, eyes, mouth, and ears choking in snow. In a daze I rubbed my shoulder—my head. Thanks to a thick parka I was not much hurt but in the blue light of that hour, with the wind spewing snow off the top of every ridge, I felt as if I had been thrust into a tomb to be buried alive by the blustering furies of this unrelenting domain. It was sure a weird scene—impossible to believe it was summer—the first week of June— June!

What a satisfaction it would be if we could terminate the difficulties of the trail as easily as we can do so on paper. We did, after a trying series of more ups and downs—around this pressure ridge and that, finally come to smooth trail again. A broad highway of smoothness spreading out before us and before a sky marshalling its colors for the dawn. So we lifted the exhausted puppies onto the sled where they rode until we reached Point Barrow at three in the morning.

> "Point Barrow, Alaska.
> "June 14, 1925.

"Dearest Ones:

"A kiss to you from the top of the world. Just a minute! That would be the Pole, wouldn't it? Well then, the top of the continent, and if the Boothia Felix Peninsula were an island, I could truly boast of Barrow as being the farthest north point on the continent. However, it is the farthest north village with a church, a school, a hospital and two trading stations, (the Cape Smythe Whaling and Trading Company and the Native Co-operative) and this year eleven white people call it home.

"I arrived here on the eighth and every day has been filled up to the brim with exciting and happy events. And by the way, my calculations were correct about the date after that experience I had with the clock stopping. My watch was forty-seven minutes off according to the best time-piece going around this place, which happens to be the Missionary's many jeweled wonder. But I digress—to continue I must go back to my arrival in Barrow. At 3 A.M. we found the entire population astir and out of doors. They crowded up to the sled to shake hands, running toward us from every direction. Presently I was drinking hot milk in the warm kitchen of the hospitable young school master, Peter Vander Sterre, who is in charge here. Mr. Vander Sterre had just returned from the whaling camp where he had been taking pictures of a large whale, one with twelve foot bone, somewhat rare in these waters of late and he had speedily developed the negatives and was then busily printing.

"In the afternoon I called at the Manse, a fine commodious home, well furnished and comfortable. The Missionary M.D. was in his office writing, his wife busy with dressmaking, while two comely native girls went in and out from kitchen to dining room stirring a spicy fragrance of newly baked goodies about the place.

"It was at the hospital, however, where I found the sterling worth of a Mission's work in progress. Two nurses and a housekeeper[19] were the good angels here. Showers of blessings on the brave souls who serve national missions in remote localities like this. And the work they do! They told me this was their 'light season.' Compared to the epidemic, when they were up night and day, I suppose it did seem *light*. You would have loved the two wee Eskimo toddlers snugly wrapped in parkas, sitting in high chairs out in the sunshine, little tubercular suspects. They had just finished their bread and milk and the junior nurse was getting them ready for bed again, as tender of them as a mother. In the woman's ward, sitting up in a chair, was my own Wainwright patient, Aveanna's wife. News of her children filled her with joy. It was astonishing what care and treatment had done for her. The sled trip home was thought too strenuous as yet, so she was patiently waiting for the Government ship to take her back to Wainwright. It seemed a long time to wait, but in the mean-

---

19 Florence Dakin, R.N., Auguta Mueller, R.N., and Miss Ann Bannan.

time she was learning how to knit, and had made several
pairs of fur boots for her children.

"The senior nurse was occupied with sterilizing dressings, the housekeeper at her baking in the kitchen. The
windows were gay with lettuce and nasturtiums growing in tin cans. They told me the soil for these had been
sent up in bags from the States—wonderful display
for a so far north garden. Next time you are enjoying
a crisp head of lettuce, think of how delicious I found
one tiny leaf of green (I simply can't add the word lettuce) laid on our salad plates the evening I was entertained at dinner at the hospital. How good it was to
sit down with company and to food I had not prepared!
What impressed me most was the way these three women
had combined the gracious amenities of living with the
strict and exacting routine of hospital regulation. The
Hospital[20] is small but well planned and nicely situated
on the south slope above the shallow lagoon which
divides the village in the summertime.

"Next day I borrowed a pair of hip boots to cross this
lagoon. It was mostly deep slush. I was on my way to
the Cape Smythe Trading Station where I was to have
dinner. From the slope on the north side this place presented strange contrasts. The natives are hauling great
loads of whale meat from the frozen ocean, sledding in
and out immense pressure ridges so much higher along
the coast at Barrow. The low flat inland country re-
sembles a swamp with its hundreds of little lakes and
ponds, islands of brown oozy tundra between. The
Station is in charge of a veteran whaler and trader,
Charles D. Brower, who has lived here for over forty
years. Here too, lives Fred Hopson, the cook at the

---

[20] This hospital burned in the early spring of 1937.

Station and a pal of Mr. Brower's through the years. His dinner was good and the conversation breezy. Sailing and tales of the sea! Australia—around the Horn—the Falklands—Mozambique! Sailing since the age of eleven —where hadn't he been? Mr. Hopson's home is in Wales. 'Oh, God love us, there is none of my family there now. I sailed out o' Penzance—I tell ye thim was sailing days. None of thim auxiliary engines put-putting you into port. My father been a whaler before me. Up in Davis Straits and the cargo in thim days! I nuvver come home in a 'clean ship.'[21] Say, I'm forgettin' to pass the cake. Thim's a few raisins in it—I'm runnin' short of 'em, what with the good fox catch and the stuff the natives fished out of the wreck, the trade has been for the fancies, and none any too much of thim have we left.'

"After dinner we had a walk around this end of the village. Back of the warehouses two old Eskimos were cleaning whale bone, scraping and scrubbing a mess of thick grease from the strips. Nineteen whale have been killed. The old native meat pits are full. Piles of the meat are heaped up back of the village, waiting for new pits to be dug. The whaling season was almost at an end and there was much ado over the big feast, the 'Nelauk' kittuk,' which follows the whaling. The women are busy sewing new artigas, not only the gingham and calico ones they wear over the fur garments, but handsome ones of fur, trimmed with ruffs of wolf and wolverine. Here in the large room of the station, where I am writing, a native woman is handling strips of wolf with a knowing eye and much bargaining is going on. With her is her pretty daughter, and I fancy the ruff is for her. Like white women at the counters of our own

---

[21] A ship without a cargo.

shops: a mother, with her mind on the budget, and a
daughter to be pleased, with a length of satin between
them. In Barrow it is a strip of soft fur and the exchange
will be in whale bone or a fox skin. Now I hear you
asking, 'Why don't the natives use the fox fur?' And
I'll tell you that fox skins do not wear well; the hair
felts up and becomes mangy and molty looking in a
short time. Wolverine fur does not collect frost and is
nearly always used next to the face. The long hair of the
wolf protects a nose and cheeks from winds and frostbite, thus the two furs are usually combined to make
the ruff which so softly halos an Eskimo woman's face.

"The true Point Barrow is twelve miles north of here.
The Eskimos call it Nuvuk, or 'the end of land.' A
little south of the village is the Cape Smythe of Beechey's
charting. Because he did not wish to endanger his ship
in the ice, Beechey did not proceed up this coast in the
Blossom, so sent his Lieutenant, Mr. Elson, in the small
barge to explore it. In Beechey's narrative we read, 'he
(Mr. Elson) proceeded to the latitude of 71° 23′ 31″ N.
and to 156° 21′ 30″ W., where the coast formed a low
narrow neck beyond which it was impossible to proceed
to the eastward, in consequence of the ice being attached
to the land, and extending along the horizon to the
northward.' I walked along this 'low narrow neck' of
land today, and though it lacks two months of the time
of year when Elson first saw it, the outlook is the same.
The ice is attached to the land and extends along the
horizon to the northward: a thousand miles of it to the
Pole, a curiously lambent field of ice.

"While the resident pioneer traders of this coast have
for many years exerted a wide and far reaching influence
for good over these primitive people, (their ilk is so rare

I take pride in naming them: Mr. A. James Allen,[22] formerly of Point Hope, now of Wainwright, and Mr. Charles Brower of Barrow)[22] it was in the Government Schoolhouses where true civism was being developed and carried on among the Eskimos. I saw it at its best in Barrow. The teacher's quarters were, at all hours of the day, (and at this season I may add night) a hive of incessant activity. Natives went in and out, the patience and kindliness of Peter Vander Sterre apparently inexhaustible. Men and boys came in to consult about the reindeer herds, about supplies for the herder boys; and the co-operative store—the reorganization of which was in progress—had come in for the discussion of many problems. The older men of the village were intensely interested in this project. Sitting in a circle, as grave as any Board of Directors, they managed the affairs of the company, their thoughtful faces indicative of the effort they were making to insure the success of this new venture they had undertaken. Occasionally they sought the advice of the school teacher. Observing his methods, I thought of how important it is to appoint the right men to these school positions. Here was a situation ideal. A young and enthusiastic fellow, throwing all of his splendid strength and exceptional abilities into the problems of these people. Helping them to solve their independence, guiding them with wisdom in the purchases of their supplies, admonishing them tactfully to guard against debt, and in many other ways proving himself to be the true and ardent student of their needs. And to top all this, he engaged in all of their activities of sports, hunting and driving deer, with a whole hearted

---

[22] Mr. Allen died in 1944—is buried at Wainwright. Mr. Brower died early in 1945—buried at Point Barrow.

joy and zest that made him an idol among these people.

"Yesterday morning, after the church services, I walked out to the place of burials. Through years of up-heaving frost, the shallow graves had given up their dead. Bones and skull and matted hair and fur, these could be seen within the broken coffins. The exposed wood of these rude boxes had been deeply scored by the snow blast. The abrasion produced showed strange lus-trous patterns in relief, as if old hieroglyphics had been embossed in silver over the gray wood. Bleached bones rattling in bleached wood—what stories they could tell! Surely an interesting ground for some anthropologist. And speaking of anthropologists, it was enlightening to learn from Dr. Ales Hrdlicka that the worst diseases of the Eskimo came to him only seventy or eighty years ago and were clearly brought by the white man. Earlier skeletal remains show none of the ravages of the 'white man's scourges.' 'And despite these scourges of tubercu-losis and social diseases,' he says, 'the natives are *not* dying out.'

"Some years ago, before I learned what stories disease could write in bone structure, stories which have given us an index to character, minds and lives of ancient races, I used to wonder why men like Hrdlicka and Boaz studied the dead, when the living were here and so much more interesting. From their researches however, we now have knowledge of the splendid racial strength of these Eskimos, their freedom from physical and moral pollution in times past; comes also the inspiration to carry on our pedagogic programme of sanitation and hy-giene in the face of flagrant opposition, such as, 'the average life span of the Eskimo has decreased to but twenty years,'—'that 97.3 percent give positive evidence of tuberculosis,'—'that the Eskimo has the mentality of a ten year old child'—and a few other gross and misleading statements made by those who have taken little time and no effort to ascertain the truth. Why no race in the world is so worthy of preservation as the Eskimo. Witness: what Denmark has done for her Greenland Eskimos.

"I spent most of the night celebrating their feast and dance, the 'Nelauk'kittuk.' I sat in the shade and out of the wind, under one of the large skin canoes propped up on its side. Beside me, and as many as the canoe could shelter, sat the older men and women of the village. In front of us was the orchestra, six men with their fan-shaped drums. Placed in a semi-circle were other canoes and in their shelter, more old people. In the open space in the center, the dancers performed. The flags of the oomaliks fluttered in the breeze, attesting the valor of the crews. Everyone was in holiday mood and as for holiday garb, you've never seen the like. Bright-colored gingham and print tigas, lustrous fur parkas with trimming of mink tails, tassels that rhythmically tossed to and fro as the dancer directed his ardour and animation to his feet. What realism these men could bring to their interpretations of the wolf, the loon, a seal hunt and other pantomimic performance! The women danced with more constraint. Theirs was a demure presentation, a graceful waving of arms and expressive hands, their neatly booted feet close together, like a stem supporting a wind blown flower.

" 'Nelauk'kittuk' means 'white walrus skin.' Near the dancing area one of these, a fine bleached skin, was stoutly stretched, raised three feet from the ground, anchored to poles of driftwood. About it the natives circled, bringing it to firmer tautness by grasping the handles or slits which had been cut in around the skin. A dancer bounced upon it and was tossed high in air, once, twice—again and again until he failed to land on his feet when another dancer tried his luck. In this exhibition, the women carried off the laurels. Not surprising, since they practice this jumping from the time they can walk. Almost every day, on every loose board in the village of a length that can be used for a teeter, you may see little girls jumping on each end, sending each other high into the air, their tiny feet landing squarely on the end of the board.

"After the tossing contests came the feast. Platters were heaped with pie-shaped pieces of whale *muktuk,* looking for all the world like rosy sections of watermelon and tasting like it too, like a greasy seedless watermelon with a black meaty rind. There were great mounds of biscuits too, all shapes and sizes, fried brown in seal oil and pails and pails of tea set before the people. Everybody fell to, heartily. It was one of the jolliest buffet affairs I had ever witnessed. While the old folks were feasting, the walrus skin was lowered so the children could enjoy their young grasshopper talents. Their childish laughter filled the air whenever one of them took a tumble. Back of one of the canoes the young lads were wrestling. Tooruk was in his glory, as expert in this sport, if not excelling, the Barrow boys. Later I saw him pridefully strutting about the village surrounded by a group of young boys, like any hero, the girls shyly admiring him from a distance.

"The nineteen dead whales in whale heaven, must certainly have been impressively appeased with this propitiatory ceremony, this feasting, these games in their honor; and no doubt were well content to have sacrificed their bone and *muktuk* for the welfare of a people who could be so happy, having provided them with sustenance and their igloos with warmth, for yet another season.

"This morning Tooruk came to the schoolhouse. I surmised he was ready to start home. I was just about to mix a cake, the usual occupation of a guest teacher in the north.

" 'When do we go home, Tooruk?'

" 'We goes now. My dogs is good now.'

" 'What's the weather going to do?'

" 'Oh, that fine wind. Is head wind behind.'

" 'All right, Tooruk, you get the sled ready and I'll make biscuit.'

" 'Say Missus Eva, I tell you something. That man is name Utchik is go now to Wainwright. He have plenty dogs. Plenty fox-skins. He have igloo near Point Halkett. He fine man, Utchik. You like wife. You many like children. He fine man.'

"In a few hours I will be Wainwright bound, and it seems that a fine Eskimo family will accompany us. I am posting this letter at Barrow, so it may bear the postmark of Uncle Sam's farthest north postoffice. And as I began this, so do I end it. A kiss to you from the top of the world."

June 16

We left Barrow 6.30 P.M. All the white folks came out to say good-bye with clicking cameras. So on the trail again. As far as the wreck of the *Arctic* it was well packed. The natives had been salvaging everything they could carry away from it, and the traffic of loaded sleds

had served to make a smooth trail. But beyond the wreck
—let me forget the pinnacles we climbed over. At Sinaru we took on our box and the things we had cached.
The river was running high and Tooruk had no end of
difficulty, climbing the slippery banks to get the stuff.
Here too, we adjusted tiny *mukluks* on the feet of the
dogs. Utchik was now far ahead of us. We could just
make out his two sleds, his wife driving the small one.

To our left was the long highland, brown and bare,
with here and there a furrow filled with snow debris. It
is a landscape of blue-greens in ice and water, sepia
browns of land with dried tawny grasses fringing the
edge of the bluffs. To the north the midnight sky was
a poem. The rose tints were reflected in the water path
our sled runners cut in the thin ice. To the south—
words falter to describe this marvelous phenomena of the
Arctic—a radiant parhelion rose, like a watch fire above
the horizon, a wonder of lighted mist haloes and shafts—
a mock sun at every intersection—glowed like a neon
emblem of Eastern morn in the sky, until the sun rising
to the east, dimmed its light.

At three in the morning we came to Kekolik, where
the reindeer herders come to make their camp at this
time of the year. The dogs bounded toward it. What
cared they for the heavy load or bleeding feet? It was
a wild ride for a few yards, endangered too, by open
water along the shore. Tooruk shouted "You all right,
Missus Eva" but he never let go his hold on the sled. It
was a great relief to have the team's mad dash halted by
the sandy shore. "They smells the deer, Missus Eva."

Our sled and canvas shelter was soon erected and the
primus going. About thirty yards away, on another
knoll, were the tupeks of the herders. One of the women,

Kelerak, came right over to tell us they had fresh reindeer meat and that their fire was hot. So on their improvised camp stove we soon had steaks broiling to a turn.
There are many impressions in my mental journal of
memorable meals. This one still holds first place as the
most enjoyable. To tell about it I must go back to Barrow, where I discovered one evening that corn now was
canned on the cob, and was mighty well pleased when I
found I could buy a can or two at the station. Then
when Mr. Hopson[23] came out to take pictures of our
sled, he brought an apple pie he had baked especially for
us, together with a jar of his famous pickled whale *muk-
tuk*. (Every person who has been ashore at Point Barrow
has tasted Hopson's "tried and found famous" Pickled
Whale.) We stowed the quart jar safely in one of Tooruk's boots. And the pie I held on my lap until—well,
until you get tired of holding pies on your lap. I do not
know what happened to it after that but Tooruk produced it when we sat down to our delicious steak at
Kekolik. So you see us now at Kekolik, dining on broiled
steaks, corn on the cob, and apple pie. And to top it off,
Tooruk told me we were halfway home.

I always think of Kekolik as Arcadia. It is a favorite
place for the herders every summer, when their herds
come to the coast to escape the scourge of the inland
mosquitoes. Their tupeks are small but well made of bent
willows covered with skins. On top they store the usual
collection of Eskimo household effects, rolls of skins, dog
harness, bags of clothing and wooden platters filled with
fresh reindeer tallow. Their sleds were set up, one on top
of the other, and from the runners hung braces of ptarmigan. Their reindeer meat was in cold storage—a snow

---

[23] Since writing this Mr. Hopson died of influenza at Point Barrow.

drift at the foot of the bank. Back of this dry sandy slope a small stream sings its way to the sea. Its clear cold water was for us a real luxury. The herd was contentedly grazing on the far side, a peaceful pastoral scene of the Arctic enhanced by a backdrop of colorful sky.

Kelerak at once started making dog *mukluks* for Tooruk from a few old and greasy pieces of denim. Would there be enough of these, I wondered, with the needling ice cutting them to shreds in a short distance? There was the blanket lining to my bag. No sooner thought of when I pulled it out and Kelerak cut and together we sewed dog shoes until every scrap of it was used, and with it almost all of Kelerak's sinew thread. I presented her with four needles from my sewing kit. Someday I'll be able to describe her joy.

By six o'clock we were ready for another night's travel. The herder and one of the boys helped us down to the trail. Just as we were about to embark, (what is the word for boarding a sled with dog team?), a white reindeer came over the hill and wandered out on the ice. Every dog on our team pricked up his ears, their bodies twitching for a meal. It was all Tooruk could do to hold them while the herder sent his faithful shepherd dog out to round it back to the tundra. He told us it was a female deer searching for her lost fawn. Poor animal, there was a poignant lilt to her head as she paused and lifted her nose, then trotted off again. On the crest of the hill she paused, turned to lift her head again, every motion one of pathos. When I expressed sympathy for the distracted beast, the herder said, (with a philosophy born of experience perhaps) "That female is forget dead fawn —that female is plenty forget when is rutting time. That female is plenty happy for fawning time come."

Sledding on the trackless wastes again. No, not quite trackless, for the dogs swiftly picked up Utchik's trail. A few miles south of Kekolik the coast bluff drops gently, gradually sloping off to assume the flatness that is so characteristic of tundra country. The southern horizon was miraged, a mirage layered with lines of azure blue and rose, the earth opening its accordion folds to meet the sky. A tranquil calm settled over us, broken only by the musical chinkle of the ice as the dogs traveled on, a tranquility that was soothing—that invited introspection. I entertain no thoughts of the chilling halts we made to mend a dog's collar or to replace tattered little *mukluks* on plodding feet; nor the dark ice crevasses we bridged with the sled and gingerly crossed on hands and knees, filled with exciting moments of helping the dogs across; nor the milder discomforts of chapped hands and wind-burned faces. These are all a part of trail travel and as such, accepted without question. What a pity that we are prone not to accept the difficulties of life's trail with the same grace, the same determination to conquer the rough places and get on to the next, until by stumbling and rising again, being bruised and healed, we come at last to a smooth trail— shining and lovely—a boulevard it might come to be, to heaven.

When we reached the head of Peard Bay, where was our small igloo tavern of the up-journey, we found Utchik encamped there. Already he had been out on the ice, had killed a seal and a large number of ducks. This was my first meeting with this family: Utchik, his wife and their three children. A daughter, Samaruna, was about Tooruk's age and the two little boys, (so alike they could easily have been twins) were around five or six years. They were very happily disposing of the bits of blubber their mother was scraping from the sealskin. Utchik was a fine type of Eskimo—an independent. Community life was not necessary to his happiness or prosperity, nor did he waste his heritage by imitating white man's ways. He went right by Point Barrow with one of his sleds loaded with furs, beautiful pelts of fox and ermine. Yes, he had visited the trading stores, but he said he could not eat a "song box" (phonograph), and his wife and daughter would freeze in silk stockings. (Utchik pronounced it *sil-lik*). He did not believe a flannel shirt was warmer than his reindeer parkas, nor would a pair of logger boots be superior to the very fine seal boots his wife could make for him. He owned two sleds and twenty-two dogs—a truly well-to-do Eskimo. What's more, he owned a fine gun and two good hunting knives. Where had he traded for those? "Oh, that many long time, maybe two year. Catch 'em gun at place is say Rumputt, big igloo place." What a time I had learning this was Rampart House, until he told us that he had gone up a river from Herschel Island and then "he is go inland river. That time he is trap much muskrat." The following winter he had returned to Nigaluk and had trapped up the Anaktuvuk River. You may be sure I was glad that so enterprising a citizen of the Arctic was seeking our Wainwright.

He inquired of Tooruk if he could trade for good sled wood. And he knew that at Wainwright there was "good walrus hunting." He wanted the ivory for sled runners, he said, turning his small sled over to point out his need and his wife must have new handles on her seal knife and sewing knife. She was still scraping fat, the blood from the seal was in a wooden vessel by her side, a congealed mass of maroon custard. Samaruna was pulling fibres from the back sinew of a caribou, rolling them over her cheek, carefully twisting them, one by one to make a skein of thread. She was a beautiful Eskimo girl. I secretly hoped that Tooruk was not missing any of her shy glances. Perhaps his admiration of Utchik had included Samaruna, and if not, I rather suspected this hour of visiting had.

We went on to Keowuk's igloo but found it too full of half-melted snow for comfort. We explored the sand-spit for a dry camping place. It was like walking on a sponge, oozing water filled our every step. We finally made a camp of sorts, where once again the sled and canvas shelter provided a cooking place. Our meal was almost ready when Tooruk spied two brant on a near tundra lake. Utchik spied them about the same time and the two men went off with their guns. Small chance for those birds, I was thinking, when I saw the brant lifting their wings, the water dripping from them like jewels, to gracefully make good their escape towards the north. The disturbance brought up a number of smaller birds, all a-chitter-chatter with alarm, the tundra whirring with wings, a thing alive.

Southwest by south across Peard Bay, was the beautiful level ice field on which we had again become a going caravan. Only now it wasn't so beautiful, for there were vast water stretches, looming dark and deeply menacing, but they proved to be really quite shallow. We were not so gay as we had been on the north crossing. Mugwa made every effort to return to the coast, the other dogs seconding the effort, and Tooruk had to resort to the whip again and again to keep the team in order. How much intelligence this good animal displayed we were to learn later, when, as we approached the overflow of the Koogarock River we found the bay a vast sheet of water. Tooruk went ahead on a reconnoitre but soon waded back with the news that in many places he could find "no bottom." There was but one thing to do, turn about face, get back to the coast and strike out for all its miles, to the west spit, Pingashoogooruk. The Seahorse Islands in mirage, the sun hidden by gray clouds, these provided the only restful vistas for our eyes on that long monotonous and circuitous route. Seven hours of trail we had not counted on. Our bodies winced their protests, and this time I can with truth include Tooruk. We were wearied to exhaustion when we reached the driftwood region on Pingashoogooruk. How we did work, pulling the sled and dogs over the sand! Poor animals! They dropped like dead as soon as we had reached a dry spot. A dry spot? Yes, *dry*, because here at least we were not boot-deep in water. The very sands were soaked as though a tide had just gone out. With the canvas to kneel on, we went about removing the soppy rags from the small bleeding feet which had carried us this far and adjusted the last of spare blanket boots. As soon as we had made the dogs comfortable, we started the primus to bolster ourselves with hot chocolate. There were still those miles to Attanik ahead of us.

"Did you say Attanik, Tooruk?" I had been asleep.

"Yesh, Missus Eva, the dogs is smells the village." But what a changed Attanik! The igloos had emerged from the deep drifts, rather I should say, the natives had emerged from the igloos. Summer tupeks were flapping on every knoll. Heaps of walrus skulls with clean ivory tusks, rusty cans, driftwood, a rack of glistening bear

skins, and then Keruk's igloo. But for the familiar
interior of this, Attanik had not been Attanik. What
a difference the continuous sunshine of ten days and
nights can make in the contour of wind-drifted snows;
and in the appearance of the igloos! What mournful
looking earth mounds they were now, standing apart in
desolate aloofness, the peat removed from the sides of
each to quicken the drying! If you ever come to Attanik, (you may have the urge to hunt polar bears some day)
come in the time of white snows. It is more in the Arctic
mood to step down clean ice steps and crawl through
a snow passage into an igloo, than it is to step over a
greasy-green pool of wet refuse to enter its rude low
doorway. But whatever the season or weather you will
find the same cheery smiling natives whose hospitality
knows no compass or weather vane. Keruk and her family deserted their igloo that Tooruk and I might rest in
quiet slumber all of this blessed day.

The trail was especially kind to us as we sped toward
Wainwright. Perhaps our longing to get back home had
something to do with it. One less sentimental would say
it was the lay of the country itself. There are no great
rivers between Attanik and Wainwright to impede sled
traffic, and the overflow of the smaller streams served to
make our way more beautiful; bright mirrors to reflect
the glories of the sky. At times it seemed as though we
were approaching pools of molten rose-colored glass.
Sometimes the pools were bordered in black jet, bits of
coal, the wash debris, that had come down with the small
stream. For long distances we passed through pressure
ridges banked high against the shingle, where now we
found smooth sledding between them and the shore. This
offered something of a novelty and we rested more than

once in the shadow of these temporary mountain ice ranges, and tried to imagine the terrific crash of impact that occurs when two meeting fields of ice are jammed up by a capricious wind.

We met great flocks of ducks, flying so low that in less time than it takes to write it, Tooruk had his gun out and was bringing them down in great numbers. His first shot brought down nine. They fell all around the sled. I picked up a beautiful King eider from this lot and with the next shot secured fine specimens of the Pacific and Spectacled eiders. Tooruk threw one apiece to the dogs. Feathers, claws and beaks disappeared in a flash. Two more shots and we had one hundred pounds extra on the sled. You may be sure the dogs were instantly revived by this excitement. And by the time their excitement had subsided, we had come up to the place where they could "smells the village." From then on they showed some mettle and our final dash to Wainwright was an exhilarating triumph.

Suddenly and happily we had arrived! I was in the midst of my people—my village! Oh, this glad homecoming! Laughing and crying, shaking hands with a whole village of hands at once! It was good to be home, the best part of any journey.

The natives came to the schoolhouse all that day, in twos and threes, in family groups to shake hands, to talk, to sit awhile. Yes, everyone was well. They had caught another whale. All the canoes were in now.

"You see my brother, Ahnaktuk, in Barrow?" "You see my cousin, Patookak? He have fine canoe." "You see Sukluk? He my fadder's brudder." And so went the conversation, each wishing to learn of someone they knew, or someone dear to them because of blood ties.

Nasholook came in to say that the weather had been so
fine he had thought best to take off all the storm sash.
Oyalla had helped to store them in the attic loft. And
Kittik, dear faithful Kittik, had kept the home fires
burning and had washed the floors. And when I paid
them for their good services, Kittik cried and said, "*Na-
ga* sugar, *Na-ga* tea, I plenty happy teacher come."

During my absence most of the families had opened
their winter igloos. Here too, the tupeks were the popular summer residence. Some families were living in the
open under their skin canoes. Doors and skin windows,
as well as the peat blocks, had been removed from the
igloos, the interiors exposed to the purifying rays of the
sun and the clean drying wind; house-cleaning time or
perhaps I should say house-drying time. The village
came in for it too. One day the men and boys armed
themselves with curious-looking rakes and marched like
a small town army to the north end of the village. Here
they spaced themselves about fifteen feet apart and
combed the village, raking up bones, cans, and refuse all
the way to the south limits where it was collected in one
great heap and taken out, far out, on the ice. They raked
the path leading from the schoolhouse to the sea. They
filled up the low puddles with the accumulated ashes,
making it all smooth and clean with several loads of
coarse sand from the beach.

Midsummer night was a poem. The sun at midnight
trailed fully six diameters above the horizon, a blazing
disk of gold. Rose and mauve clouds, floating from the
zenith, curtained it for that hour like some diaphanous
fabric veiling the Holy Grail. The pools over the sea ice
mirrored the splendor in magnificent Lumiere intensity,
the long, long night, lovely, lovely!

In the bright sunshine of the evening the village was a hive of industry: Papiglook feeding eight fat puppies; Okilyuk making arrows for the children; Tuzroak moving the peat from his igloo, his wife crimping boot soles, her white teeth biting the dark skin; Ashagak teaching her baby to walk. Segavan was mending a walrus spear, his wife scraping hair from sealskins with ashes, Artisarlook doing the same, both women kneeling on the skins, the pan of ashes between them. Agalo's family were picnicking in the shade of their oomiak feasting on duck soup—smells good. Agalo's wife dips a large bone in it and gives it to her smallest child, saying, *"na-gooruk!"* Nowlik was blowing intestines; Tigalook and Mayuenna festooning them all over the village. There were no economic worries or ills in Wainwright.

When I returned from my sight-seeing tour I went out of my way to dig my boots into the slush of what was left of the high snowdrift on the south side of the building. Wouldn't you think I had had enough of snow? It was just my way of putting off going to bed when everybody in the village was having a good time at something or other.

The next morning I attempted to portray the flamboyant beauty of the King eiders in water color. My specimens had remained well frozen in the icehouse. Some of the children spent the day flattening their noses against the window looking in on my efforts.

The oldsters were playing ball—football—kicking all over the Arctic a bag stuffed with reindeer hair. There were no rules to the game—no pre-arranged cabalic signals—no penalties—nothing to it but good sport, keep the ball in the air and going. I looked for them to wind up in Labrador—so bent were they on getting that ball as far from the village as their nimble legs could take it. Good thing the ball was just a skin ball—rip!—poof—a shower of reindeer hair! My village was home again.

Towards the end of June the days were like honey. I had blankets, comforts, furs, and pillows on the line, cleaned the medicine chests, washed ointment jars, folded gauze dressings. Evenings at the organ in the schoolroom playing "Oh Promise Me," and "At Dawning." June wouldn't be June without these sometime, somewhere. I nearly always finished up with, *"Godim naku nilukput aitchok toigatigut naku-tuktuani-su, Angun iknik ilitkossik."* Amen—in my language, the "Doxology."

The last day of June Nasholook and some of the younger men came in to discuss plans for the glorious fourth. If the wind holds out there will be enough open water for a kayak race. For the older men, a fire-making contest with their primitive old bow drills; for the older women, crimping a pair of sealskin soles for boots or converting a section of back sinew into thread. For the small boys, a bow and arrow tournament, and the usual 100-yard dashes for all ages. We were working out the details of this programme when Ahlulak's husband came in. *"Eee-lee-legah electa."* All right Kungasoona. I picked up my little black bag and left the committee to work out their own details.

Same Day. 9 P.M. I have a heart full of praise for the native women who have their babies in the lovely summer. A tupek isn't roomy to work in, but it is light and airy and clean. Our newest citizen of Wainwright is a lusty boy and no doubt as to his being a little Eskimo. He bore the tiny blue spot at the base of his strong little spine like a thoroughbred. You may be sure I do not mistake it for a birthmark or a bruise any more. It took several births to acquaint me with the fact that all Eskimo babies are born with it. I am told this is also true of the babies of a number of the Asiatic races. With oyster stew for my supper, I took a big bowl of it to Ahlulak. She was up, arranging the furs around her baby, a stew of seal meat bubbling in the pot.

(From my journal) July 2. At midnight Okreesuk walked in. All the way from Attanik to tell me that Ozuaruk had shot two of his fingers off. "That hand plenty bad—that Ozuaruk he very sick man." The men of the village immediately organized a party to go to Attanik and bring him back to Wainwright. Surely an unfortunate accident to happen, worst possible time of the year. Sea ice rotten. Tundra a soaking swamp, take forever for a sled to make the trip. And scarcely a mile of open water, let alone twenty-five miles, so that a boat could be used. Twenty-five miles up for the men, and the same back with their burden—an anxious time.

July 4. We have been waiting for hours, the natives standing in quiet little groups, I making ready for the task ahead, an amputation certain. Just before noon we sighted the party. All night and half a day, they had taken turns carrying the injured man on a stretcher. A bed in the schoolroom was ready. Dressings and solutions waited. But all too late. Gangrene had done its dreadful work. Shortly after I had made him comfortable he fell into the coma from which he never wakened. The accident occurred while he was hammering in a shotgun cartridge with his knife. "I plenty mistake," he said, as the men were carrying him. *"Muck-eee, muck-eee."*
Another shallow grave was picked out of the tundra,

the flag lowered at half-mast, and the women gathered up his few effects and burned them back of the village. No one mentioned games or races, but many talked of a fine man, a good hunter, "that Ozuaruk he killed maybe 'undred polar bear. Maybe is plenty more. He is fine hunter for walrus spear. That Ozuaruk is fine man."

July 16. A brisk northeast wind is taking the ice out in its teeth. Stranded bergs line the shore, and for the first time it looks as though we might see a ship again.

Saints of the North! What feverish excitement can prevail in this village! Three days and nights of it, all because a school of beluga whale were driven too close to shore by their dreaded enemy, the killer whale. The frantic beasts fairly leaped themselves ashore in their blind efforts to escape. Canoes, guns, spears, and Eskimos piled up on the beach with amazing alacrity and still more amazing chaos. Men and boys scrambled over each other getting into the boats. The terrorized animals thrashed the waters to foam, foam crimson with blood. Canoes spun around in circles—no one thought of steering—every man or boy shooting or plunging a spear into some live or dying whale. Some of the wounded animals were washed ashore in the melee. Natives waded out to fasten a line to them, lest they should suddenly revive and dash out to deep water again. Many of them were killed from shore, the natives running up and down the beach, shooting and whooping it up in thrilling joy over each kill. When it was over we counted thirty-three belugas on the beach.

A beluga weighs between fifteen hundred and seventeen hundred pounds. Its skin is milk white, less than an inch thick, protecting about four inches of fat or blub-

ber, warm insulation for the red meat. The largest one
of the catch was a male, fifteen feet long with a spread
of flukes of over three feet. The females were a bit
smaller. Two babies, with every evidence of being newly
born, were five feet long and slate gray in color.

Determined to try everything in the line of native
food, I stewed the white skin with onions, to eat something that tasted like mushrooms, bites like fresh cocoa-
nut and looks like it. The tough back sinew of this whale
is the best ever for sewing the heavy skins for the canoes.
Every strip of it was saved, the women treasuring it
highly.

The natives worked all night to clear away the messy
butchering debris from our village green. The meat was
divided into forty piles, representing the number of
families in Wainwright, and they lost no time getting it
stored in their ice pits before another warm day. Temperature was 46° yesterday.

With a lunch in my knapsack, I went off to have an
intimate day with the tundra. I shed my furs for this
jaunt, and wore forest-green cloth knickers and shirt,
with knee-length sealskin water boots to keep feet dry
and warm. Summer was in full swing on the tundra with
lush grasses, tiny flowers and birds by the thousands
sweeping into the air. It was a day of golden warmth,
of meandering around the larger lakes, and wading
through the shallow pools with eider ducks and black
brant and golden plovers, flinging themselves for a whirl
on high to settle down ahead on some shining pond or in
the fringe of moss and grasses surrounding. The dainty
phalaropes scattered out before me like grasshoppers in
the dry fields at home, uttering their quaint little cries

of *soo-weep, soo-weep, plee-eep, plee-eep,* only to flutter down with twirling grace a few paces ahead. The way the brilliant female courts her shabby mate, swimming round and round him to display her charms, is an unforgettable bridal of the tundra.

Mile after mile to the eastward I wandered with a wonder as to how far this bird world extended, this enchanting land of wings, with its mottled eggs and pale green eggs, and down nests and grass nests, and winged love wheeling to high heaven in mad glad ecstasy. Turning to the southward I came to the edge of an ancient tundra lake, its bed quilted with thick moss and starred with bright Arctic poppies, their fragile flaxen heads nodding to every little breeze. Here was most certainly a place "where the recluse may sit upon the ground and read sad stories of species extinct and epochs barely decipherable." If ever like the poet, I left a city to be lost in some boundless heath, this was that time. On the blufflike rim of this place I ate my sandwiches, and found I had sat me down beside a nesting longspur. Her beady black eyes followed my every move. Twice she fluttered over the nest, fussing up her mottled brown plumage in her agitation, but soon settled down to her calm brooding quite satisfied that here could be no enemy.

I returned by way of the Kuk River, following its course to the inlet, then north to the village. On a south slope, about halfway home, I came to the ruins of several old igloos, caves with roofs of bone that had fallen in. They might have been moved from Sinaru, so alike were they in ruin and general demolition. The tundra here was laced with the Arctic willow creeping over the ground, none of the plants more than six inches in length, the tiny new leaves spread out like baby hands, lending another shade of green to the tundra. I filled my hat with purple Pedicularis, Arctic poppies, arnica, and many of the dainty Senecios. Surely a botanist's rare paradise!

And just when the village tents hove in sight I discovered the soft nest of an eider duck with nine pale green eggs half hidden on the far side of a small pond, and even as I stood, trying to decide from where best to sketch them, the female bird whirred by and was soon billing the feathers of her breast to mingle them with the down of the nest. I was amused by the queer little quacks which accompanied this performance. She seemed not at all disturbed at the strange creature who stood before her putting colored marks on paper. The sketch finished, I sat on the edge of the tundra to watch white ice floating like a dream across the iridescent bight at evening. On the shore a flock of least sandpipers were bobbing up and down on their chopstick legs, making cross stitch patterns in the sand.

Tooruk helped to wash the plant specimens. He wanted to know the names of the flowers. He told me the Eskimo names for the birds I had seen, and for feathers and gizzards and such things. Afterwards we had tea, and for Tooruk there was always a heaping bowl of sugar. Tooruk liked sugar, but best of all he liked to talk in English with his teacher. So we talked about birds— and their nests—and we always came round to the trip we had made to Barrow—the two of us in the fog with the floundering dogs and the stinking meat we fed them —all in a heap together. And that igloo at the head of Peard Bay! Whew! The smelly place where we lay side by side, talking about everything that night, too!

"You learns Eskimo for that swan that time, Missus Eva."

"Yes, I went to sleep saying *Kook-ruit*. You remember how we laughed next morning when I said I would always think of it as *Kook-mush*, for that's what we had to do for breakfast."

"Yesh, you remembers sometimes Eskimo say *Kook-rook*—that time swans has the jung ones." Tooruk would write the English words while I put down my lessons in Eskimo. "Words is like birds sing on paper tonight, Missus Eva."

Bird—*Tinga-meek*
Birds in a flock—*Tinga-merek*
Birds nest—*Cap-poo'kee*
Brant—*Look-lu'ik*
Black Brant—*Neg'a-lik*
Crane—*Tah-tis'a-rook*
Curlew—*Shoo-oop'tuk*
Eider (Pacific)—*Amau-lik*
Eider (King)—*King'a-lik*
Eider (Steller's)—*Mit-tik*
Goose—*Nak-we'chook*
Goose (White fronted)—*Kanga-yuk*
Gull, Black headed—*Kook'ar-rook*
Gull, Jaeger—*E-chung'mook*
Gull, Black tipped wing—*Nak-cha-bar'rook*
Gull, Burgomaster—*Now-yuk*
Gull, chick—*Chari'ko-gah*
Hawk—*Kil-rook*
Hawks—*Kil-rah*
Loon—*Kok-so'it*
Loons, a pair—*Kok-a-ro'it*
Loon (King)—*Too-lik*
Owl, white—*Ook-pik*
Owl, chick—*Ook-pik-e-lo*
Owl, tundra plumage (brown)—*Ik-na-sa-hoy'ik*
Owl, small—*Ah-took*
Phalarope—*Ok-villa-too'mik*
Pintail duck—*Kook-a-ruk*
Plover—*Na-shat-too-oo'lik*
Plover (Golden)—*Too-lik*

Plover, black belly—*E-lak-tal'lik*
Ptarmigan—*Kah-wah*
Ptarmigan, (when in covey)—*O-kog-lik-pee-rook*
Ptarmigan, hooded—*O-kah-ri-goo'ik*
Sea Parrot—*Kee-lung-gook*
Snipe—*Noo'a-look*
Swan—*Kook-ru'it*
Swan, when with young—*Kook-rook*
Tern (Arctic)—*Too-rit-ko'yuk*
Old Squaw Duck—*Ah-hol'lik*
Snowbird—*A-mau'look*
Snowbirds in flock—*A-mau-tok'puk*
Snowbirds in flight—*Oo-kuk-tow'ruk*
Warbler (?)—*Oo-wul'look*
Breast of a bird—*Kot'kah.* And Tooruk explained
   that the Eskimo women make "sitting places"
   of breasts of birds, feather mats to protect
   them when fishing or sealing on the ice.
Feather—*Mit-koo'nik*
A bird's flight—*Tinga-roo,* or *Tinga-wunga*
Bird's innards—*Nak-moo'tah*
Eider down—*Mau-nah-nah*
Wing—*Ee-choo'kah.* When used as a broom to
   sweep up the floor in an igloo it is shortened
   to *'Choo-kah.*

Thus ended our lesson on birds. One aspires to be an ornithologist, a botanist, an anthropologist—yes, every kind of an "ologist," to fully and richly appreciate the wealth of fauna to be found in the Arctic.

Along about three this morning I lay awake listening to a peculiar barking that I knew at once was no barking of canines. A short half-smothered cough-like bark, unlike anything I had heard before. So I up and lost no time getting into boots, and out of doors to come up with Eskimos and canoes all mixed together on the beach. Walrus! Walrus! was the cry, and a delirious frenzy they were in, for here again was food to kill. The fickle wind was sweeping the ice pack back to shore. Out on the ice pans, dark pods of these animals lay, apparently asleep, with here and there a great bull, head uplifted as if on watch, calling an all's well in his hacking bark far out to sea. The men and boys snatched up their weapons and paddles. The walrus hunt was on! The women of the village and I watched the canoes threading their way through the ice until the thin fog hid them from view, but the muffled barks persisted and we knew some walrus would soon be *pee-chook.* The fog drifted over the village thick and cold, driving the women to the shelter of their tupeks and me shivering back to my bed.

At noon the sun was making every warm effort to penetrate the thick soupy mist but it wasn't until late afternoon that the women began gathering in groups at the edge of the bank to await the return of the hunters. Soon I saw them meandering down to the south of the village, just the cue I needed to bank the fires and breeze down to join them.

If you are curious to learn something new in the way of oral expression for joy, you should hear a group of Eskimos returning from a successful walrus hunt. Far from the south, borne on the wind, came their hunting song of victory, *"Oooooo-lah, oo-lah, oo-lah, oooooo-lah!"* In the distance, we could see the canoe with sail up billowing up the bight. Then again came the glad chorus, *"Oooooo-lah, oo-lah, oo-lah!"* The small children on the beach repeated the cry as if in echo. Some stranded ice pans near the shore provided a clean landing place for the gory cargo. But first the men must eat and drink tea, and already the women were carrying down the bubbling pots of soup and hot water. The hunters sat themselves down in a circle there on the shingle and talked long hours of the chase. The canoe was heaped with hacked-up chunks of red meat, walrus heads and tusks on top of the load.

The walrus are killed with rifles. If the natives can kill the barking one without arousing the inert animals lying on the ice, they are fairly certain of securing the entire pod. The hide is thick, most unwieldy and stiff, and does not lend itself to easy manipulation. For canoe coverings it must be split, or thinned, a painstaking job for the native women. It is only when the natives are short of bearded sealskins that they use the walrus hides for their boats. The ivory is sold in trade at about one dollar per pound, an average pair of tusks weighing from fifteen to twenty pounds.

Otoiyuk's crew had killed sixteen walrus, Anakak's fourteen, Angashuk had killed more "but we is not know how many that Angashuk is get," and Tuzroak came in with five. More pits to be dug in the frozen tundra; more meat to be preserved, so that men and dogs may not want during the long dark winter. Summer days are the harvest days and Eskimos must "make meat." Otoiyuk and his men have gone out again. The ice pans are drifting lazily in the bight, "good that wind for walrus."

July 28. My hand at my throat this morning! The ground was white! It had snowed during the night! Thin flakes were still flying. Oh, it can't be! The ship must come!

Kootook came bounding to the schoolhouse this morning, swinging his small daughter through the halls on a breakneck run into my rooms, breathless, gasping out his excited stream of Eskimo words as he took up his daughter's arm, pushed back the sleeve of her parka to uncover a lumpy ball of dirty gingham, blood soaked and dripping. She had been helping with the cooking— the knife had slipped, taking the fleshy part of her thumb off in one slice. The slice still held by a shred of skin. Between Kootook's rapid fire sentences and the frightened child, I had an anxious time enough with antiseptic towels and bandages and adhesive tape. All through his sign language I shuddered every time he started to lay his oily fingers on the fresh wound. He picked up the dirty rag a dozen times to show me just how he had wrapped it, and would have put his finger on the bleeding cut again had I not held his hand from doing so. Such a festering mess Eskimos can make of their simple cuts, infecting them the way they do.

All day I was boiling instruments and making sterile dressings and that night—but why tell of it. A clinic record speaks louder than words.

Clinic Record July 28.

Name	Age	Sex	Diagnosis	Treatment
Nanaoruk	12	F	Corneal Ulcer	Warm water irrigation. Yellow Oxide Oint.
Walook	37	M	Infected Hand	Lanced and Dressed.
Nutak	45	F	Lame back	Liniment and Hot Water Bag.
Kaligiluk	40	M	Infected finger	Lanced and Dressed (pus green)
Papiglook	Old Man		Stomach ache (too much walrus)	Epsom. Sal. Lax.
Kavik	8	F	Under nourished	Codliver Oil. Food.
Manuluk	4 months	M	Thrush	Bor. Acid Wash.

Elusina	35	M	Knee Sprain (Slipped in canoe)	Ep. Sal. Pack and bandaged.
Nasholook	28	M	Sliver in finger	Removed and Dressed.
Papiglook	Old man		Acute Gastritis	Enema at 1 A.M. (Whew!) Enema at 9 A.M. Broth at 4 P.M.
Kavik	8	F	Under nourished	Codliver Oil. Food.
Nanaoruk	12	F	Corneal Ulcer	Treatment repeated.
Manuluk	4 months	M	Thrush	Bor. Acid Wash. Mother's Breast, same treatment.

Papiglook has recovered, but its a merry dance he leads me every time fresh meat comes into the village. Whale or walrus or seal, he simply stuffs until his belly is distended like a balloon. He came in this morning rubbing his stomach and smiling, saying, *"Aregah, aregah nagooruk,"* happy and all set for another feast. Three cheers for Epsom Salts, I suppose.

When I weighed little Kavik today—and it is just six months since I started her on cod-liver oil—I found she had gained seven pounds. I suspect her father too of being tubercular and there are three other children in the family who will bear weighing and watching.

Nutak returned the bottle of liniment today. Just for good measure I gave her shoulders and back another good rub. She was sewing boots in the shelter of a canoe, she told me, and did not realize the wind was at her back when the sun had gone around. Next morning, *"Ar-rah,* that back is much sick."

Up to August 1, the clinic record shows, treatment

was given in 1574 cases. About one third of these have been for digestive disturbances in one form or another. Infections come next, and then sprains. During January and February, the months in which the influenza epidemic raged (1925), nearly 700 clinic cases were recorded with over 100 visits made to the igloos (soup or medicine). Twelve babies were born to bless as many village igloos and there have been four deaths. In the daily cod-liver oil column, there are three cases, two adults and one child.

With the beautiful sunshine of April and May came the painful and wretched snow blindness. Four adults and about thirty children were treated for this. The Eskimos guard their eyes with snow glasses of home manufacture, made of ivory or wood with narrow slits cut out for vision. Among the medical supplies are included several pairs of dark glasses for eye treatment. And bless the genius who first thought of "fine-tooth combs," now provided by the department. These were distributed for the populated scalps at the opening of school. At the first meeting held for the mothers, I talked myself hoarse stressing the need for their use. You should have seen the slick little heads that appeared from out of the parka hoods the next morning! One mother thought the "fine tooth" method a bit tedious, so she clipped the heads of her two small sons and asked for soap to complete the job.

The recent snow has melted and once again the country shines like summer. Loose ice fills the sea. Temp. 48°. Walked into the empty schoolroom this morning, wondering, as I've done so often of late, how long before it will be the busy warehouse of supplies again. Only a

TAKPUK.

Eva Louise Richards.
1925

TOOLIKELO.

Eva Louise Richards.

month to go before another school year must begin. Would the next year go as quickly—and the next? The thought swept me into a mood of nostalgia.

"August 1

"Dearest Ones:

"With this letter I fly to your arms to escape the Blue Devils which have suddenly come in to torment me. I have filled every minute of this long day with work to banish them but with no success. Tonight they sit grinning on every shining window, behind clean curtains, and on the freshly blackened cannon-ball heater. It's the ice. If it would only go away, if the winds of Heaven had some tender regard—could at least be kind and blow this subtle menace to navigation back to the North Pole so that a ship—*our* ship, could come to us.

"A few days ago when the thermometer dropped to 28° and our world was white with snow, I went around, in no quiet state of mind, checking supplies, planning— against a broken rudder or something—to spread my dwindled stock over another twelve months, but how in the world was I going to distribute three cans of tomatoes (all I have left) and five cans of corn, and so on down the meagre list, so as to assure a balanced ration. And flour, what I have on hand whittles the Staff of Life down to a mere crutch. Of medicines there is a shortage, too, as I have told you, but for these I harbor no apprehension since the Department would find some way of sledding them up. Surely the gods who have endowed a few of us with courage enough to come to the Arctic, will not be unmindful of the spiritual whale-bone necessary to stay our peace of mind, which for me at the moment depends on the ice; a vast ocean of barrier ice still crushing against our shore here at Wainwright."

My eyes and nose were still red when I crumpled this
letter to the waste basket. What I needed was a pail of
hot suds.

August 4. A fresh south wind blows. Temp. 40°.
Ripped my old blue wool dress and turned it. Looks like
new. Tonight I'm knitting collar and cuffs for it, of
scarlet wool. Bright color! Knitting! Foot-dragging
hours! It is my turn to discover how well they go
together.

Kungoona accompanied her husband to the coal mine
on Monday. Today (Wednesday) comes word that her
baby was born at Herd No. 1 Camp. She came back on
a load of coal as far as the inlet. From there Opiksoon
with his sled and dogs gave her a lift to the village. Both
mother and small son are none the worse for their long
chilly journey.

Each day now sees families arriving from Icy Cape or
Point Lay. A narrow stretch of open water has opened
along the shore, like a river between ice banks, running
south to where the bight begins to taper to its shallow
crescent tip beyond the inlet. Alulik paddled up this
stretch in his kayak this morning, skimming the light
waves like a wild bird. He landed on the beach below the
bank where I was sketching.

Now a kayak is the most graceful thing in a seacraft
you ever saw. It does in the water what a swallow can do
in the air. It is Eskimo genius expressed in a streamlined
covered canoe, with a round opening in the top to fit the
man who paddles it. Driftwood and sealskins go into its
making. They are called one-man boats. They are more
than that. They are like a magician's silk hat from which
come seven rabbits.

When round-faced Alulik stepped out, his wife popped up from the opening, as if she had been conjured from a brown butter crock. Reaching down into the canoe she pulled out a small child who blinked his eyes at the too sudden daylight, and after him came rolls of skins, a few poles, a tin pail, and then, cradling the kayak from side to side, out rolled two puppies.

Before my eyes the poles and skins became a tupek and homemaking was in order. Kayak magic!

The young boys and girls of the village had a gay time in the schoolroom this evening, singing songs and playing games. "Teacher's games," they call them. Did you ever play games with young Eskimo girls and boys? No? Gracious what a time you've missed. You should have seen them "Marching around Jerusalem." I am certain their gales of laughter were heard at Barrow. "Button, Button," proved the most popular. I believe they would have played this game all night if I had not suggested another. They were still shouting hilariously after passing the button an hour and a half. "Pinning the Tail on the Fox" elicited shrieks of delight. Such doubling over with mirth when the blindfold was removed, to discover where they had pinned the "tail." I had hoped to serve chocolate while it was yet daylight, but they had another round of "Jerusalem," and we lighted the lamps, the first time since whaling time, at 10 o'clock. A colorful sunset had lighted the room until then.

August 10. Kavaringa, the oldest woman in the village, came in today to bestow upon me the name of Elagak, for her husband's sister who died here three years ago. This was so unexpected, so unusual a gift, I scarcely knew what to say or how to accept it.

"Kavaringa is full of crying to give teacher present," she said, "now many days old pains in hands—my heart is full of liking to make boots—old pains cannot make boots—teacher like sister's name—Kavaringa give teacher Elagak." It was a gift straight from her good old heart.

Her eyes were like twin stars when I invited her to have tea with me. I spilled it too, moved as I was when she bowed her old gray head to give thanks before touching a spoon. Kavaringa had gone to school to Dr. Stevenson.

I resolved on some good resolutions when I learned that Kavaringa's sister had been highly respected and loved in this village of Wainwright, and as Nasholook later told me, "that Elagak is fine woman, all the time happy." There must be no more blue devils and red noses—not for Missus Eva Elagak.

The village heard the news of this gift very early, for when Walook came in to have his hand dressed at the clinic hour, his greeting surprised me, "How you, Elagak." And on the last strip of adhesive, "*Kwayannuck,* Elagak." (Thank you, Elagak.)

Bless my eyes! Did I see Kootook waving his telescope run by the window just now? Snatching a sweater from my chair I made a dash (Merciful heavens, one hall would have been enough!) out to join him, but where had he gone? Into the native store, of course. No, he wasn't there. Around the north end of the building. Bump! Thump! Of course, the ladder! Dear God, is it the ship? I dashed around to the east side to find Kootook on the third rung, taking his time. Clump—clump. "Oh, hurry Kootook, hurry, tell me what you see." Would he ever reach the ridgepole? Eternity of Eternities! Was an Eskimo ever so slow? There now, but no, first he must adjust that telescope. At last, but no, he must adjust the thing again. "Kootook, what do you see?" Oh, Saints on high! Would that telescope ever be adjusted? Kootook scans the ice fields to the south, slowly moving the telescope, closely examining the horizon, slowly, slowly—dear God, is a ship so small?

Tooruk came, breathless, around the corner. "Missus Eva, that something is burn on stove." Would my heart go on beating—lift my feet—move my body? There is no ship. Back into the house, numb with cold. What was it I was doing? Oh, yes, a cornstarch pudding. Milk boiling over. I wiped up the stove, all the while my eyes on the window. Natives were everywhere, every igloo alive. I could hear them scrambling to the roof. I'll go out again, perhaps by this time— I met Kootook in the hall. What was he saying? Oh! The ice is going out? Maybe tomorrow, ship come.

A day of taut nerves, of breathless anticipation at the window. Tomorrow dawns, the ridgepole is crowded, men and boys clumping up and down the ladder. Kungoona comes in quietly with her new-born son.

Another morning. One-half of me ignores the apathy of the other half and takes time to make toast without burning, to sit quietly eating stewed prunes and rolled oats, when suddenly—the excited whole of me is at the window, a cup of coffee spilling in my hand.

That's where I was, at the window, when I heard the first leaping shout, the thumpety—clump! down the ladder, banging doors—glad breathless Tooruk, Oyalla at his heels, "Sheep come! *Oomiakpuk!* Sheep!" A village gone mad, natives banging through the halls, running to their tupeks, *Aiyah, Oomiakpuk! Aiyah!*

"Please Missus Eva, I ring school bell?"

"Why yes, Tooruk, run and ring it." (All new to me how to welcome a ship.)

And then Nasholook, "Maybe now that flag," and someone dashes in to take it off the schoolroom wall, and oh! such a fumbling with stiff halyards until the flag, *our* flag, flutters up in a chorus of *ah-regahs,* to wave its taut salute.

Still a mere dot on the horizon, this ship, but already exercising a magical influence over this village. Everyone is running somewhere, to the beach and back again, into the tupeks and out, pulling clean snow shirts over their heads while on the run. Kootook shares his precious telescope; canoes are carried to the water; children shouting and laughing as they trundle old Ageepaluk to the edge of the bank. The women have blossomed out like gay flowers, bright plaid and pink and blue ginghams hurriedly donned over their furs. And on the peak of all the excitement, Segavan serenely walks in with his diary. "See Missus Eva," says he, "here I write, 'Government ship *Boxer,* August 15.' I write 'Captain Whitlam' name here." And I glance at the page with my mouth full of hairpins.

Out in the bight under a radiant sky, a little gray ship comes to anchor, *our* own tiny Bureau of Education ship, bringing supplies for the school, supplies for the teacher, freight for the natives and freight for their store, and mail, sacks and sacks of mail to make glad our northern station.

Buoyantly and eagerly I rode out with my natives to board her. Up the familiar little ladder, calling out a glad word to the captain on the first rung, to everyone else from the third, and a swing to the deck from the last.

"Well, what kind of a year did you have? I hear you had a bad time with the flu. Say we got a lot of stuff for you. You must be going to spend the rest of your life here. You want to look over these bills of lading?" I take the sheaf of papers while we all talk at once.

Then up the companion way came Barney, the same old Barney, "Weel, weel, 'tis a bit stouter ye are, and look'a the roses in thim cheeks, and last year—and I mind yer kindness and me finger and all—ye was that thin ye could ha' blowed through a goose quill. Shure 'tis glad I am to see ye lookin' so foine." Now some of the children had come aboard with their mothers and they crowded round him, so—"What is noo ye wee beggars? Ho, Ho! plums is it? Weel, git doon to the galley," and away he went to fill small fists, his rich brogue bouncing all over the British Isles.

The winches rattled a din, for there was much to unload, and the canoes went to shore with their burdens of freight. The radio operator breezed by with the mail. "Six sacks," he said, "all for Wainwright. Keep you busy till Christmas!" How could he know it better than I, or what those bulging parcel-posted packages might hold of scarlet wool to banish the lonely hours of the coming year?

When the mess gong silenced the winches the Eskimos came aboard for coffee and Tooruk was with them. "That schoolroom is now much full, Missus Eva—all the boys is works good today." It was then I remembered that Tooruk was keeping the tally of lighterage time for the men. Already the barter goods for their pay was piled on the deck. Tooruk would be helping the first officer with this, using his English words proudly.

Soon the winches were rattling again—this load and

then another and I would be going ashore. I would be going ashore with Tooruk and Sungaravik and Oyalla and the others. Together we would unpack and store and make ready for another year. It was going to be a good year and I was eager to begin it. For one thing the native store was moving into its own building. That meant more room for my older boys and girls. Both schoolrooms were to be painted. And new blackboards! *Ah-regah!*

And then I knew somewhat of the language. Interpreted conversations were all very well but they used up too much time. Now with my knowing the Eskimo for stomachaches and backaches and "that leg is plenty pain," the clinic hour would last *that* long and not run bandages and ointments into my dinnertime. Nasholook was so pleased with this spare time that he was planning a river trip with intention of routing a trapping line for the winter. And I, well for me there might be time to read those books I had chosen so carefully, seeing as eight of the ten were still waiting an Arctic mood, one that would at least deign a glance at the titles.

Best of all the health of the village was good. The ship's arrival had been the means of a clean bill. It was astonishing how the "plenty pains" had *pee-chooked*. And Anakok's son was home again, his arm as vigorous with the paddles as any boy's in the village. What's more, the ice was drifting in pans to a prosperous walrus season. *Ah-regah naguruk!*

As I waited near the pilothouse, waxing enthusiastic over all this, I was singularly aware that what the explorers had said of the Arctic was true: the North had gathered me to its heart—the warm heart of its little people— and would never let me go: that here among these primi-

tive Eskimos, whose simple lives had revealed to me a love
and contentment for living such as I had never known, I
was ready to spend the rest of my days.

What of the future years? Well . . . "in my Father's
house are many mansions"—an igloo must be one of
them.

ADDENDA.

U.S.M.S. *Boxer* Personnel. 1924-1925.

S. T. L. Whitlam . . . . Captain

O. J. Hansen . . . . First Officer. ('24)

Arthur Friend . . . . First Officer. ('25)

Elsworth Bush . . . . Second Officer

Herman Selwick . . . . Chief Engineer

Emil Holland . . . . Second Engineer

Billy Woodruth (Eskimo) . . . . Asst. Engineer

Abraham McGamet (Eskimo) . . . . . . Asst. Engineer

Duff Barney . . . . Steward ('24)

J. S. Clark . . . . Steward ('25)

Alphonso Manuel . . . . Asst. Steward

Carl Madsen (Eskimo) . . . . Asst. Steward

Harry Anakok (Eskimo) . . . . Asst. Steward

Eskimo Sailors and Deck Hands.

Ray Barster—from Barrow, Alaska.

George Porter—from Wainwright, Alaska.

Robert James—from Wainwright, Alaska.

Isaac Washington—from Kotzebue, Alaska.

Jack Jones—from Noatak, Alaska.

Dwight Tivick—from Wales, Alaska.

Roy Coppock—from Noatak, Alaska.

Sweeny Uluk—from St. Lawrence Island, Alaska.

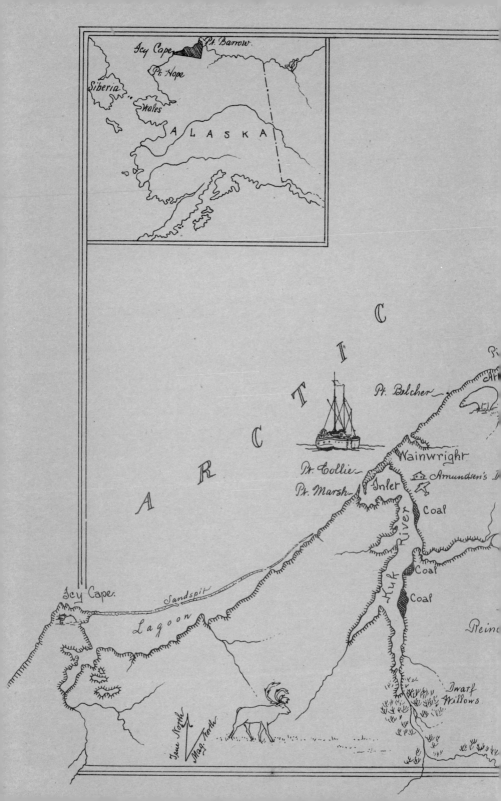